Fifty Years On:
The Case for Catholic Schools

)

Errata

Page 33, reference **should read** (Richmond, 1945).

Page 149, reference in endnote 40 **should read** Jeynes, W. H.
(2000; 2003).

Page 164, **should read** In 1976, James Callaghan …

Page 198, references **should read** Jeynes, W. H. (2000) and
Jeynes W. H. (2003).

Fifty Years On:
The Case for Catholic Schools

ANDREW B MORRIS

Matthew James Publishing Ltd

First published in Great Britain 2008 by:
Matthew James Publishing Ltd,
19 Wellington Close,
Chelmsford,
Essex CM1 2EE
www.matthew-james.co.uk

ISBN 978-1-898366-92-8

Cover design by Gill England
Printed and bound in Great Britain by Cromwell Press, Trowbridge, Wiltshire

Contents

Acknowledgements

This book draws heavily upon the work of many distinguished writers - specialists in their own fields. I have noted those sources either in the text or in the extensive footnotes. There are a number of others, however, who also deserve my thanks for their expertise, help and support in its preparation.

My first thanks must go to my wife, who painstakingly proof-read, and re-read, each chapter in their many guises and revisions. I am most appreciative of the help and support she has given me over many months.

I must thank, also, Fr. Marcus Stock for allowing me to make so much use of his knowledge and understanding of Catholic education; Ruth Armstrong, a partner in the law firm HJB Gateley Wareing, and Paul Barber, Barrister-at-Law and Director of Schools for the Archdiocese of Westminster for reviewing and advising on the accuracy of the legal content of chapters 6 and 7; Prof. John Sullivan of Liverpool Hope University and Dr. Petroc Willey of the Maryvale Institute, Birmingham, for reading and commenting so helpfully on the initial manuscript; and to the many colleagues in the various diocesan Schools Commissions in England who encouraged me to presevere and seek its publication.

In particular, I must thank the Archbishop of Birmingham, the Most Reverend Vincent Nichols, for his helpful comments on the text, in particular those sections that referred to the Church's dealings with government, and for his agreeing, so generously, to provide the foreword to the case that I am making for Catholic schools in England.

However, while expressing my wholehearted thanks for all the help I have received, I must make it clear that the views and opinions expressed in the book, any omissions, misinterpretation or errors that it may contain, are my own sole responsibility.

Andrew B. Morris
Liverpool Hope University
8th September 2008

Foreword

I am very pleased to be associated with the publication of this book.

The public debate about schools of a religious character is often to the fore at this time. Sometimes it is driven by those who are ideologically committed to the separation of all religious belief from education. This means that as Catholics we always have to be ready not only to defend our schools but also to give a positive and systematic account of their character and achievements. Values which shape education should always be explicit. There is no such thing as 'value-free' education.

For this reason I welcome Dr Morris' scholarly and methodical approach to the case for Catholic schools. He has gone to great trouble to assemble and establish an evidential basis which describes in detail the history, the legal situation and the achievements of Catholic schools over the last fifty years. Evidence as presented in this book is a good antidote to rhetoric and gratuitous assertions.

All who are interested in the debate on the place of schools of a religious character will find this book of great interest. This will include those who lead, teach in and support our Catholic schools as well as those who are interested in the issues that feature in this debate and who are prepared to take on board the evidence and detail which should inform that debate itself.

I thank Dr Morris for his work.

✠ Vincent Nichols
Archbishop of Birmingham
8th September 2008

Preface

At the beginning of the twenty-first century, most members of the Catholic Church take the existence of its state maintained schools (almost) for granted. It was not always the position. The creation and continued existence of a state supported Catholic sector has at different times been a matter of some considerable controversy.

The sector's current character and distribution can be attributed, arguably, to two key decisions of the Catholic bishops of England and Wales taken some ninety years apart. The first, taken as a collective body after the restoration of the hierarchy in 1850, was to make the provision of Catholic elementary schools their highest priority. The second, in response to the political settlement of 1944, was to pursue voluntary aided status for their existing and future schools. The underlying rationale for both decisions was their concern to provide an effective mechanism for the transmission of Catholic faith and culture for a predominantly poor and working class Catholic community, and secure control over the style and content of religious instruction. Catholic schools were to be the places where people learned their Catholicism becoming, with the home and church, a tri-partite self-sustaining community structure.

The decision to build such schools has involved the Catholic community in considerable capital expense over the years, and the acceptance of an on-going financial responsibility for their maintenance and improvement. In so doing, the Church has become a net contributor to the cost of providing the national education system. Catholic schools seek to provide an education that is appropriate to any civic institution, but taught within a religious context that permeates all aspects of their day-to-day activities. They are expected to provide high educational standards and exercise a particular duty to care for the poor and disadvantaged. That concern for the poor and under privileged is not new but has formed a central element of the bishops' educative mission for over 150 years. Initially, it was expressed in the drive to build elementary schools before churches. Today, it is reflected in their espousal of voluntary aided and comprehensive status for diocesan schools, together with a rejection of pupil selection by ability or aptitude.

The commitment of the Catholic Church in providing schools is evidence of the value it has always placed upon education. As such, it argues that, in serving the common good,[1] it is right and proper for Church schools to receive state support[2] for their role in providing an appropriate enviroment for parents who want a Catholic education for their children; especially since those parents are contributing to the education of others who prefer some other type of state supported school.[3]

However, the Church's view has not always received universal approval. Partly because of the political landscape in England since the Reformation, the role of religious belief in state sponsored education became a particularly thorny issue during the period leading up to the passing of the 1870 Education Act that established the dual system of education in England. It also formed the basis of Non-conformist opposition to the Education Act of 1902 which reorganised education on a municipal basis. The Education Act of 1944 appeared to overcome much of the sectarian rivalry that marked the passing of its 1870 and 1902 predecessors. It seemed to offer new opportunities for the development of a national education system that could accommodate differing religious opinions and provide both equal opportunity and greater social equity.

During the next fifty years, for the most part, that early promise seemed to have been fulfilled. The previously bitter controversies over the place of Catholic schools within the newly entrenched dual system certainly diminished and they became an accepted and unremarked feature of state maintained provision, almost ignored in the major government reports on the future development of education written in the late 1950s and 1960s.[4] Clearly, their expanding presence had not become a focus of any social conflict and they were no longer regarded as an actual or potentially divisive influence. Indeed, it is perhaps apposite that, in recognition of the general acceptance of the Catholic sector, the first major sociological study of the sector, published in 1978, was entitled 'Catholic Education: The Unobtrusive Partner'.[5]

Nevertheless, significant obstacles remained. The new secondary schools that were required under the provisions of the 1944 Act created severe financial difficulties for the bishops. In all their dealing with government both in the period leading up to the publication of the bill and following its enactment, they had sought, unsuccessfully as it turned out, for equity in the financial support provided by government when building schools for the Catholic population. Their position was set out in pamphlets published in the early 1950's [6] when the actual and potential cost of school provision seemed as if it might be too much for the Church to sustain.

Since then financial, social and political circumstances have changed. The financial burden has reduced as the level of government grant aid towards the capital costs of providing voluntary aided schools has risen over the years, from the initial 50% in 1944 to 75% in 1959, 80% in 1967, 85% in 1975 to its current 90% level in 2002. In contrast, socio-political disputes about the continuing role of the Catholic sector within the state system have returned, especially so in recent years,[7] following the present government's policy of using diversity in educational provision as a mechanism for raising standards, and encouraging different church or faith groups to establish schools as a way of achieving that objective,[8] particularly in the secondary sector.

The thrust of much popular criticism seems to be directed at perceived problems associated with the provision of schools for minority ethnic faith communities, established as a result of mass immigration starting in the 1950s. The arguments in favour of, so called, minority faith schools within an increasingly secular and pluralistic society, closely parallel those of the Catholic bishops over a century earlier. The antagonisms these new schools seem to have generated have once again made the role and existence of Catholic schools a controversial matter. Consequently, fifty years on from those early arguments setting out the bishops' case for equity in the degree of financial support given to Catholic schools within the state system, it is, perhaps, time to re-present the Catholic position.

Unlike the original, however, this new 'Case for Catholic Schools' is not concerned with arguments about financial equity, though that remains a matter of concern. Instead, in a series of connected essays, it will draw heavily upon the work of specialists in various areas - philosophical, historical, sociological, educational, political, legal and theological – in an attempt to explain to both proponents and sceptics of religiously based educational provision, how the maintained Catholic sector originated, what it seeks to do and how it makes a positive contribution to society.

As in the 1950s, there is a case to be made. It will, of course, be partial but also seek to be fair and balanced. The intended audience is general rather than scholarly (but with extensive explanatory notes provided for those who may wish to pursue the basis for the propositions put forward). The context is the diminishing understanding and practice of religion in an English society that is sometimes sceptical about the Church's presence within the educational system. It is hoped that the case being made will be of particular interest to those who value Catholic schools in particular, and church schools generally. It may also be of value to the Church's traditional partners in local and central government with whom we share a responsibility for the successful education of current and future generations of children, but who possibly have a limited understanding about the genesis or purposes of Catholic schools.

Most importantly, it seeks to provide a summary of supportive arguments for the Catholic sector that may be of use to those whose task it is to present the case for Catholic schools in their local circumstances to others who may not have much sympathy with the existing dual system as seen from the perspective of voluntary sector providers.

NOTES

1 This concept is regarded by the Catholic Church as having universal application and is defined as the sum total of social conditions which allow people, as groups or as individuals, to reach their fulfilment more fully and easily. There are three essential elements within the concept: i) respect for the individual and the natural freedoms that are indispensable for their personal growth; ii) social well-being and development of the group, and; iii) peace and justice. For a fuller explanation see the *Catechism of the Catholic Church* (1994) §§1905-1912.

2 Gravissimum educationis [Declaration on Christian Education] (1965) in: A. Flannery (ed) (1981) *Vatican Council II: The conciliar and post conciliar documents*, Leominster, Fowler Wright, pp. 725-737.

3 The bishops' argument that the state should provide financial support for the Catholic sector equal to that given for non-denominational schools was a consistent element in their discussions with government from the earliest times of state education, see, *The Catholic Attitude on the Education Question*, (1906) and *The Catholic Attitude on the Education Question*, (1929) both published by the Catholic Truth Society. It is neatly summarised in the bishops' Declaration on Education of 1928 – see the Acta [minutes] of their annual Low Week meeting, Tuesday April 17th, 1928 - *"That precisely the same facilities of education should be given to those who regard definite religious teaching as an essential part of education as those who attach no such importance to teaching of that character."*

4 For example, neither Catholic education nor Catholic schools appear in the index and glossary of the Central Advisory Council for Education Report *'15-18'* for the Ministry of Education (Crowther Report, 1959). The CACfE Report *'Half Our Future'* (Newsom Report, 1963) is similarly lacking. Its only recognition of the sector is a short description to social conditions of a Catholic community in Lancashire and, in another section of the Report, comments that, concerning the spiritual and moral education of 13-16 year olds, *"For Church of England and Catholic schools the situation will be markedly easier in some respects"*. The CACfE Report *'Children and their Primary Schools'* (Plowden Report, 1967) also sees no need to acknowledge the existence and implications of a dual system of education despite the fact that some 30% of the schools they were studying were Church schools.

It is also noticeable in all three reports how little input there was from official (or unofficial) representatives of the Catholic sector.

5 Written by the sociologist Michael P. Hornsby-Smith, himself a Catholic with, perhaps, a partisan interest, without which such a book would not have been contemplated by academics of the period.

6 *The Case for Catholic Schools* (1951; 1955), London, Catholic Education Council; *The Cost of Catholic Schools* (1955) London, Catholic Truth Society.

7 In recent times, questions about the place (if any) of religiously based education within the state maintained system has been the subject of much scholarly debate – see, for example, Gardner, R. et al., (2005) *Faith Schools: Consensus or Conflict?* London, RoutledgeFalmer; Judge, H. (2002) *Faith Based Schools and the State: Catholics in America, France and England*, Oxford, Education Symposium Books; Parker-Jenkins, et al., (2005) *In Good Faith: Schools, Religion and Public Funding*, Aldershot, Ashgate, – as well as more polemical contributions in the popular press and other media outlets attacking religious belief. For example, see articles by Polly Toynbee, P. (2001) 'Keep God out of class', in *The Guardian*, Friday November 9th; Toynbee, P. (2006) This is a clash of civilisations – between reason and superstition, *The Guardian*, Friday April 14th; Beckett, F. (2001) 'Holier than thou', in *The Guardian*, Tuesday November 13th; Dawkins, R. (2001) 'Children must choose their own beliefs', in *The Observer*, Sunday December 20th (presented in the form of an open letter to the then Secretary of State, Estelle Morris); Porteus-Wood, K. (2004) Scale down religious schools or face a disaster for race relations, *National Secular Society*, 9th June, http//www.secularism. org.uk (accessed 9th June 2004); National Secular Society (2007) The public don't want more faith schools, and they will be divisive, *http//www.secularism.org.uk* (accessed 10th September 2007).

8 See, for example, Department for Education & Skills (2001), *Schools Achieving Success,* London, Her Majesty's Stationery Office; Treasury Minutes on the Nineteenth Report from the Committee of Public Accounts 2003-04, *Making a Difference: Performance of maintained secondary schools in England*, presented to Parliament by the Financial Secretary to the Treasury, June 2004 (Cm 6244), § 25.

Chapter 1

UNDERSTANDING CATHOLIC SCHOOLS
– HISTORICAL CONTEXT

THE CATHOLIC COMMUNITY IN ENGLAND[1]

Using the term Catholic to define one specific social group in England can be problematical. There are members of the established church who use the term Catholic of themselves in the sense that they "belong to the universal Christian Church". In doing so they distinguish themselves from 'Roman Catholics', i.e. those Christians who acknowledge the primacy of the papacy in religious affairs. Since this document is concerned, essentially, with the latter group, for the sake of clarity throughout this document they will be termed 'Catholic' and their ecclesiastical institutions will be titled as belonging to the 'Church'. Where referring to the former the term 'Anglican' and 'Church of England' will be used. It is hoped that the convention will not give any offence.

Like all communities, that of the English Catholics has changed over time in response to differing political, social and demographic circumstances. From the Reformation to the early nineteenth century they comprised a community almost entirely excluded from the social, economic and intellectual life of mainstream society. But despite the violent disruption of medieval piety and religious practice that accompanied the break from Rome by Henry VIII, the resultant ascendancy of the Elizabethan episcopacy and subsequent severe restrictions of penal times, small pockets of recusant Catholic aristocracy, lesser gentry and common laity, retained their traditional religious allegiances, beliefs and, as far as was possible under the changing circumstances and religious influences at home and abroad, their Catholic practices.[2]

During the half-century between 1778 and 1829, the structure of anti-Catholic legislation that had developed since the Reformation was dismantled. By 1820, the social leadership of the Catholic aristocracy had ceased to be of real significance in the composition and activity of the Catholic community at large which was beginning to be concentrated in the emerging industrial cities, swollen by Irish Catholic immigrants from the 1790s onwards and the gradual population drift from the countryside. It has been estimated that in 1770 there were about eighty thousand Catholics in England and Wales. By 1850, that figure was nearer seven hundred and fifty thousand, approximately a tenfold increase. About a quarter of those were living in the northern cities of Preston, Wigan, Liverpool and Manchester.

Over the next one hundred years there was a gradual but steady increase in the size of the Catholic population. In 1912 it numbered some 1.7 million; by 1962 it was 5.6 million.[3] Following the pattern of the previous century, the Church was strongest in Durham, the North Riding of Yorkshire, Cumberland, Northumberland, Lancashire, Cheshire, Warwickshire and London. In Lancashire and Durham there were large rural Catholic populations, but the rest were mainly urban, working class and still relatively poor. By the time of the outbreak of war in 1939 there were indications of a gradual movement from the inner cities to the suburbs and the emergence of a more affluent and educated Catholic middle class. However, for the most part, Catholic communities remained concentrated in relatively small urban parishes each with its own church and elementary school. As populations expanded so, more or less, did the associated buildings, and in doing so they retained a measure of religious insularity. For example, it was not until the succession of John Heenan as Archbishop of Westminster in 1963, just after the Second Vatican Council began, that there were any significant ecumenical encounters with other churches.

The strength of religious self-identification also fostered a degree of social separation. As such, it could be argued that English Catholics formed a recognisable minority subculture with its own religious, social and moral norms of behaviour, value systems, attitudes and beliefs well into the 1950s. The following description of a Catholic working class community in Lancashire is, perhaps, a fairly typical example of Catholic social circumstances more generally during much of the first half of the century.

Family Life and General Social Behaviour

"The (Roman Catholic) parish clergy hold a unique position in dockside parishes, however relaxed some parishioners may be in religious observance. The parents are amenable to quite slight pressure from the school, perhaps

because the school has been under the Sisters for nearly a century, though the general moral standpoint that we all share has a good deal to do with it. People are decent and good-living; there are strikingly few broken homes and illegitimate children. Families are still fairly large, and there is a great family sense so that, even when mothers are out at work, there is always some relative, usually the grandmother to turn to ... Although there is a great deal of talk of "murdering" and "battering", I have only come across two cases in six years of girls severely beaten by father or mother. The parents are foolishly generous and quite inconsistent in their treatment of the children who are adept at evading consequences. The bad language shrieked from the top balcony of the tenements sounds appalling but appears to be rather a maternal safety valve than a heart-felt threat. Indeed, the children are very much loved and secure in their family affection. Every new baby is welcomed to an extra-ordinary extent. The girls are very kind to little ones and to the old. I have never come across an instance of rudeness or unwillingness to oblige an old person, though this may be due to caution, since grandparents are still powerful. They are rude to neighbours, carrying on family quarrels with gusto, and fights are common. I have much work in keeping fights out of school, and it is horrifying how even "good" girls all flock to watch a fight anywhere. The girls will fight as fiercely as the boys if they get the chance. Most girls stay up very late but few stay out. Those who do, stay on the tenement landings in the semi-darkness with the boys. Their main amusements are gambling, singing or cat-calling, horse-play and some sex-play. Sexual laxity is rare in this district under school leaving age. I have had no schoolgirl mothers and only three girls who have tried their hand at soliciting or got into the company of a prostitute by choice. Girls marry very young, so, whilst doing all we can to deter them from marriage before 18, we do our best in the Fourth Year to give them some training for their career as wife and mother."

(Central Advisory Council for Education, 'Newsom Report', 1963, §56)

In the years immediately after the war Catholics retained their ascribed and recognizable identity as a religio-ethnic subculture. By the 1950s they had become a significant, but still minority, community, representing nearly 11% of the population. A decade later, numbers had risen to 5.6 million, just over 12% of the total. From today's perspective, those years represent a numerical high watermark which, in their history since the Reformation, was something of an anomaly and the expansion of Catholic numbers that lasted into the 1960s was to be followed by a relative decline that could be seen in a whole range of indicators, for example, in lower mass attendance, fewer numbers of active priests, fewer marriages and a reducing birth rate.[4]

Many commentators cite the 1960s as the start of quite dramatic and profound changes in social attitudes in England. The Catholic community was not immune from them. Somewhere around the late 1950s and early 1960s there was a distinct shift in the Church. Some saw the Second Vatican Council as the defining moment of change since it legitimated a new and distinctly different way of looking at the nature of the Church, which had significant consequences in every sphere of its activities from worship and liturgy to its relationship to the world. Others argued that an older ideological homogeneity of an authoritarian Catholicism began to break up earlier with the death of Pope Pius XII in 1958. The precise date, if it is possible to be definite about a process, is, perhaps, irrelevant. What is important is that the laity's sense of what it meant to be Catholic fundamentally changed.[5] A Catholic identity today is much less a communal and ascribed mark as it was in pre-war years, but is to some extent chosen, a result of individual, voluntary choice. Between the pre- and post-war generations, Catholic social identity has been transformed as the distinctive sub-cultural solidarity of the first part of the twentieth century has begun to dissolve. In particular, the attitudes of younger generations of Catholics have converged with the mores of the wider and increasingly secular society, albeit retaining some tribal-like cultural and religious allegiances.

At the beginning of the third millennium precise numbers for the Catholic population in England and Wales are difficult to establish. Estimates made by individual parish clergy of the number of Catholics known to them give a figure of approximately 4.14 million, close to 8% of the population. It is not generally regarded as being particularly precise and is probably an underestimate of the real numbers. For example, it takes no account of the existing and sizeable ethnic Catholic communities[6] served by chaplains to foreign immigrants. It will not include significant numbers of people who regard themselves as Catholics but whose attendance at mass in any particular parish location may be intermittent or very infrequent. Nor will it have accurate data about economic migrants from central Europe arriving in Britain as a result of the extension of European Union borders, simply because central government has no adequate monitoring mechanism in place. Anecdotally, many thousands are Polish (and presumably in most cases Catholics). Whether they will settle permanently, or simply be part of a transient migration is, as yet, unknown. The Catholic Directory for England and Wales for 2006 suggests that Catholics comprising approximately 12% of the total population.[7] However, the accuracy of the Directory's statistical data has been severely criticised[8] and, given the known decline in the numbers of Catholic youngsters enrolled in Catholic schools over the past thirty years, it appears an unduly optimistic assessment. The truth may well be found somewhere between these two figures.

THE NATIONAL EDUCATION SYSTEM IN A CHANGING SOCIAL CLIMATE

The beginnings of the national educational system were set within a predominantly Christian culture. For the most part, a mutually supportive linkage between education and Christianity was accepted as part of the natural order. Areas of dispute tended to be denominational in character. For the majority population religion adherence was important, though there were many, particularly city dwellers, for whom religious practice was minimal. For those with political and social authority, however, disputes about the nature and role of religious belief and instruction in state supported schools were central during the period leading up to the passing of the 1870 Education Act. They also formed the basis of non-conformist opposition to the Education Act of 1902 that reorganised education on a municipal basis.

The co-ordinated national system introduced by the 1902 Act was largely a compromise, retaining a dual system having, broadly, two different types of school. Those provided by the newly created local authorities were maintained by government grants and local rates. Voluntary, or non-provided schools as they were designated, were funded, mainly, by Christian denominations and maintained by them with the assistance of some Government grant, but not by local rates. Secular instruction in both types of school was under the directions of the local education authority. Religious instruction was in accordance with the voluntary school's trust deed but strictly non-denominational in local authority schools.

Whether Britain could be regarded still as a Christian country during the fifty years leading up to the next great reform of the educational system following the Second World War is debateable. Despite the seeming strength of the established church and evidence of Christian practice during that period, there was also widespread religious apathy. However, an underlying assumption that the practice of Christian religion remained the societal norm is implicit in the provisions of the Education Act 1944 concerned with religious education (sections 23-30) and made explicit in schedule 5 of the Act that set out the procedure for preparing a locally agreed syllabus for religious education to be taught in state provided 'county' schools.[9] But during the 1950s presumptions about a Christianised Britain, and the extent to which Christianity should underpin the educational system became less tenable.

A report prepared for the Ministry of Education in 1959 noted the shared common spiritual heritage of the 15 to 18 year olds whose future education it was considering, but argued that while they needed a faith to live by:

> *"they will not all find precisely the same faith and some would not find a faith to live by"* [but] *"would be aware of the different metaphysical assumptions that are made in different circles … ."*
> (Central Advisory Council for Education, 'Crowther Report', 1959, §§66; 75)

Four years later a second report for the Ministry of Education was more equivocal about the school's role in contributing to the spiritual and moral development of pupils.[10] It recognised the decline in religious sensibilities, noting:

> *"the existence in any particular county school of teachers of various [Christian] denominations would be less likely to affect their ability to co-operate in the school's task of religious and moral upbringing than had been the case a generation ago."*
> (Central Advisory Council for Education, 'Newsom Report', 1963, §158)

It also acknowledged the developing plurality of attitudes within the country that could create difficulties for schools, arguing:

> *"… a hundred years ago nearly all good men would normally have given the same answers to the problems which beset the young immediately in their courtship habits and prospectively in their conception of the marriage relation. Today Christians and agnostics would still agree in their attitudes but it would be stupid to deny that there are profound differences."*
> (Central Advisory Council for Education, 'Newsom Report', 1963, §163)

On the other hand, the report suggested:

> *"… there will be much common ground which Christian and agnostic may travel together … [and] support the concept of natural law."*
> (Central Advisory Council for Education, 'Newsom Report', 1963, §164)

Despite their concerns, members of the committee felt able to agree four recommendations supporting the role of Christian religious instruction and worship in local authority schools as a potent force for good.

In contrast, the Plowden Report on the primary sector, submitted to the Secretary of State for Education and Science just three years later in October 1966, was unable to come to a unanimous view. Symptomatic of their concern was its preference for the term Religious Education rather than the phrase Religious Instruction (as used in the 1944 Act). While a majority of the members were in favour of mainly Christian education and worship in schools, their recommendations were more concerned with resolving perceived problems than providing wholehearted support. They advocated flexibility in interpretation of the existing law allowing pupils to be withdrawn from religious lessons and worship (though not suggesting any change). They wanted better parental advice about withdrawing their children from such activities, improved religious education training for teachers and an enquiry into the way religion should be presented to primary school pupils. In addition there were two minority reports. One was supported by just two of the twenty-five members. They were particularly concerned about the difficulties facing parents who wished to exercise rights of withdrawal when no alternative programme of moral or ethical education existed and drew attention to (unspecified) difficulties in drawing one up. They concluded:

> *"... the attempt should be made to determine what it is that we wish our children to learn in ethics in a society which is increasingly rejecting the sanction of supernatural revelation."*

(Central Advisory Council for Education, 'Plowden Report', 1966, pp. 492-3)

(Extract from a 'Note of Reservation on Religious Education')

The more significant minority opinion, supported by six members, including A. J. Ayer, the eminent philosopher, came to the conclusion that religious education was not a suitable subject to be taught in primary schools, arguing that the necessary involvement of theology in Religious Education made it both too recondite and too controversial a subject for inclusion in the curriculum. In doing so they acknowledged they were not in accord with mainstream public opinion and, in seeking an alternative which might address public concerns, they accepted that it was:

> *"... not easy to see what form the syllabus of moral and social education could take [and] far from wishing to deny the importance of this branch of*

education [thought] it should arise out of the general life of the school."
(Central Advisory Council for Education, 'Plowden Report', 1966, pp. 489-92)

(Extract from a 'Note of Reservation on Religious Education')

Given their analysis of mid-1960s Britain which led to their minority view, it is difficult to see how they expected the hoped for generalised Christian life might be generated and sustained. In the event, during the last forty years, English society has seen an accelerating trend away from any specific Christian underpinning of its cultural attitudes, values and practices. The secularisation of society, with its predominately humanistic, liberal and materialistic values has become the new orthodoxy. No longer do government and its agents look to Christian principles for their guiding principles for determining public policy. At the beginning of the third millennium, the general consensus is that, for good or ill, we live in a liberal, pluralistic and secular society where, in the name of tolerance, governments of different political persuasions have adopted an attitude where all lifestyles that are not positively harmful to the state are accorded equal status. In today's political discourse, truth seems to have become relative and any claims to the contrary, including religious views, are deemed to be strictly matters for private consideration.[11]

THE CATHOLIC COMMUNITY AND ITS SCHOOLS

Schools provide one of the major formal ways in which the knowledge, understanding and achievements of one generation are handed on to the next. They are an important mechanism for developing and transmitting values, attitudes and a vision of the very nature of humanity which, in turn, impacts upon the society in which they function. To understand and evaluate the significance of any school or school sector, it is important to understand its cultural background. This is probably especially relevant in England where schools have traditionally been regarded as communities in their own right, with implicit and explicit values, attitudes and practices that define their general culture. In other words, to understand today's Catholic schools we need to know something of their origins.

Schools have always played an important part in Catholic life. From the earliest times the Church regarded them as one of the chief instruments for catechising and civilising society. Until the severe legal restrictions on the teaching and practice of Catholicism in England were repealed, the survival of an educated Catholic community owed much to schools established outside the country. Subsequently, for the Catholic laity, what we might now describe as secondary education was centred on Catholic independent schools established, mainly, by religious orders. This chapter is, however, not concerned with their educational activities, important though they are,[12] but with the provision made by diocesan bishops in response to the difficult economic, social and political realities facing a mainly working class and immigrant Irish community during the latter part of the nineteenth century. This was a community that was particularly vulnerable, not just because of its poverty but also because of its ethnic origins and Catholic allegiances.

Partly because of the administrative structure of the Church, it could be argued that the bishops have never been able to establish a single comprehensive coherent and co-ordinated strategy for Catholic education in England.[13] On the other hand, their intentions have been clear. The existence, nature and distribution of Catholic maintained schools in England at the beginning of the 21st century can be attributed, arguably, to two decisions of the English Catholic bishops taken some ninety years apart. The first, taken as a collective body after the restoration of the hierarchy[14] in 1850, was to make the provision of Catholic elementary schools their highest priority.[15] The second, in response to the political settlement of the 1944 Education Act, was to pursue voluntary aided status for their existing and future schools. Both required the bishops to make a huge financial commitment to education. The rationale for both decisions was the need, as they saw it, to provide an effective mechanism for the transmission of Catholic faith and culture for the Catholic faith community.

Between 1770 and 1850 there had been a dramatic increase in the numbers of Catholics living in England, caused, mainly, by the influx of Irish immigrants from 1790 onwards. Their need for employment, coupled with a general drift away from the countryside caused by the rapid industrialisation of society, led to the concentration of large numbers of poor working class Catholics in the inner cities. It was against this background that the bishops first made their commitment to build Catholic elementary schools.

They were determined to compete with the schools provided by local School Boards following the Education Act of 1870 despite the latter being better equipped, larger and more efficient. Their central purpose in so doing was to secure control over the style and content of religious instruction. Catholic schools became the places where people learned their Catholicism. Together with the church or chapel they served as an essential focal point, providing stability, a sense of belonging, of pride and self-assertion and solidarity with the wider Catholic community. In 1869, Education Councils were set up in each diocese to further the building of elementary schools. There were three hundred and fifty Catholic elementary schools in 1870. A decade later there were over seven hundred and fifty, established mainly through the Education Councils and provided through the financial support of a predominantly poor working class community.

As the Catholic population in England steadily increased and the state took a greater role in educational matters, the bishops responded to the provisions of the Education Act 1902 and accepted a great financial burden in order to achieve their aim of providing sufficient places in Catholic schools to meet the increasing demand. While meeting the costs of adapting, improving and extending existing schools, they also found the resources to build new ones. Ninety-six were built between 1914 and 1930.

During this period the Catholic population was still mainly located in the major industrial cities. The following description of a Lancashire community in the late 1950s is perhaps typical of many during much of the first half of the century.

> "The girls are all drawn from the immediate neighbourhood within an area of a half square mile, all of the same racial and religious stock, Irish and Catholic, and almost all are the children of unskilled labourers who are in full employment. The community is very stable despite slum clearance and most of the children are descended from former pupils."
> (Central Advisory Council for Education, 'Newsom Report', 1963, §55)

Though the pattern of Catholic settlement remained much as it had been throughout the period from 1850 to the first part of the twentieth century, at the outbreak of war in 1939 there were indications of a gradual but persistent move from the inner cities towards the expanding suburbs. This trend was to continue and accelerate in the immediate post war period. The extension of secondary education following the 1944 Education Act encouraged the breakdown of insularity as Catholic secondary schools drew their pupils from several parishes, often many miles apart. On the other hand, the priority still given by the bishops to a distinctive Catholic education, provided in its own schools, helped the Catholic community to preserve some sense of its own religious identity and doctrines and a feeling of membership of an extra-national religious society.

The 1950s saw an expansion of Catholic educational provision in response to the rapidly rising post war birth rate, renewed Irish immigration and significant numbers of Catholic refugees who had been displaced by the war choosing to settle in England. As a result, arguably, of successful Catholic schooling in the post war years, a more extensive and wealthier Catholic middle class developed and in the mid 1960s the existing gradual dispersal of Catholic families into the suburbs accelerated. That demographic movement was accompanied by changes in patterns of belief and adherence to traditional values and practice that had been features of Catholic life for generations. There was also the start of a general and rapid decline in the overall pupil population. The trend has been reflected in the Catholic community.

The number of Catholic pupils in Catholic maintained schools peaked in 1974 at 0.94 million. In 1980 there were approximately 0.76 million, in 1990 some 0.68 million and in 2003 there were 0.63 million Catholic pupils attending Catholic schools in England and Wales.[16] That gradual decline has led, for the first time for over a century in many parts of the country, to the number of available places in Catholic schools exceeding demand from baptised Catholics. Some, but not all, of the now surplus capacity has been removed by reorganising, closing or amalgamating schools.

Those trends, together with the repeal of legislation introduced in the 1980 Education Act designed to secure the religious character of Catholic schools by limiting their intake to baptised Catholics, and the popularity of church schools with parents generally, has led to an increase in the proportion of non-Catholic pupils on roll in many Catholic schools. In addition to the more disparate intake there were significant cultural changes accompanying the renewal of the Church following the Second Vatican Council. Coupled with the rise of a market oriented educational climate, these developments have created tensions both within and for Catholic schools as they grapple with twin roles as both religious and civic institutions working within an increasingly secularised post-Christian society.[17]

The bishops' policy statements have adjusted to the new circumstances of falling school rolls and an evolving multi-cultural, multi-ethnic society.[18] In some individual cases, responding to the immediate social circumstances where the school is located, Catholic schools have changed their role, seeking to be a benefit to the community as a whole, sometimes in collaboration with other Christian denominations in joint church schools, rather than providing education solely for the faith community of baptised

Catholics.[19] Nevertheless, the educational vision of a place in a Catholic school for every baptised catholic child, so clearly articulated some 150 years ago, continues to be the prime reason given by the bishops for providing and supporting Catholic schools.[20]

However, debates about the role and purpose of Catholic schools in the current market driven economy raise questions about the ways, if any, that Catholic schools are different and distinctive from other state supported institutions.[21] Both Christians and those who reject the validity of using God as the basis on which human activity and education should rest, acknowledge that if schools do adopt Christianity as a rationale for their educational aims, such a religious stance must, necessarily, impact upon the nature and style of the curriculum provided and the emphasis schools place on the purposes of the pupils' studies.[22] Cardinal Basil Hume put the case most strongly when he argued at the Catholic Education Service National Conference in Birmingham that, in current English society:

"Disputes over the purpose of education reflect a much deeper conflict in our society over what it is to be human. We are in fact in a battleground of competing ideologies, fighting for the minds and imaginations of the young, offering rival views of human fulfilment and happiness"

(Hume, B., 1995, p. 3)

THE STATE MAINTAINED SECTOR IN THE THIRD MILLENNIUM

Currently, some 35 percent of primary and 16 percent of all secondary schools in England and Wales are defined by government as having a religious character. The vast majority have been provided by the Church of England and the Catholic Church, but there are also a small number provided by minority Christian denominations, some Jewish, Muslim and Sikh schools, together with a few joint ventures by different Christian denominations working together in a variety of partnerships. The Catholic maintained sector in England and Wales provides education for some 0.79 million pupils in 2,203 schools.[23] In England, the Catholic sector educates approximately 0.72 million children representing approximately 9.6 percent of the pupil population.[24]

One might have thought that, given the well-documented decline in formal religious practice during the latter part of the twentieth century,[25] there would be a lessening of public interest in religious-based schools and an increase in those sharing secular educational goals. This is clearly not the case. The reality of today's educational world sees an increase in disagreements about its fundamental purposes and greater parental demand for choice as to where and, perhaps to a lesser degree, how their children are educated. In our secular, pluralistic and avowedly tolerant society, this reality probably guarantees some form of diversity of provision as a philosophical and political necessity.

The Education Act 1996, section 11(2), placed a duty on the Secretary of State for Education to "… exercise his powers with a view to (among other things) improving standards, encouraging diversity and increasing opportunities for choice." Recent documents have expressed the current Government's intention to encourage diversity of provision, particularly in secondary education[26] culminating in the Education and Inspection Act 2006, section 2, which places a duty on local authorities to secure diversity of provision and increase parental choice. The expressed political rationale is that diversity promotes innovation and higher educational standards. Nevertheless, a commitment to diversity cannot be open-ended and is not necessarily a self-evident social good. On the contrary, many argue that diversity of provision is undemocratic, discriminatory and a source of social unrest.

In one sense, perhaps, it is inevitable that the dual role of Catholic schools, supporting Catholic parents in transmitting Catholic culture but also working for the common good of a post-Christian and highly secularised society, will highlight tensions between secular and religious values. It has been the subject of comment by Catholic bishops on a number of occasions. The following statements, some twenty years apart, are typical:

> *"In our own time, there is much in the law and in the behaviour of people which is quite contrary to the teaching of the Gospel. Our Catholic communities must quite deliberately reject much of what is described as progressive in our society."*
>
> (Mullins, D., 1981)

> *"Multi-cultural Britain cannot be negotiated in purely secular terms … nowhere is this more important than in education …"*
>
> (Nichols, V., 2002)

Bishop Mullins argued further that, in providing Catholic schools, the Church was not simply rejecting and condemning what it observes in civil society, but showing religious activity to be a normal part of everyday life.

... the Catholic school should ensure that its very nature is proclaimed like a beacon to the world at large so that the very act of attendance can be seen as a significant religious activity".

(Mullins, D., 1985)

This is a view that needs to be reaffirmed and articulated in contemporary circumstances against those who argue that religion must only exist as a private activity and others who are, once again, questioning the right of parents to send their children to schools that are in conformity with their own philosophical and religious beliefs, on the basis that to do so might promote social disharmony.[27]

Throughout, reference has been made to Catholic schools as a sector, implying a degree of uniformity of purpose and character. However, while there may be many similarities that justify doing so, it must be recognised that there will be significant variations between schools, both in their understanding of their mission and the pupil population they serve; perhaps more so today than in previous decades. The degree of religious understanding and adherence to the Catholic faith shown by parents will vary. School governors, appointed by the Church to secure and develop the religious character of the school, will have varying levels of personal adherence and may differ in their understanding of, and commitment to, the religious dimension of Catholic education as defined by the Ordinary of the diocese. Catholic teachers are also likely to have different levels of faith commitment. While such differences may not impinge upon their pedagogical competence, their ability to contribute towards developing and sustaining the Catholicity of the school may be affected. In addition, not all teachers in Catholic schools are themselves baptised Catholics. This is particularly the case in the secondary sector where some 46 percent of the teaching staff are not Catholics; in the primary phase it is much lower, approximately 19 percent (Catholic Education Service, 2003). The same will be true of the pupil population where numbers of non-Catholic pupils have risen when places became available because of the declining birth rate. Significant numbers of non-Catholic pupils may have an influence on the nature of the school and the education it can provide though implications for pupil attainment, if any, have not as yet been empirically tested to any great extent.[28]

NOTES

1   This section is a very simple summary of a complicated story. For those who require a much fuller description of the changing Catholic community in England there are a number of excellent general histories which have served as sources for this chapter, for example, Battersby, W. J. (1950) *Secondary Education for Boys*; Battersby, W. J. (1950) *Educational Work of the Religious Orders of Women*; Gwynn, D. (1950) *The Irish Immigration*, and *Growth of the Catholic Community*; Hughes, P. (1950) *The English Catholics in 1850*; all to be found in: G. A. Beck, (ed) (1950) *The English Catholics 1850-1950*, London, Burns Oates.

Other sources include, Bossey, J. (1975) *The English Catholic Community 1570-1850*, London, Darton, Longman & Todd; Evennett, H. O. (1944) *The Catholic Schools of England and Wales*, Cambridge, Cambridge University Press; Norman, E. (1986) *Roman Catholicism in England*, Oxford, Oxford University Press; McClellend, V. A. & Hodgetts, M. (eds) (1999) *From Without the Flaminian Gate*, London, Darton, Longman & Todd; Hornsby-Smith, M. P. (ed) (1999) *Catholics in England 1950 to 2000*, London, Cassell; Kennedy, P. (ed) (2001) *The Catholic Church in England and Wales 1500-2000*, Keighley, PBK Publishing Ltd.

More detailed local histories, particularly of immigrant Irish communities, also provide some fascinating details of the social deprivation that the Catholic bishops sought to alleviate. For example, see various essays in R. Swift & S. Gilley (eds) (1985) *The Irish in the Victorian City*, London, Croom Helm; R. Swift & S. Gilley (eds) (1989) *The Irish in Britain 1815-1939*, London, Pinter; and R. Swift & S. Gilley (eds) (1999) *The Irish in Victorian Britain*, Dublin, Four Courts Press.

2   Descriptions of lay people's experience of religion before, during and after the Reformation and the subsequent penal years are given in, for example, Duffy, E. (1992) *The Stripping of the Altars*, New Haven & London, Yale University Press; Matthew, D. (1950) *Old Catholics and Converts*, in: G. A. Beck, (ed) (1950) *The English Catholics 1850-1950*, London, Burns Oates; Norman, E. (1986) *Roman Catholicism in England*, Oxford, Oxford University Press.

3   Though there was a real and significant increase in the Catholic population, some have argued that the startling rise in numbers over this period can partly be explained by new statistical techniques - see Norman, E. (1986), *Roman Catholicism in England*, Oxford, Oxford University Press.

4   Estimates suggest that, largely as a result of high levels of Irish immigration in the late 1950s, the Catholic population increased from 4.7 million or 10.7% of the total population in 1951 to 5.6 million or 12.2% in 1961. In the early 1960s one in eight marriages was solemnized in a Catholic church and the proportion of Catholic infant baptisms as a proportion of total live births had risen to 16.1%. In the two decades after the end of the war the number of parishes increased by one fifth from 1,910 to 2,320 and the number of priests by one quarter from 6,257 to 7,808. In the early 1960s a whole string of indicators peaked: Mass attendances around 2 million; child baptisms around 134,000; receptions (conversions) around 15,000; confirmations around 81,000; and marriages over 46,000 with 50 per cent between two Catholics. The corresponding figures thirty years later are 1.1 million; 75,000; 6,000; 46,000 (for 1985); and 17,000 (with the proportion of marriages between two Catholics around one third).

An illustration of the rapid changes in Catholic numbers in at least one part of the country can be seen in the case of the Diocese of Middlesbrough. It was created, together with the Diocese of Leeds, when the Diocese of Beverley was split into two in 1878 because of the increasing Catholic population, particularly in the cities of Hull and Middlesbrough. Numbers continued to increase into the second part of the twentieth century with churches and schools being provided to meet the resultant demand. In contrast, at the beginning of 2005, the bishop issued a consultation document on possible parish reorganisation in 2006, noting a one third drop in Sunday Mass Attendance over a period of twelve years, from nearly 30,000 in 1992 to under 20,000 in 2004.

5   For a much fuller discussion of this phenomenon, see Hornsby-Smith, M. P. (1999) English Catholics in the New Millennium, in M. P. Hornsby-Smith, (ed) (1999) *Catholics in England 1950-2000*, London, Cassell; also Hulmes, E. (1999) Faith in Crisis: From Holocaust to Hope 1943-2000, in: V. A. McClellend and M. Hodgetts (eds) (1999*) From Without the Flaminian Gate*, London, Darton, Longman & Todd.

6   Afro-Caribbean; Albanian; Austrian; Belorrusian; Brazilian; Chaldean; Chinese; Croatian; Czechoslovakian; Eritrean, Filipino; French; German; Ghanaian; Goan; Greek; Hungarian; Iraqui, Chaldean and Syrian; Italian; Keralan (Latin and Syro-Malabar Rite); Korean; Latin American; Lebanese; Lithuanian; Maltese; Melkite; Nigerian; Polish; Portuguese; Slovakian; Slovenian; Spanish; Tamil; Ukrainian; Vietnamese.

7   See *Catholic Directory of England and Wales* (2005) Manchester, Gabriel Communications Ltd, pp. 924-26.

8   See Spencer, A. E. C. W. (2006) *Facts and Figures for the Twenty-First Century – An assessment of the statistics of the Catholic community of England and Wales at the start of the century*, Taunton, Pastoral Research Centre.

9   Those who wish to obtain a greater understanding of the social conditions and public attitudes of the period up to and including the implementation of the 1944 education Act would do well to read Barnard, H. C. (1947) *A History of English Education from 1760*, London, University of London Press; Beales, A. C. F. (1950) The Struggle for the Schools in: G. A. Beck (ed) (1950) *The English Catholics 1850-1950*, London, Burns Oates; Bossey, J. (1975) *The English Catholic Community 1570-1850*, London, Darton, Longman & Todd; Curtis, S. J. (1948) *History of Education in Great Britain*, London, University Tutorial Press Ltd; Evennett, H. O. (1944) *The Catholic Schools of England and Wales*, Cambridge, Cambridge University Press; Finan, J. (1975) *Struggle for Justice*, Stoke-on-Trent, Catholic Teachers' Federation; and Norman, E. (1986) *Roman Catholicism in England*, Oxford, Oxford University Press.

10   The Newsom Report was concerned with the education of pupils aged 13-16 of average and less than average ability attending (mainly) the secondary modern schools of the time.

11   In theory, social liberalism is agnostic about moral truth. So, for the state, promoting the common good consists in legislating to establish instrumental conditions for harmonious living based on the maximising of individual freedom and access to material welfare. This is not, of course, the understanding or teaching of the Catholic Church – see *Compendium of the Social Doctrine of the Church* (2004), London, Burns & Oates.

12   Battersby, W. J. (1950) Secondary Education for Boys, in: G. A. Beck, (ed) (1950) *The English Catholics 1850-1950*, London, Burns Oates; Evennett, H. O. (1944) *The Catholic Schools of England and Wales*, Cambridge, Cambridge University Press.

13   For example, in recent years there have been differing responses by dioceses to such government initiatives as Grant Maintained Schools, its desire to establish Academies, and its Private Finance Initiative. Some dioceses have established, or plan to establish jointly owned schools with other Christian denominations, others oppose the very concept or have withdrawn from existing arrangements. Some dioceses have well developed tertiary systems for post-16 education; others prefer 11-18 schools. Some dioceses encourage their schools to adopt local authority policies and procedures for their own use, others take the view that, in order to protect the autonomy of

their schools, it is important for the appropriate diocesan authority to provide diocesan schools with model policies for governing bodies to adopt that are specifically tailored to their Catholic character.

14 The term *hierarchy* is used here in the technical ecclesiastical sense and refers to the distribution of ordained orders and ministries within the Catholic Church, namely deacon, priest and bishop. It is often used generically, though inaccurately, of the Pope and bishops. It is useful here, perhaps, to explain a little about the administrative structure of the Catholic Church. It is generally perceived by those outside the Church, including colleagues in the local authority educational services, as a sort of monolithic bureaucracy with authority delegated by the papacy to the Cardinal Archbishop of Westminster and then cascaded downward via the bishops to the priesthood and laity. That is not the case. Authority within each diocese is vested in the individual bishop or Ordinary, of whom there are 19 in England and 3 in Wales. In educational matters, as in all other, each is autonomous (even if the Archbishop of Westminster may be accepted as their 'leader' in many of the Church's dealings with government). The bishops meet in conference from time to time, normally in Low Week after Easter. They are advised on educational matters by officers of the Catholic Education Service. This is the vehicle through which the bishops interact with government officials. It was established as the Catholic Poor School Committee in 1847. Its twenty-four members comprised a clergyman and two lay members from each of the then eight ecclesiastical districts of England and Wales. It changed its name to the Catholic Schools Committee in 1888 and in 1905 it was converted into the Catholic Education Council when it included secondary education within its remit. At that time it had eighty clerical and lay members. In 1991 it was reorganised, given a wider brief, including tertiary education, and was again renamed, this time as the Catholic Education Service.

15 Province of Westminster, 17th July 1852, in: R. E. Guy, (1886) *The Synods in English: being the texts of the four synods of Westminster*, London, St. Gregory's Press.

16 Statistics are provided by the Catholic Education Service.

17 This reality has been explored in a number of essays, studiers, theses and books. For example, see Egan, J. (1986); Egan, J. & Francis, L. J. (1986); Arthur, J. (1995); McLaughlin, T. (1996); O'Keefe, B. (1999); Hornsby-Smith, M. J. (1999; 2000); Fulton, J. (1999; 2000); Grace, G. (2002; 2003); Storr, C. (2007). For details see bibliography.

18 In response to the Catholic Church's understanding of its relationship with other faiths originating in the conciliar and post-conciliar documents of the Second Vatican Council, the developing multi-racial character of many parts of England and Wales, and the position of Catholic schools situated in areas with sizeable minority faith communities, a document *Catholic Schools and Other Faiths* was prepared in 1976 by a special Commission established jointly, at the request of the Bishops' Conference of England and Wales, by the Committee for Other Faiths, The Committee for Community Relations and the Department for Catholic Education and Formation. Its conclusions, recommendations and guidance make clear the need to respect other faiths and to work with parents and spiritual leaders of other faith communities whose children attend or may wish to attend a Catholic school in order to develop mutually beneficial and creative relationships. A more recent report, O'Keefe, B. & Zipfel R. (2003) *Ethnicity, Identity & Achievement in Catholic Education*, London, Catholic Education Service, reflects the Church's commitment to, and success in, supporting youngsters from minority ethnic communities attending Catholic secondary schools in a variety of ways that reflect the particular circumstances in which the schools operate.

19 It is not always clear to what extent such collaborative arrangements are pragmatic solutions to individual circumstances and/or political encouragement (such as the current government's Academies programme) where it is not possible to have the traditional form of Catholic school or

whether they are new forms of religious solutions to the church's understanding of its educative role. Whereas in some areas of the country some collaborative enterprises have flourished, others have floundered. The issues have been debated, for example, in Caines, J. (1994); Chadwick, P. (1994); Arthur, J. (1995); Hyper, P. A. (1996); Murray, V. (1996); Grace, G. (2002); Murphy, A. J. (2005). For details of these references see bibliography.

20 Cardinal Hume (in 1994 and 1995) and bishops Worlock (1995), Konstant; (1996), Nichols (in 1995 and 2002) and Regan (2004) have all made statements over the last decade re-iterating the message that the prime educational aim of the Catholic Church is, as far as is possible, to provide a Catholic education in a Catholic school for all baptised Catholic children. The Catholic Education Service, acting on behalf of the Bishops Conference of England and Wales, has made the same case in 2003 in: *Catholic Education: A CES Position Paper on Catholic Education in Schools and Sixth Form Colleges*, London, Catholic Education Service. This does not mean, however, that the means to achieve that primary goal will be the same in every diocese. For details of the above references see bibliography.

21 This issue was first raised by Hornsby-Smith, M. P. (1972; 1978). It is discussed within the context of contemporary educational climate by Grace, G. (2002). For details of these references see bibliography.

22 See, for example, Eliot, T. S. (1939) *The Idea of a Christian Society,* London, Faber & Faber; White, J. P. (1982) *The Aims of Education Restated,* London, Routledge & Kegan Paul, pp. 76; 88; 89.

23 The total number of institutions given in the Catholic Education Service statistics collected in January 2004 includes primary and secondary schools (modern, comprehensive and grammar) and sixth form colleges. None of the seven Catholic Grammar schools are diocesan institutions. All are owned by religious orders and conducted according the their particular trust deeds.

24 DfES (2004) *Statistics of Education, England*, London, HMSO.

25 See, for example, analyses by Davie, G. (1994) *Religion in Britain since 1945*, Oxford, Blackwell; Gilbert, A. D. (1980) *The Making of Post-Christian Britain*, London, Longman; Brown, C. G. (2001) *The Death of Christian Britain*, London, Routledge; Bruce, S. (1995) *Religion in Modern Britain,* Oxford, Oxford University Press; Bruce, S. (2002) *God is Dead: secularisation in the west*, Oxford, Blackwell; Ashworth. J. & Farthing I. (2007) *Churchgoing in the UK*, Teddington, Tearfund.

26 See DfES documents, *Schools Achieving Success,* (2001); *Education and Skills: Investment for Reform,* (2002); *A New Specialist System: Transforming Secondary Education,* (2003) ; *Faith in the System,* (2007) For details see bibliography.

27 See, for example, Passmore, B. & Barnard, N. (2001) Voters oppose expansion of faith schools, *Times Educational Supplement,* 30th November; Hansard (2002) *Report of the debate on the Education Bill 2002*, Columns 577 to 587, London, House of Lords 17th June; Local Government Association (2002) *Education Bill*, Education Policy Review Meeting, March 2002, London, Local Government House; Office Of The Deputy Prime Minister (2004) *Social Cohesion: Sixth Report of Session 2003-04*, Vol. 1, 23-29, London, House of Commons; Porteous-Wood, K. (2004) Scale down religious schools or face a disaster for race relations, *National Secular Society*, 9th June, http//www.secularism.org.uk (accessed 9th June 2004); Association of Teachers & Lecturers (2007) *Faith Schools Position Paper*, http://www.atl.org.uk/atl_en/images (accessed March 26th 2007); National Secular Society (2007) The public don't want more faith schools, and they will be divisive, 10th September, *http://www.secularism.org.uk/thepublicdontwantmorefaithschool3.html,* (accessed 14th September 2007).

28 Bishop Konstant has argued that *"unless Catholic schools comprise, in some meaningful way, communities of faith they will be unable to carry out their religious functions of catechesis and evangelisation. Consequently, the questions of who and who should not be admitted to Catholic schools is a fundamental problem, the solution to which will differ depending upon the specific local circumstances"*. See, Konstant, D. (1996) 'Master Builders' – The Role of Catholic Teachers, in: *Partners in Mission: a collection of talks by Bishops on issues affecting Catholic education*, London, Catholic Education Service & Briefing. See also, Nichols, V. (1995), The Church's Mission in Education in a Multi-Faith Society, in: *Partners in Mission: a collection of talks by Bishops on issues affecting Catholic education*, London, Catholic Education Service & Briefing.

In his book, *The Ebbing Tide* (1995), Leominster, Gracewing, James Arthur has hypothesised three 'types' of Catholic school each having its own characteristics that affect the way in which it works and the form of education it will provide.

Donnelly C. (1999; 2004) has noted, in the context of Northern Ireland, how staff and governors of joint church schools find it difficult, if not impossible, to create a 'joint-school ethos' and that such schools have the potential to create conditions that maintain or harden boundaries between different Christian faith traditions rather than dilute them. Donnelly's observations about Northern Ireland are confirmed in a report of a seminar *Integrated Schools and Faith Schools* held by the Nuffield Foundation, Friday 5th July 2002. However, it must be remembered that Northern Ireland is, in many ways, its own special case and it may be unwise to extrapolate such findings into differing cultures. On the other hand, similar observations have been made in a study of the impact on a Church school in England operating within a federation of different types of school, see, Image F. (2005) Unpublished M. Ed thesis (details in bibliography).

An independent study commissioned from the National Institute for Christian Education Research based at Canterbury Christ Church University, Kent by the Archdiocese of Birmingham found a positive association between pupils' examination scores at age 16 and high proportions of Catholic pupils on the school roll. It was most evident for pupils attending schools located in very deprived areas and who, within their particular schools, were academically weak. See Morris A. B. & Godfrey R. (2006) *A statistical Survey of Attainment in Catholic Schools in England with Particular Reference to Secondary Schools Operating Under the Trust Deed of the Archdiocese of Birmingham*, hppt://www.bdsc.org.uk and also hppt://www.nicer.ac.uk.

Chapter 2

OBJECTIONS TO CATHOLIC SCHOOLS – THE FAITH SCHOOL DEBATE

BACKGROUND

The current debate encompasses a great deal that is not always immediately obvious. It touches upon fundamental issues about the nature of humanity, the purpose and meaning of life; about religious belief and practice; the nature and aims of education; the human and legal rights of parents and their children; the nature of the state and its role, if any, in the education of children. Political discussions and conclusions about such issues are complicated by a number of factors. Perhaps the most important being the heavy involvement of churches in the provision of schools before education became a matter for state legislation. The development of that 'dual system' may have been a pragmatic solution to the complex situation existing at the time, but it has proved remarkably resilient and adaptable to the country's needs following its creation by the Education Act of 1870 and entrenchment in the Education Act of 1944 and all subsequent education legislation.

However, that does not mean that the integration of schools having a religious character within a comprehensive state system was universally accepted in the years immediately following the end of the Second World War. One writer, clearly not a supporter of faith based education, noted regretfully *"the decrepit 'Dual System' escapes unscathed"* (Richmond, 1965). Nevertheless, he looked forward to the provisions of the Act producing a thriving secular and (almost) religion free national education service.

> *Some of the old Church schools will eventually, like rotten fruit, fall into the State bag. By gentlemanly agreement they will be known as 'Controlled ' but in everything else but name they will become secularised. The others will carry on, in premises falling into further disrepair, peddling catechisms and formularies under the name of religion to children whose general education will have been compromised to purchase this Bill's safe conduct. But the final verdict will be that it [the 1944 Education Act] was worth it."*
>
> (Richmond, W. K., 1945, p. 171)

In retrospect, perhaps, its most worthwhile achievement was the seeming resolution of the religious antagonisms that had plagued educational development for so long. For almost fifty years, and until very recently, the debate about the place of church schools within the national state maintained system became notable for its absence. They became an accepted and totally acceptable element of the state system. It has only been in the last decade that their existence and value has again become a matter for heated public discussion. It is arguable that the renewed interest has been generated mainly by the prospect of a rise in the number of state supported Muslim schools but, whatever the reasons, once the debate was re-ignited, objections have been focused on a generalised concept of 'faith schools', as if they all have the same character and fundamental purposes. It is not at all clear why that is the case. It may be simply a lack of understanding or, possibly, evidence of an increasingly aggressive secular ideology. However, rather than pursuing the intricacies of the debate as they apply to all the differing faith based schools, this chapter focuses on the main elements in relation to the maintained Catholic sector.

A SUMMARY OF OBJECTIONS

Objections to Catholic schools in England come from a variety of ideological, philosophical and social perspectives. Some argue that religious belief is an irrational delusion, inimical to a liberal society and, consequently, harmful to individuals and the integrity of the state. In its most extreme form this argument claims that religion is the cause (or at least a major determinant) of war and conflict.[1]

Others, less dramatically, do not attack religion *per se* but argue that religious belief and practice, and therefore religious education, should not have any place in the public affairs of a secular liberal society; that it is solely a private matter.[2] Arguments are put forward to the effect that religious education is a form of indoctrination and, consequently, confessional schools should have no place in any educational system.[3] Further objections include claims that Catholic schools erode social cohesion and/or enhance social division,[4] limit the personal autonomy of children,[5] seek to entrench parental authority over children's human rights,[6] damage other schools through their admissions practices,[7] deny social justice for atheists or those adhering to other faiths[8] and enjoy unjustified privileged financial support from government.[9] This chapter will attempt to give an outline of those arguments and briefly comment on the points that are raised; the most important of which will be considered in greater detail in later chapters.

RELIGIOUS BELIEF – UNIQUELY DANGEROUS AND IRRATIONAL

There are those who assert that religious belief is irrational, a danger to (rational) society and, therefore, undesirable. Consequently, schools having a religious character must also be undesirable and, if they are already in existence, should be suppressed or so constrained as to prevent them fulfilling their religious purposes. An extreme form of this argument was espoused by the totalitarian regimes established in the names of bolshevism, fascism, national socialism and communism. In order to sustain the charge that religion is uniquely dangerous to either individuals or the state, it must be shown that other world views are necessarily benign. Yet, as the history of the twentieth century has shown so clearly, states espousing secularist or atheistic ideologies have proved just as capable as theocracies of causing untold harm to their citizens and neighbours.[10]

Even if one abandons the claim that religion is an inherent danger to human existence and well-being, the charge associating theism with irrationality remains present. However, it is difficult to see how it is possible to sustain an argument that all theist philosophers from the Greeks onward have been irrational. It is true, for example, that some may not find the five ways to demonstrate, or 'prove', the existence of God described by Aquinas intellectually convincing, but to claim they are the product of an irrational mind is nonsense. A belief in God can be as much a rational conclusion derived from the evidence available to our senses and reason as non-belief; each as 'provable' in the scientific sense as the other. On that basis, the claim that religious belief must be actually, or potentially, harmful to our, or any, society is just as suspect. A less extreme position accepts that while religious beliefs are not necessarily irrational, schools should not involve themselves in inculcating any unproven and/or unprovable forms of understanding. Since theistic (and atheistic) beliefs cannot be proved in any scientific sense, it continues, they should not form part of the school curriculum and, therefore, Church schools having a confessional approach to religion are suspect. Provability is, however, a particularly weak criterion on which to base an argument for singling out Catholic education as being uniquely problematic. Much of what is generally regarded as appropriate to teach in schools cannot be proven in any scientific sense and can be highly subjective or contentious, for example, history, literature, any form of artistic appreciation and all value judgements. Some might even exclude science on the basis of Popper's view that scientific knowledge is not true, simply not yet found to be false.[11] To exclude all contentious matters from schools would ensure a very impoverished form of education.

RELIGION IN A SECULAR SOCIETY

Given the fact of diverse views and understanding about the nature of humanity and the purpose (if any) of our existence, the secular perspective argues that, to avoid social disintegration and conflict, all world views should be regarded as having equal value. This form of social pragmatism does not imply, of course, that all world views have moral equivalence or that the state's neutrality requires individuals to hold a similar view. It is a perspective demanding that a particular social or religious doctrine should not be imposed on those who do not share that opinion. (While this position would be accepted in most plural democracies, it appears to come under strain wherever people do not share all the doctrinaire propositions of secular liberalism).

In respect of education, the secular argument for state neutrality towards religious belief can result in a range of relatively benign policies intended to enhance mutual understanding and sustain social cohesion. One such approach advocates excluding any form of religious education from state schools. Another requires state schools to teach about religions generally but to refrain from inculcating any particular religion. Each has their champions. Both these versions depend upon on two key contestable assumptions: that education is a matter of public concern while religion is entirely private. A third policy option is for the state to support schools, either fully or partially, of differing philosophical and religious persuasions.[12] This is the policy currently in place in England that is now under attack from some sources.

> Those who make education policy have a duty to promote inter-communal understanding, social cohesion and good citizenship by vigorously supporting integrated schools, and the shared values and multi-belief religious education that are common in good community schools
>
> (Mason, M., 2001, p. 2)

However, the truth of the underlying assumptions for the above view is not self-evident but open to serious challenge.

[The secular argument's] premises include that education is a matter of interest to the state and not to parents, even though parents may have important transcendent beliefs to pass on to their children; that education be narrowly defined in the interests of the state; and that religion per se is not desirable. Failure to accept any one of those three premises makes the secular educational project suspect.

(Holmes, M., 1992, p. 86)

EDUCATIONALLY DEFICIENT

There are two main stands to this argument. One is that, in schools with a religious character and purpose, the time devoted to religious instruction and practice must detract from the subject areas that form the secular curriculum so inhibiting pupils' education progress. The second is allied to, and often underpins, the assertions that anything other than teaching *about* religion, much in the manner of that an anthropologist might utilise, cannot be an educational experience but *must* be a form of indoctrination.

If it were true that pupils attending Catholic schools were consistently failing to achieve the educational standard expected by the state, and that the time devoted to religious matters in Catholic schools could be proven, without qualification, to be the reason for such a lack of educational progress, then the objection might carry some weight. While it is the case that individual Catholic schools have not always provided a satisfactory standard of education, reports from the government's inspectors show that this particular objection to the sector as a whole is entirely without foundation. On the contrary, the evidence shows that Catholic schools, on average, are less likely to have unacceptably low educational standards than do secular community schools.[13]

The more serious assertion is that Catholic schools are educationally deficient because their pupils are subject to indoctrination. Because of a lack of hard data, the merits of this claim are harder to evaluate than those of low educational standards. The main difficulty is that indoctrination is a concept for which it is extremely hard to formulate a universally accepted definition.[14] This has not, however, prevented its use against religious based schools. In its starkest form, the argument can be put as follows:[15]

(1) faith schools teach children to believe in religious propositions;

(2) no religious proposition is known to be true;

(3) teaching for belief in propositions not known to be true is indoctrination;

(4) under no circumstances should any school indoctrinate its pupils; therefore

(5) faith schools should not be tolerated.

However, to make the charge of indoctrination stick, opponents of Catholic schools need to go beyond the rather simplistic argument outlined above and show more precisely what is objectionable. This will involve consideration of lesson content, pedagogic methodology and/or the teachers' intentions.[16]

A balanced perspective would probably acknowledge that in respect of lesson content and methodology every teacher in every school at some stage in the educational process has, to some extent, to indoctrinate in the sense that they do not and cannot always produce sufficient reason for every statement or proposition they put to their pupils. Valid reasons may, of course, exist. The teacher may not fully understand or know the reasons themselves (for example, much of quantum physics); the pupils may not be intellectually able to grasp the reasons at that period of their development and, since there is insufficient time available to explain everything, some things have to be taken on trust when stated by a recognised authority. As a matter of necessity and practicality, good teachers (and parents) will use indoctrinatory methods with infants for most of the time; with more mature, reasoning young adults hardly at all.

Further, it should be recognised that teaching is not solely a didactical process. Teachers cannot help but display actions, attitudes and values that may not be expressed in words but still impact upon the pupils. It is simply not possible for them to refrain from using anything other than reason in their interaction with their pupils and so, in those terms, the charge of indoctrination can be levelled at every teacher in any school. Indeed, it can be argued that some societal values and moral norms must be accepted as given, in order that a child can begin to make sense of the social environment in which they are growing up.[17] The process of socialisation cannot be achieved solely through the child's own individual and uninfluenced reasoned evaluation of the available evidence. Perhaps the argument is really about which attitudes and beliefs are inculcated in this way.

In terms of curriculum content and pedagogic methodology employed in schools, the claim that they must necessarily indoctrinate their pupils is not so clear-cut as their opponents sometimes assert. Nor is it obvious that the purpose or intention of teachers in such schools must necessarily be intended to treat pupils in such a way as to actively prevent them develop open and questioning minds.[18] This is not to deny, of course, the possibility of unacceptable indoctrination in religious based schools, but the possibility does not imply actuality, and it must be remembered that secular schools are open to exactly the same objections.

> *Secular schools ... are not ideologically free zones. Secularism has its own ideological assumptions about the human person, the ideal society, the ideal system of schooling and the meaning of human existence. While these assumptions may not be formally codified into a curriculum subject designated 'secular education' as an alternative to 'religious education', they characteristically permeate the ethos and culture of state-provided secular schools and form a crucial part of the 'hidden curriculum'.*
> (Grace, G., 2002, p. 14)

> *Our everyday reality is constructed for us out of a lengthy social history ... the most powerful effect ... [of which] has been the dominance of an array of metaphors for reality... [that are] sufficiently great in contemporary industrial Europe to act as an unintentional indoctrination [and] these pictures of reality are often taken ... to be absolute statements, indeed, true doctrines.*
> (Hay, D., 1985, p. 140-41)

> *We can of course point to clear cases of indoctrination, examples where people have been bullied into accepting propositions or practices whose meaning they may not understand but these show that indoctrination cannot be explicated simply by reference to content or to methods. We may see what is unacceptable in the particular case but this cannot be generalised into a set of defining (necessary and sufficient) conditions. Presenting false or even incoherent claims may not be indoctrination (consider physics teaching a century ago) and nor may the unreasoned inculcation of truths (consider language teaching at any time). Some forms of religion are [indoctrinatory] but it does not follow that all are unless one simply insists on regarding any imparting of religious beliefs and practices as educationally unacceptable.*
> (Haldane, J., 1986, p. 168)

PERSONAL AUTONOMY

Closely allied to the charge of indoctrination is the claim that Catholic schools violate the child's personal autonomy both through the religious education curriculum they employ and the everyday attitudes, values and practices they adopt by virtue of their religious character. In respect of religious education, the 'autonomy argument' makes the point that children are unable to make fully informed choices between different and essentially contentious world views. Thus, it continues, any attempt to provide religious instruction for young children must tend towards unacceptable forms of indoctrination.

> *... given the importance of fundamental religious and value commitments to a person's life, such commitments should be entered into only subject to all the normal requirements for valid consent: in particular, competence, full information and voluntariness. Religious schools ... are likely to violate these requirements, partly because of (younger) children's lack of autonomy and partly because of the nature of such schools' missions. ... teaching about different religions is acceptable according to the autonomy argument. What is not acceptable is religious instruction ...*
>
> (Humanist Philosophers Group, 2001, p. 10)

The same charge could, or course, be made of any form of introduction to differing world views, whether coming from a theistic, humanistic or other philosophical perspective.[19]

In making the claim that personal autonomy is the supreme good, the opponents of Catholic schools are, it can be argued, placing complete faith in the value of human reason as the sole route to truth. This is an act of faith on their part, directly comparable to the religious belief they oppose, since there can be no conclusive empirical support for it.[20] Indeed, a case can be made that personal autonomy, as understood in its ordinary or philosophically technical senses, cannot constitute a viable educational aim.[21] Even if the contention was true, it is difficult to see how the necessary conditions for personal autonomy, in the sense of enabling people to make totally free choices, can be established - unless one lives in complete isolation from all external influences. That is not the human experience.

The contrary argument is that young children cannot help but be initiated into an existing culture (whether religious or otherwise) which provides the framework references without which their acquisition of useful knowledge would be impossible.[22] Consequently, children have to simply accept many things in order to progress towards a level of personal autonomy where they can accept or reject through reasoning that which they have formerly taken on trust. This argument seems to imply that the debate about the desirability or otherwise of Catholic schools is not about a clash of polar absolutes, autonomy or indoctrination, but a question of degree and definition. If that is accepted, the debate can be characterised as differing pedagogical views about how schools manage the gradual process from intellectual dependence to independence as the child matures over a period of several years and how best to ensure that progression.[23]

Proponents of Catholic schools could argue that the general and religious curriculum, together with the religious environment they provide, enables pupils to experience a faith community which may be essential to the achievement of a level of understanding that makes autonomous, informed consent, or rejection, possible.[24] Opponents might still argue that the experience offered by Catholic schools is a unique mixture of direct and more subtle forms of indoctrination that negate personal autonomy. However, the dispute would then be centred on the acceptability or otherwise of the specific educational practices actually employed, rather than a general assertion of the superiority of philosophical and theological beliefs. If it were moved onto that ground there might even be the possibility of an agreed resolution.

HUMAN RIGHTS

There are a number of arguments that highlight the rights of parents to determine the form of education their children receive. Within the context of the faith school debate, their general thrust is that if parents are responsible for the well-being of their children, and they believe that education within a religious faith to which they adhere is beneficial for their children's growth, then they should be able to send them to schools that provide an education in accordance with their convictions.

There are two main objections to this position. One accepts the central proposition of parental rights in the matter of their children's education, but argues that the state should not be expected or required to support such schools. If parents want a religious based education they must finance it themselves. The second points to tensions between parental rights over their children and the human rights of the children themselves. The case is made that parents do not own their children and that education is for the child's benefit not that of the parents. This argument, however, begs the question as to the content and methodology involved in an appropriate form of education, and who is to determine the answer.

As discussed above, there is a view that religious instruction is incompatible with the development of personal autonomy. If autonomy is to be regarded as the highest possible good arising from compulsory education, and if the development of autonomy depends on authority being removed from religious parents then, some may argue, that authority should be removed. Clearly, there are forms of child rearing and educational practice that are totally unacceptable, and in such instances it is right for the state to intervene because the child's human rights should 'trump' those of parents. Legislation outlawing corporal punishment and determining a national curriculum are examples of such intervention. Others include, in extreme cases, taking children into care or restricting parental access. However, simply transferring control from parents to the state does not, of itself, ensure a resolution of the problem. There is no guarantee that the state will necessarily be a benign or unbiased influence. In England, the state has rightly been very wary of intervening in such matters simply on the basis of the form of religious instruction as practised in Catholic schools. To do so would be the first steps towards secular totalitarianism.

DIVISIVE AND EXCLUSIVE

When considering these two particular charges, it is important to clarify the meaning attached to them before coming to a judgement as to whether they are true. If the claims are proven within the context of an agreed meaning, then it can be seen whether assertions that such attributes are socially damaging are supported by the available evidence.

If, by divisive, the claim is that all children do not all attend the same school, or type of school, and therefore do not meet children of all other social, cultural or religious backgrounds and do not receive the same sort of education, then the criticism is trivial. Used in this sense it merely acknowledges the reality that no two schools can possible serve the same constituency. To take an extreme example, it is unlikely that are very many Yorkshire children in Cornish schools and vice versa. Even if it were the case that all schools did have a national representative mix of pupils, no two children can ever be exactly the same so the experience of any one individual would still differ depending on the particular school they attended. The fact that all children do not attend the same school cannot be shown to be the cause of actual societal harm. The opponents of Catholic schools seem, however, to be making much more serious charges; namely, that their existence actually generates societal discord, or that they are a manifestation of a form of inter-communal difference, of potential rivalry, that is of itself harmful. While these latter objections are more substantial, they simply articulate a theory that social differences are intrinsically harmful and, in the case of Catholic schools and the Catholic community, they still require an evidential base if the claims are to be sustained.

In response to argument that there is no empirical evidence to support the charge that Catholic schools in England cause social disharmony, opponents may point to Northern Ireland to support their case. To sustain the charge, however, they still have to show that the different types of school in Northern Ireland are the primary cause of community rivalry. Many would argue that they are not. In a similar, but less contentious way, opponents of Catholic schools may wish to argue that their very existence is a public mark of religious differences which (again pointing to Northern Ireland as a malign example) highlight and sustain incipient social discord. A counter view might suggest that such claims are not so much an argument that religious based schools are themselves harmful but that the very existence of different religious (or social, racial or cultural) groupings within a single state is problematical.[25] There is also an argument, of course, that in anything other than highly homogeneous countries, acceptance of human diversity may be generally beneficial. Neither proposition is, however, capable of empirical proof.

In contrast to the above, the charge that Catholic schools in England are not inclusive can be subject to empirical investigation. Nevertheless, there is again the question of the meaning ascribed to the term 'inclusive'. Traditionally, schools have been, or attempted to become, communities in their own right serving particular populations. Community is a complex concept but can be regarded as a discernible entity, often delineated by location or by cultural values and practices, in which individuals derive a sense of identity and worth. Cultural communities tend to share values, attitudes and practices; are often socially homogeneous; tend to be family orientated, nurturing and interactive in a variety of mutually reinforcing ways. Religious faith can be one of their main and most potent forming elements.

In the school context, especially since attendance is a matter of legal compulsion, the existence of shared values among parents or pupils does not necessarily imply that there is a community in the normal sense of the word, or that they necessarily help generate social coherence within the school population. It depends entirely upon the nature and context of the values. In order that a particular school population develops into a community there must be a willing adoption of a set of formative values[26] that generate a shared understanding of what comprises a good education and an involvement in common activities or projects that sustain and develop that communal understanding.

People who share such formative, or constitutive, educational values know what schools should be trying to achieve and how it might be morally accomplished, precisely because they agree on the essential character and purpose of human existence and the contribution that education makes to human flourishing. This description could almost be a paradigm of the history of voluntary educational provision in the U.K. where a clear example of constituent values in operation can be seen in the Catholic sector.[27] No organisation, institution or community that holds the sort of constituent values set out above can be totally inclusive. In one sense, therefore, the charge that Catholic schools are not inclusive is clearly upheld. Once again, however, that they cannot be totally inclusive does not mean that they are necessarily damaging to the state, but simply that the existence of different cultural communities is problematical in a pluralist society.

A second claim of lack of inclusiveness relates to the pupil intake of Catholic schools. The objection comes in two forms; either that preference in admissions is given to baptised Catholics, or that non-Catholics are not allowed to attend. The first version is manifestly true, as can be seen in the model criteria of admissions prepared for Catholic schools by their respective diocesan authorities. The second is demonstrably untrue.[28] However, given that successive governments have only allowed Catholic schools to be built where there is a proven Catholic demand/need, and that regulations require schools to have clear and unambiguous admission criteria in the event of over-subscription, it may well be the case that non-Catholics who apply for a place in a Catholic school are not admitted because of insufficient available places.[29] Where there are places, Catholic schools accept and educate significant numbers of non-Catholic pupils, though the basis of the educational enterprise and its activities inevitably remains rooted in a Catholic understanding of the nature and purpose of human existence. If they do not, then the school will not be Catholic, irrespective of the religious adherence of its pupils.

DISCRIMINATORY

A further, connected, objection claims that the existence of Catholic schools is a form of discrimination against non-Catholics, either because their admissions processes favour baptised Catholics or because their ethos, values, attitudes and practices are Catholic in character. In one sense the claim must be true, though a counter argument would assert that to deny baptised Catholic parents and their children the opportunity of a Catholic education in the existing Catholic schools is also discriminatory. The fact that they may discriminate in the senses outlined above does not, of itself, necessarily make them unacceptable in a liberal democracy.

FINANCIAL PRIVILEGE

Finally, the complaint is sometimes made that state support of faith schools places an unfair financial burden on those who do not share the particular faith. As such, the argument goes, Catholic schools are being given an unfair financial privilege. On the other hand, the provision of all public sector schools are financed out of general and local taxation, and so everyone is involved in providing for the education of the young irrespective of whether they have children who need to be educated. Proponents of Catholic schools would argue that, rather than being financially privileged, they have to accept a greater financial burden in order to ensure an appropriate education for their children than those subscribing to different philosophical positions. Not withstanding the financial contribution made by the Catholic community towards the initial provision of its schools, it may be the case that, because of their dispersion and relative scarcity, over the life of the school there may be additional costs to society, for example, in providing transport to enable baptised Catholic children to have a Catholic education. This does not mean, however, that Catholic schools are necessarily more costly to maintain than similar community schools, those located in rural areas, or those serving children with particular educational needs. Even if they are **always** the most expensive, it is still not a particularly strong reason for their abolition. There are many instances where the achieving equity in outcomes for differing social or regional groups requires an unequal distribution of national resources.

SUMMARY

The purpose of this chapter has been to provide a brief but, hopefully, balanced summary of the range of objections that have been raised about

Catholic schools (and other religious based institutions) in recent years. All have counter arguments that can be made in their defence, some of which are outlined. The responses of proponents of the Catholic sector to the more serious charges are extended and amplified in succeeding chapters.

NOTES

1   These objections are grouped together because they have the same underlying view that religious belief in all its manifestations is "a bad thing". Clearly not all critics raise all these objections on all occasions. However, the government's encouragement for new faith based schools in 2001, and re-asserted in 2007, led to the publication of a number of these opinions, or variants of them, by, among others: Grayling, A. C. (2001) Keep God out of public affairs, *The Observer*, Sunday, August 12th; Toynbee, P. (2001) Keep God out of class, *The Guardian*, Friday November 9th; Beckett, F. (2001) Holier than thou, *The Guardian*, Tuesday November 13th; Dawkins, R. (2001) Children must choose their own beliefs, *The Observer*, Sunday December 30th; Gillard, D. (2002) Glass in their snowballs – the faith school debate, *Forum*, 44. 1. 15-23; Porteus-Wood (2004) Scale down religious schools or face a disaster for race relations, *National Secular Society*, 9th June; National Secular Society (2007) The public don't want more faith schools, and they will be divisive, *http// www.secularism.org.uk* (accessed 10th September 2007).

2   See, for example, Copson, A. (2006) Why education should not divide on faith, Westminster Forum, 24th April, *http://Ekklesia.co.uk/content/features/article_060428faithschools.shtml,* accessed 14th December 2006; Humanist Philosophers Group (2001), *Religious Schools: The Case Against,* London, British Humanist Association; Grayling, A. C. (2001) Keep God out of public affairs, *The Observer*, Sunday, August 12th 2001

3   See, for example, Hand, M (2003) A Philosophical Objection to Faith Schools, *Theory and Research in Education*, 1. 1. 89-99; Toynbee, P. (2006) This is a clash of civilisations – between reason and superstition, *The Guardian*, Friday April 14th.

4   See, for example, Passmore, B. & Barnard, N. (2001) Voters oppose expansion of faith schools, *Times Educational Supplement*, 30th November 2001; Hansard (2002) *Report of the debate on the Education Bill 2002*, Columns 577 to 587, London, House of Lords 17th June 2002; Local Government Association (2002) *Education Bill*, Education Policy Review Meeting, March 2002, London, Local Government House; Office Of The Deputy Prime Minister (2004) *Social Cohesion: Sixth Report of Session 2003-04*, Vol. 1, 23-29, London, House of Commons; Porteus-Wood, K. (2004) Scale down religious schools or face a disaster for race relations, *National Secular Society*, 9th June, http//www.secularism.org.uk (accessed 9th June 2004); National Secular Society (2007) The public don't want more faith schools, and they will be divisive, *http//www.secularism.org. uk* (accessed 10th September 2007); September Association of Teachers & Lecturers (2007) *Faith Schools Position Paper*, http://www.atl.org.uk/atl_en/images (accessed March 26th 2007).

5   See, for example, Humanist Philosophers Group (2001), *Religious Schools: The Case Against,* London, British Humanist Association; Marples, R. (2006) Review: Faith Schools; Consensus or Conflict, *British Journal of Educational Studies*, 54. 2. 250-251; Leahy, M. (1990) Indoctrination, evangelization, catechesis and religious education, *British Journal of Religious Education*, 12. 3. 137-144.

6   See, for example, Mason, M. (2003) Religion in schools: a rights-based approach, *British Journal of Religious Education*, 25. 2. 117-128; Marples, R. (2005) Against faith schools: a philosophical

argument for children's rights, *International Journal of Children's Spirituality*, 10. 2. 133-147; Parker-Jenkins, M. (2005) The legal framework for faith-based schools and the rights of the child, in: R. Gardner, J. Cairns & D. Lawton (eds) *Faith Schools: Consensus of Conflict?*, London, RoutledgeFalmer.

7   See, for example, West, A. & Hind, A. (2003) *Secondary school admissions in England: Exploring the extent of overt and covert selection*, London, Centre for Educational Research, Department of Social Policy, London School of Economics and Political Science; West, A., Hind, A. & Pennell, H. (2004) *School admissions and 'selection' in comprehensive schools: Policy and practice*, London, Centre for Educational Research, Department of Social Policy, London School of Economics and Political Science; West A. (2006) School choice, equity and social justice: the case for more control, *British Journal of Educational Studies*, 54. 1. 15-33; Chamberlain, T., Rutt, S. & Fletcher-Campbell, F. (2006) *Admissions: Who goes where? Messages from the statistics*, Local Government Association Research Programme Report 4/05, Slough, National Foundation for Educational Research; Gibbons, S., Machin, S. & Silva, O. (2006) *Competition, Choice and Pupil Achievement*, London, Centre for the Economics of Education, London School of Economics; Association of Teachers & Lecturers (2007) *Faith Schools Position Paper*, http://www.atl.org.uk/atl_en/images (accessed March 26th 2007).

8   See, for example, Mason, M. (2001) Faith Based Schools: The Humanist View, debate at the Royal Society of Arts, 18th October, *http://www.humanism.org.uk/site/cms/contentarticle=1272*, (accessed 14th December 2006); McMahon, A (2002) in: *Hansard Debate on the Education Bill 2002*, column 919, 6th February 2002; Brighouse, H. (2003) Faith-based schools in the UK: an unenthusiastic defence of a slightly reformed status quo, *Philosophy of Education Society of Great Britain Newsletter 2002-2003*, 31-32.

9   See, for example, Willis, P. in: *Hansard (2002) Official Report, Standing Committee G*, 10TH January 2002; Dawkins, R. (2004) *Appeal for an end to state-subsidised faith schools*, London, National Secular Society, http://www.secularism.org.uk/32999.html, accessed 30th June 2005; Association of Teachers & Lecturers (2007) *Faith Schools Position Paper*, http://www.atl.org.uk/atl_en/images (accessed March 26th 2007).

10   See Burleigh, M. (2005) *Earthly Powers*, London, Harper Collins; Burleigh, M. (2006) *Sacred Causes*, London, Harper Collins.

11   Popper, K. (1959) *The Logic of Scientific Discovery*, London, Routledge.

12   See, for example, the educational systems in Holland, Belgium and Australia. An outline of these systems and for opposing views on state support of denominational schools is well made by De Jong, J. & Snik, G. (2002) Why should states fund denominational schools? *Journal of Philosophy of Education*, 36. 4. 573-587.

13   Evidence available from government and other sources is outlined in chapter 8.

14   See Theissen, E. J (1993) *Teaching for Commitment: Liberal Education, Indoctrination and Christian Nurture,* Leominster, Gracewing, which defends religious nurturing and instruction against the charge of indoctrination by, among other means, formulating *"a new ideal of liberal education … a new lead definition of indoctrination"* (see preface). Theissen argues that the initiation of children into a particular religious tradition should not be pejoratively labelled indoctrination in the sense of an immoral and indefensible activity and that, while some forms of faith based upbringing and schools can indoctrinate children, that they actually do so is not as evident, inevitable or even as probable as opponents claim.

15 See Hand, M. (2003) A philosophical objection to faith schools, *Theory and Research in Education*, 1. 1. 89-99. Also the associated correspondence, Short, G. (2003) Faith schools and indoctrination: a response to Michael Hand, *Theory and Research in Education*, 1. 1. 331-341; Siegel, H (2004) Faith, knowledge and indoctrination: a friendly response to Hand, *Theory and Research in Education*, 2. 1. 75-83; Groothuis, D. (2004) On not abolishing faith schools: a response to Michael Hand and H. Siegel, *Theory and Research in Education*, 2. 2. 177-188; Hand, M. (2004) The problem with faith schools: a reply to my critics, *Theory and Research in Education*, 2. 3. 343-353: Mackenzie, J. (2004) Religious upbringing is not as Michael Hand describes, *Journal of Philosophy of Education*, 38. 1. 129-142; Tan, C. (2004) Micheal Hand, indoctrination and the inculcation of belief, *Journal of Philosophy of Education*, 38. 2. 257-267.

16 See, for example, the discussion of the nature of indoctrination in Barrow R. & Woods, R. (1975) *An Introduction to Philosophy of Education*, London, Methuen, chapter 5, pp. 63-78. The necessary conditions concerning content, intention and methodology are discussed using as its context an imaginary description of Catholic education which the authors call "a paradigm case of indoctrination" (§3, p. 64). The discussion that follows shows, quite clearly, that the influences Catholic Church expects its schools and their teachers to bring about in its schools (see endnote 18) does meet the paradigm they present. *"To influence is not in itself to indoctrinate. Provided that children are ultimately brought to examine for themselves the various moral values that are adhered to within a society and which they have been initially brought to conform to, they have not been indoctrinated"* (p. 74). See also, Thiessen, E. J. (1993), particularly chapter 4, pp. 87-110; Mitchell, B. (1900) *How to Play Theological Ping-Pong: Collected Essays on Faith and Reason*, London, Hodder & Stoughton, chapter 6, pp. 88-97.

17 The philosopher Roger Scruton argues that there are three distinct kinds of knowledge: knowledge *that,* knowledge *how,* and knowledge *what.* The first kind of knowledge is information (of which science is the systematic part); the second is skill; the third virtue. They correspond to the three inputs into a rational life: facts, the means and ends. Knowing what to do (the ends) in various circumstances is a matter both of right judgement and right feeling. He argues, that the virtuous person 'knows what to feel', and this means feeling what the situation requires: the right emotion, towards the right object, on the right occasion and in the right degree. Moral education has just such knowledge as its goal: it is an education of the emotions. This form of knowledge, or understanding, is obtained/developed within the context of the group or community. It is communal living within a common culture that enables individuals to learn how and what to feel, and in doing so raises their lives to the ethical plane, where the thought of judgement inhabits whatever they do. For a much fuller explanation of these ideas and his definition/explanation of the nature of culture see: Scruton, R. (1998) *An Intelligent Person's Guide to Modern Culture*, London, Duckworth.

18 On the contrary, documents from the Catholic Church encourage forms of teaching in its schools and institutions of higher education that conform to modern methods and seek open-mindedness in its students. See, for example, Sacred Congregation for Catholic Education (1977) The Catholic School, § 31. *"It [the school] must develop persons who are responsible and inner-directed, capable of choosing freely in conformity with their conscience."*

See also Nichols, V. (2006a) Oral Evidence taken before the Education and Skills Select Committee on citizenship education, Monday 11th December 2006, Questions 609-708, HC 147-I, Uncorrected transcript, *http://www.publications.parlament.uk/pa/cm200607/cmselect/cmduski/uc*, accessed 9th January 2007. In answer to a question put to him by the Select Committee for Education (Q646) about the possibilities for pupils to debate contentious issues in Catholic schools, the Archbishop of Birmingham stated, *"According to the age of the children I would expect this [teachers to encourage debate and controversy ... or somebody either in the class or the teachers' put(ting) an opposing viewpoint to the teachings of the Church] in any class, and certainly I would expect it in an RE class ...".*

See also the section in chapter 8 subtitled, 'Possible Beneficial School Effects - Pupil Attitudes'

19 Although philosophical disputes about the perceived clash between a religious upbringing and the liberal ideal of personal autonomy usually discuss the issues solely within the context of religious belief, it has been pointed out that the term 'religious matters' covers not simply theistic but also atheistic and agnostic perspectives of human existence. See, Gardner, P. (1991) Personal autonomy and religious upbringing: the 'problem', *Journal of Philosophy of Education*, 25. 1. 69-81.

20 Gardner draws attention to the argument that the liberal's apparent commitment to neutrality and individual searches for the 'truth' is founded, in fact, upon a pre-established agnosticism. See Gardner, P. (1991) Personal autonomy and religious upbringing: the 'problem', *Journal of Philosophy of Education*, 25. 1. 69-81, p. 79.

21 See Hand, M. (2006) Against autonomy as an educational aim, Oxford Review of Education, 32. 4. 535-550.

22 See Altena, P., Hermans, C. A. M. & Scheepers, P. L. H. (2004) Dependent autonomy: towards a contextualised and dialogic aim for moral education, *Journal of Empirical Theology*, 17. 2. 172-196.

23 Questions whether a religious based school promotes or inhibits the development of personal autonomy are discussed in much greater detail in Strike, K. (2003) – see bibliography. He makes a clear distinction between groups that share an "evaluative framework" or "comprehensive doctrine" (such as Catholicism in the USA) and those that subscribe to a "common way of life" and suggests that there is no reason why, in principle, a view of liberalism which holds autonomy as its central commitment should oppose faith schools simply because of their religious basis. He argues that the question of whether or not Catholic schools promote the personal autonomy of their students has far more to do with the character of the comprehensive doctrine that defines Catholicism than the fact they are faith-based schools. His conclusion is that Catholic schools are (probably) more capable of developing autonomous adults than their common, or public, school counterparts.

24 See the theological exploration of human freedom and autonomy in: Pope Benedict XVI, (2007) *Jesus of Nazareth*, London, Bloomsbury, pp. 202-204.

25 This view is based on the supposition that if all members of society shared the same beliefs and subscribed to the same practices there would be no divisions or rivalry between them. A moment's thought should serve to show that this is simply not the case. Think of a football or cricket 'local derby' match. Further, if an educational system is used to eliminate diversity in fundamental beliefs it would be, arguably, an abuse, because it would fail to respect the autonomy of those in their charge by indoctrinating them into a single totalitarian system.

26 It has been argued that no educational community can subscribe to a particular set of constituent values and at the same time have a neutral stance to differing conceptions of the 'good life' and a 'good education'. Liberal inclusiveness, therefore, which requires neutrality on such matters, cannot be the basis for a cultural community within a pluralistic society in any meaningful sense of that word. See Strike, K. A. (1999, 2000). Full details in bibliography.

27 The ideas developed in these paragraphs are derived from Strike, K. A. (1999) – see bibliography - who argues, albeit from an American perspective, that although many Catholic schools accept and educate non-Catholic students, the values that constitute Catholic schools as communities do not allow them to be fully inclusive in the sense understood by secular liberalism. Despite his acceptance that students accrue genuine educational benefits when they attend schools organised

around constitutive values (such as Catholic schools) he seems to accept the rationale in the USA for the allocation of such institutions having, what he terms, "high constitutiveness", to the private rather than the public education sector.

28 See discussion in chapter 8. Also, Catholic Education Service (2003) *Catholic Education: A CES Position Paper on Catholic Education in Schools and Sixth Form Colleges*, London, CES; Catholic Education Service (2006) *Quality and Performance: A Survey of Education in Catholic Schools*, London, CES; Phillips, T. (2005) *After 7/7: Sleepwalking to segregation*, speech given at the Manchester Council for Community Relations 22nd September 2005, http://www.cre.gov.uk (accessed 28th March 2006).

29 Arising from discussions between the Secretary of State for Education and Archbishop Nichols during the passage of the Education and Inspections Bill 2006, an agreement was reached that, for the first time in over half a century, would allow Catholic authorities to build schools having up to 25% additional places over and above Catholic need in the area concerned, dependent upon local political agreement. See Hansard (2006) *Debate on the Education and Inspection Bill*, 2nd November, Col. 481. Also, Johnson, A. (2006) *Letter to Archbishop Nichols from the Secretary of State*, 26th October.

Chapter 3

A CASE FOR DIVERSITY – EDUCATIONAL PROVISION IN A PLURALIST SOCIETY

INTRODUCTION

This chapter draws heavily on the work of others[1] for its arguments support-ing the ideal of diversity in the state's educational provision. They are not necessarily concerned with making a case for Catholic schools. Their ideas have been utilised here, however, because they show that, within the existing legislative structures of the existing (compulsory) English maintained edu-cational system, solid arguments can be made that it is both reasonable and sensible for the state to allow or even encourage diversity in the character of the schools it is prepared to support financially.[2] Historically, in England, such claims have been made, mainly, by different Christian denominations. In the increasingly socially diverse society found in Britain at the beginning of the third millennium, other groups, perhaps most notably Muslims, could use similar socio-cultural and philosophical arguments.

In Western liberal democracies, governments derive their legitimacy and authority from the totality of their electorate. Though it is difficult to define exactly the boundaries of that authority, it is generally acknowledged that there are limits. In some matters a government may act on behalf of an individual with or without their consent. However, it is accepted that it should not act against the individual's declared wishes[3] except for some very good reason, for example, to avoid serious harm to others.[4] Recognition that the education of children is one area where the state's powers should be limited is found in the Human Rights declarations of the United Nations[5] and the Council of Europe,[6] the principal elements of which have been incorporated into English Law.[7]

THE PROBLEM

It might seem reasonable, given the general decline in formal religious practice during the latter half of the 20th century, to assume there would be a corresponding support for purely secular educational goals. This clearly is not the case. Although religious practice generally appears to be in overall decline in western democracies, in some countries religious based schooling is thriving[8]. While in England there may be fewer people who regularly attend church than there used to be (although non-churchgoers often use religious labels to categorize themselves) and increasing numbers who claim no religious affiliation at all,[9] many parents do not accept that there is a middle way between a religious and a non-religious or totally secular education. In addition, increasing parental demand in recent years for choice as to where and how their children are educated, and the very nature of our relatively rich western, liberal, pluralistic,[10] democratic societies, seems to have generated rather than diminished major and overt philosophical disagreements about the educational process.

The existence of minority groups holding strong religious beliefs within a liberal democracy tests the state's commitment to the values of 'tolerance', 'open-mindedness' and 'rationality', especially in respect of the type of education it provides or allows. While it may favour a compulsory secular education designed to inculcate those liberal values, it is not easy to see how such a system, based on a world view that may be philosophically unacceptable to significant numbers of (religious) electors, is in any intrinsic way superior to a confessional religious education. Both face the claims of ideological indoctrination and there is no prima facie case that a secular ideology is necessarily more benign or beneficial than one rooted in particular religious beliefs.

Though some critics of organised religion deny the rationality of religious belief, it is the case that both theistic and atheistic thought can be reasonable and rational (though by definition one or other must be based on a false premise). Acceptance of this fact precludes a general attack by secularists on confessional religious education simply on grounds of irrationality. In the same way, though specific religious beliefs may be erroneous, that does not of itself provide sufficient reason to exclude them from society. It must be accepted, however, that theistic, atheistic and agnostic world-views are essentially contentious. Clearly, no religious doctrine or belief is universally agreed. They are not publicly testable in a scientific sense or beyond reasonable dispute. On the other hand, historical and philosophical enquiry, as well as personal experience, can provide cogent reasons both in favour of and against theism. None are undisputedly conclusive. Any suggested solutions to the demand for confessional religious education or instruction, will inevitably, therefore, remain matters of debate and legitimate disagreement.

It can be argued that the reality of England's liberal, pluralistic character and the history of its educational system probably precludes a single, agreed and acceptable common form of schooling. If that is so, some form of diversity of provision for minority groups remains a philosophical and practical necessity. However, a commitment to diversity cannot be open ended and, as a principle of public policy, is not a self-evident good. On the contrary, many assert that diversity of provision is undemocratic, discriminatory and a source of social unrest. Nevertheless, all western pluralistic societies offer some sort of choice in the matter of schooling they allow or provide, so perhaps the debate is not so much between common schools or diversity, but the limits and conditions of the choices that the state can and should support. The consequent political dilemma in any particular society is to find some equitable mechanism for reconciling contrary but politically acceptable world views.

DIFFERING PERSPECTIVES – SOME EDUCATIONAL IMPLICATIONS

What follows is, by necessity, a very brief exploration of the opposing socio-political positions of liberalism and communitarianism in respect of education. It does not pretend to do full justice to the complexities of their arguments. However, it should serve to highlight differing perspectives on the desirability of diversity in the state's provision.

Liberalism argues that the state should provide a neutral framework within which differing, and possibly conflicting, life-styles can exist in harmony and neither intrude nor pronounce on any of them, except to prevent harm to others. This is rooted in the idea that a community is a voluntary association of persons and that the legitimate exercise of group authority should be subject to the freedom of the individual. For those who hold that individualistic view, people must determine their values and beliefs for themselves in such a way that allows them to be adapted or changed in the light of personal experience and evidence. In respect of education, this approach would be concerned primarily with equipping children with the means of acquiring knowledge but should not involve any attempt to teach with authority about truths or values that lie beyond the actual experience and commitments of pupils. To do so, it is argued by some, would place unacceptable restrictions on their personal autonomy.

Taking that position at face value, if the sole function of education is to encourage, or oversee, the development of basic intellectual skills, the state should not seek to impose any schemes for education based on any particular understanding of what is true and good, no matter how widely held and deeply rooted such a view may be. Yet, in reality, governments do point to some underlying moral principles to justify their educational legislation,[11] and teachers cannot help but project and impose on their pupils some moral values and attitudes; if only their own. It is difficult to see, therefore, how this ideal of intellectual and moral autonomy can be realised in practice.[12]

There are two main arguments deployed against the individualistic premise. Some would argue that the emphasis on personal autonomy fails to recognise the necessary dependence of children and young people on significant others in their lives for their social and emotional well-being.[13] Even if one accepts the arguments about personal freedom, choices cannot be made in a vacuum. The greater part of a child's upbringing and education takes place in the informal surroundings of the home that is necessarily culture bound and cannot, for good or ill, fail to exert a profound influence. Again, even assuming the possibility of a culture-free upbringing, individuals can only choose from a pre-existing range of social and cultural views, each with their merits and deficiencies. This begs the question of how such potentially distinct perceptions of the good life can be available for children to choose between if not as a result of outside influence.[14] Critics also argue that individual freedom requires an assumption of a general commitment to a set of values that is not necessarily the case in a plural society.[15]

The contrasting communitarian perspective argues that liberal individualism underestimates the essentially collective nature of society in which people have rights and responsibilities towards each other. It would hold that society is more than an aggregate of distinct individuals and its character cannot simply be determined by the values and behaviour of those who comprise the majority group at any one time. While accepting that persons are distinct,[16] it would hold that individuals are bound together by shared needs, interests and sensibilities that are rooted in common traditions.

These assumptions also have implications for education. As before, schools exist to provide children with basic cognitive and practical skills in order that they may acquire, organise and express knowledge about themselves and their environment. However, the primary concern of education is with the transmission of existing culture, that is, the accumulated knowledge, understanding, attitudes and practices of a particular society. Where genuine pluralism is accepted by the state as a desirable feature for society, there may well be differing legitimate views of what is and what ought to be. Political philosophers recognise the dilemmas such contrasting perspectives may bring when applied to education, particularly so in multicultural societies where groups may define themselves in terms of their religious beliefs and practices. Some have attempted to show that faith based schools can fit either a liberal or communitarian paradigm. Others have attempted an intellectual reconciliation or, alternatively, argue that, within a liberal society such as our own, there is no straight-forward way of resolving the problem and recommend a compromise or accommodation between irreconcilable positions.[17]

For the Catholic Church the primary purpose of its schools is the transmission of Catholic truths and values. All other proper goals of education are secondary.[18] From this perspective, teachers could legitimately be expected to hold, or at least adopt, an agreed perception of 'the good life' with its concomitant values, attitudes and practices that are consistent with those of families whose children attend a Catholic school.

The above sketches are, of necessity, brief and incomplete, but the general outline of each and of their points of difference should be clear. For those who hold theistic views liberal individualism is flawed.[19] If one accepts that education is essentially concerned with the transmission of an established world view, and as such cannot fail to be committed to specific values and ways of life which are presented to the younger generation, two questions follow: what are the particular values and traditions and how should they be transmitted? Both impinge upon debates about who has responsibility for the education of children and the role that formal schooling should have in that process.

Within western democratic societies it is generally accepted that parents have the prime duty[20] to assist their children to become fully human persons and that the legitimate role of government is to provide legal force and financial support for this moral imperative.[21] For obvious reasons, society has so organised itself that parents are able to entrust part of their task to professional teachers who act in their place. Nevertheless, under the English legal system, the ultimate authority for education rests with parents. This supports the moral position taken by various churches against possible action from government that might violate a basic human right[22] and, at the same time, explains the conscience clauses in existing legislation relating to state schools. When parents exercise their rights by sending their children to independent or voluntary aided denominational schools that represent particular philosophies with which they are in sympathy or to which they adhere, it is unlikely they would want to opt out of elements of the education provided. However, the vast majority of parents send their children to state provided community schools where the benefit provided by conscience clauses are more obvious.

Where government provides or maintains schools at public expense it is right and proper that it should determine and implement public policy in respect of education. This will involve legislation, including statutory duties guidelines for local authorities and school governors but, if one accepts the arguments above, its education policies should ensure the greatest freedom for parents to have their children educated in accordance with their own philosophical and religious beliefs while maintaining the stability of the state and protecting individuals from harm.[23]

Recent parliamentary debates about diversity of provision within the English educational system illustrate political disagreements about educational purposes, its practice and the core function of a school. Some argue that it is, essentially, to serve the (economic and social) needs of a secular state. Others, that its primary purpose is to provide a service to parents.[24] The Catholic Church, while not denying the legitimate claims of the state, holds the latter position.

It can be argued that the state must maintain control over the content of education to ensure the maintenance of the liberal democratic ideal and of the coherence of the state itself. However, education is a value laden activity and if the core ideals of state sponsored schools are defined in such a way that they are acceptable to everyone, their ideological content will be minimal. They risk becoming little more than a general prohibition of intolerance, violence, and harm to others. Such limited values might allow a school to operate in a peaceful and harmonious manner but, without further development, are unlikely to generate strong parental commitment within a heterogeneous, pluralist society and so contribute little positive 'societal glue'. On the other hand, if those values are developed to give them greater content, they will inevitably become more contentious and, therefore, potentially divisive.

Those who strongly oppose the idea of a state monopoly in educational provision believe that society should value pluralism and, therefore, encourage parents to pass on their culture to their children by choosing the most appropriate school. The potential unintended dilemma arising from diversity in school provision might be a decreasing sense of identification with the nation state, so making a common, state maintained education less acceptable to tax payers.

Isaiah Berlin comments directly on the liberal-communitarian dilemma[25] when he describes how individuals might experience a lack of freedom in two distinct ways. One is to experience a lack of recognition as a self-governing autonomous individual; the second is where the socio/cultural or religious group to which one belongs is neither recognised nor given appropriate respect. In a specific comment on parental choice, he recognises their right to choose an education for their children as being an important freedom that should be preserved. He suggests that limiting their right (using the argument that it is necessary to do so in order that future freedoms might be supported) is not acceptable in a liberal society. He argues further against the notion that there is a hierarchy of human goods in which individual autonomy is accorded primacy. For Berlin, belonging can be just as important as autonomy and that human dignity does not depend solely on individual rights. He argues that belonging and autonomy are both human goods and therefore there should be a trade-off between them that will involve gains and losses. He suggests that liberals should be able to recognise the gains that can accrue from separate schools in terms of the cultural congruence and a sense of belonging they can provide and, in giving their support, they can accept the loss of individual autonomy. It only becomes problematic for liberals if personal autonomy is granted absolute status as the foundational human value. While there has to be some view about such matters, for Berlin, there is no logical necessity to accord that pre-eminent status to a culture free autonomy – even if such an ideal is attainable.

If one accepts Berlin's view, educational policy makers in a pluralistic society have to determine how schools can be provided in a way that is fair; that does not undermine the collective sense of a society; that accepts religion, culture, and language as important matters which parents legitimately wish to pass on to their children; that ensures some equality of opportunity as well as equity; that is efficient and that leads to high levels of educational outcome. Legislators could decide to impose one particular form of education through the state school system. However, such a strategy would run counter to the concept of a plural society. They may decide to allow diversity of provision under certain conditions designed to avoid damage to individuals or the state, or they may move towards a universal approach, but one that avoids, removes or circumvents any areas of contention between different groups so that it can become acceptable to all.[26]

REASONABLE SOLUTIONS

Generally speaking, western democracies have classified religion as an area in which pluralist variation is legitimate. That does not mean that anything claiming to be a religion will be considered legitimate (for example, scientology has often been excluded from the category), but the major world religions are usually accepted as such. Consequently, arguments underpinning an insistence upon a state sponsored monopolistic secular educational system hinges on two key assumptions: that education is of public concern and that religion is purely a private matter. Neither of those assumptions is universally accepted or intellectually unassailable.

If children are educated simply for the purposes of the state, it follows that any form of religious practice would be inappropriate in state provided schools, unless there was an established state religion to which the vast majority of the population subscribed or if the state were to determine that religion *per se* is desirable. In the latter instance, if there were variety in religious practice, it would make sense for them all to be equally supported. Such a decision may, of course, be unacceptable to atheists. If, on the other hand, the purposes of education are broader, for example, if they include the passing on of values and traditions from generation to generation, irrespective of their worth to the state, then the argument of the those holding strong religious beliefs that education should include the ideas that they consider to be of most worth has greater validity.

As outlined in chapter 1, the present dual system in England derives from legislation conceived and enacted within a predominately Christian mindset. As a result of the religious settlement in the 1944 Education Act, voluntary aided church schools are free to pursue religious instruction and worship in accord with their denominational norms and practices. Non-church and voluntary controlled schools are required to begin each day with a single act of collective worship and provide religious education, neither of which may be distinctive of any religious denomination.[27] Religious education was to be in accordance with an agreed syllabus. During the 1950s this was intended to be confessional in nature, that is, its aim was to nurture non-denominational Christianity and encourage civic virtue within a (nominally) Christian society. This approach proved unviable as society began to change in the following decades. Secularisation, increasing numbers of immigrants adhering to established but non-Christian religious beliefs, pedagogical challenges to the use of biblical sources in religious education and a general decline in religious practice all have had a destabilising impact on the socio-religious assumptions underlying the 1944 Education Act.

There are now in England a significant number of non-Christian communities, whose members are closely united by bonds of culture and religious faith. Many wish to establish schools in which their beliefs and traditions will be respected and transmitted to their children. The political response has been equivocal. While the present government seems supportive of their aspirations, most noticeably so in its unprecedented document *Faith in the System* (DCSF, 2007), others have argued that their perceived educational needs (and those of society at large) can best be met if their children attend the secular community schools.

If society accepts cultural and religious differences as a legitimate and/or desirable feature of a pluralistic state then such a proposition seems some-what contradictory. It does not seem realistic to argue that the educational aspirations of the religiously committed can be effectively met within a school, or by a syllabus, that only teaches children about religion as a social phenomenon. Simply learning about the differing forms of religious behaviour and worship that exist in a plural society is not the same as experiencing religious life. Furthermore, if, in an attempt to be culturally neutral, religious behaviour is presented without criticism or approval, little respect is being given to the particular religious practice of pupils or of their parents. Indeed, it could be argued that by using such an approach schools are, effectively, preventing children exploring and developing the experience they have at home, and are explicitly denying its value.

For children to learn how to worship God and develop the quality of that worship, interaction with others who experience and have experienced the influence of God in their everyday is required. These experiential conditions are not specific to religious worship, of course, but are a required element whatever the adored object. In the religious context, therefore, generalised teaching **about** religion(s) and forms of liturgical worship, almost as a form of an atheistic anthropology,[28] simply describes activities and ceremonies to children that may well be contrary to their existing cultural frames of reference, attitudes and beliefs. It will not help them worship, enlighten and deepen their understanding about what they already believe[29] or enable children from different backgrounds and beliefs to experience the acts of worship that they observe.

On the other hand, genuine respect for the beliefs and practices of a religious community does not require that everyone in society necessarily share them. It does, however, require that their real characters are recognised and accepted on their own terms in a positive and supportive manner. This implies more than simply allowing them to exist. Proper respect from the state, it could be argued, would be marked by providing mechanisms that enable communities wishing to educate their children in a relevant religious cultural environment to do so. Within the bounds of practicality, that represents the longstanding position of successive governments since 1870.[30]

Parents have a statutory duty to educate their children, but not necessarily in state maintained schools. However, where religious groups are sufficiently numerous, it has been generally accepted that the state may give appropriate financial support to help them establish suitable schools. This was the case with the Catholic Church under the settlement of 1944 and, it can be argued, should hold for other religio-cultural groups in today's multicultural society.

Religious groups, however, go beyond a minimal request for respect and have long argued that religion has an intrinsic value, not just for individuals, families, and communities, but also for the state.[31] Religion can add important substance to policy debates, particularly those, such as education, with moral connotations. Religion, it is argued, provides another perspective on human purpose and value, perhaps less materialistic and self-centred than our existing consumer society. Yet, paradoxically, even if its claims are true, the teaching and practice of (a specific) religion in state controlled schools is hard to defend because, almost by definition, a pluralist state should not impose religious doctrine. If a pluralist society is one where a variety of cultures and belief systems are present, accepted and valued, then it is impossible to imagine a monopolistic school system that can do justice to all those varied systems at one and the same time. Diversity, therefore, appears unavoidable;[32] a position that can be argued by libertarians on both the right and left of the political spectrum.[33]

That does not imply that religious communities should have an absolute right to state support to help them establish their own schools. Society has the right to prohibit activities if these can be shown to be harmful in some important ways and it is legitimate to invoke this right in educational contexts no less than in others. Thus, if a community group wish to create a school for teaching anti-social techniques or inculcating aggressively racist attitudes, or if children are deprived of basic educational needs because of an overemphasis on religious activities, the state has the right to intervene in the interests both of the children and of the wider society.

It is important to recognize that this caveat has no necessary or particular connection with Catholic schools, or other established church schools. In England, there is no evidence to show that they are educationally or socially harmful and hence there can be no general prima facie case against them on those particular grounds. Indeed, the consideration of parental rights, and the argument for the inseparability of culture and religion, suggests that there are solid socio-political and educational grounds for supporting denominational schools provided the ends towards which they are directed and the means they employ are not unreasonable.

SUMMARY
This chapter has tried to make the following case. That in a democracy such as our own:

- parents and society have a joint interest in the education of the child.
- any attempt to inculcate a state doctrine with children, irrespective of their parents' culture and religion, is to deny pluralism and to adopt a totalitarian mentality.
- the state has no right to determine the education of its citizens nor have parents an absolute right to choose any form of education for their children, especially if that choice may be detrimental for society.
- parents should be able to choose, within reasonable limits laid down by the state, an education for their children in conformity with their own beliefs and values.
- the state should not use the great power of compulsory education to eradicate (however unintentionally) cultures that do not threaten it and from which it may indeed benefit. However, it is legitimate for

the state to supervise the education of the young within a subculture, to ensure that reasonable standards and practices are being utilised.

The Catholic Church in England has always argued that the state should provide support for the education of legitimate minorities (of which it regards itself as being one) and that religious belief should be accepted as having a central role in education for those parents who wish it for their children. Just over seventy-five years ago the Catholic bishops agreed the following statement on education:

"Precisely the same facilities of education should be given to those who regard definite religious teaching as an essential part of education as to those who attach no such importance to teaching of that character." [34]

That formulation retains its potency today.

NOTES

1   For a fuller exposition of the philosophical arguments, see Haldane, J. (2004); Holmes, M. (1992); Berlin, I. (1969). Also Burtonwood, N. (1998, 2000, 2002, 2003) and De Jong, J. & Snik, G. (2002) - see bibliography.

2   Section 11(2) of the Education Act 1996 placed a duty on the Secretary of State for Education to *"… exercise his powers with a view to (among other things) improving standards, encouraging diversity and increasing opportunities for choice"*, while section 2 of the Education and Inspection Act 2006 places a similar responsibility on local authorities. The current government is actively promoting that diversity of provision, encouraging business leaders, entrepreneurs and different church or faith groups to establish schools particularly for the secondary sector. The policy has a number of detractors who argue, in particular about religious based schools, that they create or sustain social disharmony. These, and other objections to Church schools, will be dealt with in Chapter 8.

3   For some useful discussion of this important issue see 'On the Source of the Authority of the State' in: Anscombe, G. F. M. (1981), *Collected Philosophical Papers Volume III*, Oxford, Blackwell, pp .130-155.

4   Article 9 (2) of the European Convention on Human Rights, Freedom of Thought, Conscience and Religion: "Freedom to manifest one's religion or beliefs shall be subject only to such limitations as are prescribed by law and are necessary in a democratic society in the interests of public safety, for the protection of good order, health or morals, or for the protection of the rights and freedoms of others."

5   United Nations Declaration of Human Rights, article 26.

6   The Council of Europe. Protocol to the Convention for the Protection of Human Rights and Fundamental Freedoms, article 2.

7   The Human Rights Act, 1998 incorporated many of their basic principles into British law but such legislation does not necessarily place a responsibility on any government to provide a particular

type of school simply because some parents may want it. Conversely, in the UK any move to abolish existing faith-based schools against the interest and expressed desires of parents would seem to breach international conventions and conflict with current statutory provisions. These legal rights and responsibilities are debated further in chapters 6 and 7.

8   There is considerable evidence of the relative effectiveness of Catholic schools from a number of countries. The evidence will be considered in Chapter 8. In the USA, the fastest growing educational systems over the last decade have been those offering fundamentalist Christian education. In Canada, Roman Catholic schools (now fully publicly funded) are in the ascendant in Ontario and religious independent schools are growing in British Columbia and Alberta (thanks to partial government funding). In Australia, partially funded religious schools, notably Catholic schools, flourish as public schools decline and in the Netherlands, where there has been free choice among religious and secular schools since well before World War II, enrolments appear stable.

9   See, for example, analyses by Davie, G. (1994) *Religion in Britain since 1945*, Oxford, Blackwell; Gilbert, A. D. (1980) *The Making of Post-Christian Britain*, London, Longman; Brown, C. G. (2001) *The Death of Christian Britain*, London, Routledge; Bruce, S. (1995) *Religion in Modern Britain*, Oxford, Oxford University Press; Bruce, S. (2002) *God is Dead: secularisation in the west*, Oxford, Blackwell; Ashworth. J. & Farthing I. (2007) *Churchgoing in the UK*, Teddington, Tearfund.

10 In this context a pluralistic society is one in which, as an *a priori* good, differing life styles, beliefs and value systems are, in principle, accorded equal value. The state provides mechanisms that protect the various positions and refrain from giving its support to any particular viewpoint in order to promote the legal equality between diverse components of society and refrain from giving its support to any particular viewpoint. It accepts limits on its powers in order that minority beliefs and groups are protected from unwarranted state interference and, where necessary, supported to ensure equal access to the benefits that the state provides. Two differing views of the concept of pluralism are distinguished in: Dennis, N. (2001) *The Uncertain Trumpet*, London, Institute for the Study of Civil Society. One is 'strong', the other 'weak'. By strong pluralism he means situations in which definite, differing, conflicting and often incompatible positions were allowed and whose differences are acknowledged and respected; discourse between them is on the basis that some may be better than others in some ways or particulars. In contrast, weak secularism, is the view that all positions are equally valid and under which there exists a state of affairs in which no group can, as it were, 'fight its corner' or argue a case that it is in any sense better than any other. Norman argues that within a weak plural society any such attempt is usually regarded as a serious social solecism. This is despite the fact that the acceptance of any ideas or values must, logically, require a belief on some reasonable ground that they are superior to some others. If not, acceptance of any particular belief must, logically, be irrational.

11 See the emphasis that is currently placed by government upon the need to devise an educational system that is intended, primarily, to give pupils the necessary skills to increase the national Gross Domestic Product. For example see, DfES (2001), *Schools Achieving Success*, London HMSO; DfES (2001) *Schools Building on Success*, London HMSO; DfES (2003) *Education and Skills: the Economic Benefit*, London HMSO; DfES (2004) *Five Year Strategy for Children and Learners*, London HMSO; DfES (2005) *14-19 Education and Skills*, London HMSO.

12 It is not at all self-evident that the idea of personal autonomy, of which there are numerous competing definitions within philosophy, is defensible as an educational aim, despite its popularity with many educationalists. See Hand, M. (2006) Against autonomy as an educational aim, Oxford Review of Education, 32. 4. 535-550.

13 For example see Bowlby, J. (1953) *Child Care and the Growth of Love*, Harmondsworth, Penguin;

Breckenridge, M. E. & Vincent, E. L. (1955) *Child Development*, London, W. B. Saunders Company; Hostler, P. (1959*) The Child's World*, Harmondsworth, Penguin; Winnicott, D. W. (1964) *The Child, the family and the Outside World*, Harmondsworth, Penguin; Bowlby, J. (1988) Changing theories of childhood since Freud, in E. Timms & N. Segal (eds) (1988) *Freud in Exile*, New Haven, Yale University Press; Kraemer, S. (1993) Domestic Organisation and Personal Identity, *Annual Review*, Windsor, St. George's House; Whitfield, R. (1995) Educating for Family Life: from advocacy to investment and action, *The Month*, December, pp. 465-469; Whitfield, R. (1996) Security of Attachment: a necessary objective in taking ourselves and our children seriously, *Annual Review*, Windsor, St. George's House.

14 Children learn and are influenced within a social context determined by adults. Those involved might be parents, the apparatus of the state, commercial interests, the media, or a combination of them all to varying degrees. The debate is about who should have priority in the transmission of culture and how that might be best achieved. See, for example, the discussion in: Tan, C. (2004) Michael Hand, indoctrination and the inculcation of belief, *Journal of Philosophy of Education*, 38. 2. 257-267; also, Gardner, P. (1991) Personal autonomy and religious upbringing: the 'problem', *Journal of Philosophy of Education*, 25. 1. 69-81.

15 Disputes about freedom of speech and its use, as some see it, to denigrate a community's religious beliefs serves to illustrate the dilemma of two opposing general sets of values existing within a society.

16 Some challenge even the distinctness of persons, regarding them as parts of society standing to it as do organs to a body. John Haldane argues that this view is essentially incoherent, see Haldane J. (1985) Individuals and the Theory of Justice, *Ratio*, 27. 2. 189-196. For a useful survey of additional arguments supporting a social view of knowledge and value, see, Pettit, P (1986), '*Social Holism and Moral Theory*', in: Proceedings of the Aristotelian Society, Vol. LXXXVI.

17 The arguments have been debated in a number of papers. See, for example, Halstead, M. (1995) Voluntary apartheid? Problems of schooling for religious and other minorities in democratic societies, *Journal of Philosophy of Education*, 29. 2. 257-272; McLaughlin, T. H. (1995) Liberalism, education and the common school, *Journal of Philosophy of Education*, 29. 2. 239-255; Arthur, J. (1998) Communitarianism; what are the implications for education? *Educational Studies*, 24. 3. 253-368; Singh, B. R. (1998) Liberalism, parental rights, pupil's autonomy and education, *Educational Studies*, 24. 2. 165-182; Williams, K. (1998) Education and human diversity: the ethics of separate schooling revisited, *British Journal of Educational Studies*, 46. 1. 26-39; Burtonwood, N. (2002) Political Philosophy and the Lessons for Faith Based Schools, *Educational Studies*, 28. 3. 239-252; Burtonwood, N. (2003) Social cohesion, autonomy and the liberal defence of faith schools, *Journal of Philosophy of Education*, 37. 3. 415-425.

18 See the arguments to this point in chapter 15 of Haldane, J. (2004) *Faithful Reason: Essays Catholic and Philosophical*, London Routledge.

19 Government is charged with the task of maintaining a stable society. This presupposes a shared commitment to, or acceptance of, specific common values. In an essentially homogeneous state, the conformity of parental attitudes and understanding with that inherent in state maintained school provision will conceal the occasional interference with the integrity of minority belief and practice. In a pluralistic society where legitimate dissent is widespread, the partnership between the state, perhaps representing a strong secular world view, and parents adhering to a strong and definite religious faith, inevitably becomes strained. This will tend to increase the potential for social disruption.

20 Some would argue that, in spite of the fact that the Universal Declaration of Human Rights affirms the right of parents to educate their children in accordance with their own religious convictions, parents have no such moral right and that any claim by religious or cultural minorities to establish schools to provide such an education is subordinate to the child's right to autonomous well-being. For example, see Marples, R. (2005) Against faith schools: a philosophical argument for children's rights, *International Journal of Children's Spirituality*, 10. 2. 133-147; Mason, M. (2005) Religion and schools – a fresh way forward? A rights-based approach to diversity in schools, in: R. Gardner, J. Cairns & D. Lawton (eds) (2005) *Faith Schools Consensus or Conflict?* London, RoutledgeFalmer.

21 If this were not the case then the state would, logically, remove children from their parents at birth rather than leave them to be influenced by them. While no-one is advocating this approach, it is perhaps, not surprising that some are sceptical of government initiatives contained in the Childcare Bill 2006 which, however apparently supportive of parents and families, seem to encourage younger and younger children to spend increasing amounts of time in the care of state sponsored and controlled nurseries. See, for example, Kirby, J. (1996) *The Nationalisation of Childhood*, London, Centre for Policy Studies.

22 It is important to distinguish between two concepts of human rights. There is the religious understanding of universal and timeless human rights that derive by virtue of *"being created by God in his image and likeness"* and those political rights, such as freedom of expression, which while they may be rooted in Christian ethics, are culturally and historically human decisions, dependent upon particular socio-political circumstances and, therefore, adjustable rather than absolute.

23 The rights and duties of parents vis-à-vis the state are explored more fully in chapter 6.

24 See, for example, Hansard, 17th June 2002, *Education Bill 2002 debate*, columns 577-587; Hansard, 8th February, 2006 *Faith Schools Expansion debate*, columns 720-737; Hansard, 30th October, 2006, *Education and Inspection Bill debate*, columns 17-48 and 103-130.

25 See the essay Two Concepts of Liberty in: Berlin, I. (1969) *Four Essays on Liberty*, Oxford, Oxford University Press.

26 Legislators could decide to impose one particular form of education through the state school system. However, such a strategy would run counter to the concept of a plural society. In response they may decide to allow diversity of provision under certain conditions, or they may move towards a universal approach, but one that avoids, removes or circumvents any areas of contention between different groups so that it can become acceptable to all. Whether such an ideologically neutral school is possible in practice or would be acceptable to parents is another matter.

27 The use of the expression 'religious denominations' in the 1944 Act has long been assumed to refer to various Christian churches. However, while this may have been the intention of the legislators no mention of Christianity is made in this connection and multi-faith syllabuses agreed upon by representatives of various religions (such as the Birmingham Agreed Syllabus of 1975) were perfectly legal. It is important to add here that the Act includes several convenience and conscience clauses freeing schools from the worship requirement if '[their] premises are such to make it impracticable to assemble [pupils] for that purpose', and freeing individuals from both assembly and instruction if these run counter to conscience. In practice few parents invoke the latter clauses but many schools fail to comply with the worship requirement though it would not be impracticable for them to observe it. Some opponents of compulsory religious education cite this general disregard of the law as evidence of its absurdity, arguing that it is wrong for the state to require of those involved in education what they do not believe to be appropriate, and dangerous to maintain statutes once they

have been brought into contempt — particularly in an educational context where the effect may be to encourage general disrespect of proper authorities.

28 See Gardner, P. (1991) Personal autonomy and religious upbringing: the problem, *Journal of Philosophy of Education*, 25. 4. 69-81, in which he notes that within an educational context the adoption of pedagogy to promote the liberal commitment to autonomy is not, in fact, a neutral methodology but is necessarily rooted in agnosticism.

29 See Haldane, J. (1986) Religious education in a plural society, *British Journal of Educational Studies*, 34. 2. 161-181. He argues that, "the vision of those who accept the desirability of religious education, but only in some non-specific uncritical form, in the sense of providing teaching only *about* religion(s), denies the worth of any religion. The idea they seem to have is of bustling classrooms alive with the colours, textures, scents and sounds of several continents, or again playgrounds in which traditional games and folk tales of different countries are enacted. But excluded from this view is any instruction or worship in the religions that gave birth to and sustain the life of these cultural features. This image has appeal to those concerned about social division, religious intolerance, cultural domination, disaffection and indoctrination and who associate them with religious instruction, but it only holds together by trivialising the culture and religions of those involved." See also, Gardner, P. (1992) Propositional Attitudes and Multicultural Education or Believing Others are Mistaken, in: J. Horton & P. Nicholson, (eds) (1992) *Toleration: Philosophy and Practice*, Avebury, Aldershot.

30 The most recent articulation of this longstanding policy can be found in: Department for Children, Schools and Families (2007) *Faith in the System,* Nottingham, DSCF Publications. See also the speech accompanying the document's launch, Balls, E (2007) Faith in the System, speech by the Secretary of State at the British Library 'Sacred' exhibition, 10th September, *http://www.dcsf.gov.uk/speeches/speech.cfm?SpeechID=677.*

31 For an historical explanation and illustration of this claim by Catholics, see St. Augustine of Hippo (1467) in: *Concerning the City of God Against the Pagans* (in particular Books 2.19 and 19.17) translated by Bettenson, H. (1972) London, Penguin Books (2003 edition).

32 Acceptance of this position is (reluctantly) acknowledged in the House of Commons Education and Skills Select Committee Report (HC 633-1) on the Schools White Paper *'Higher Standards, Better Schools For All'* (2006) §§107, 108, 168.

33 See, for example, Hargreaves, D. (1996) Diversity and Choice in School Education: a modified libertarian approach, *Oxford Review of Education*, 22, 2, 131-141.

34 The second resolution in the 'Acta' [minutes] of the Annual Meeting of the bishops held in Low Week, and dated Tuesday, April 17th 1928.

Chapter 4

WHY THE CATHOLIC CHURCH PROVIDES SCHOOLS

UNIVERSAL CONTEXT

The Catholic Church's involvement in education is rooted in Christ's command: "Go teach all nations" recorded in the gospel according to St. Matthew, chapter 28, verse 19. However, the term Christian Education does not appear until much later, about 96 A.D., in Rome. Later, towards the end of the Second Century, it is recorded that St. Clement of Alexandria established a small school for young men in that city and that Origen was its first headmaster. He claimed that his school would enable students to combine the life of a Christian with that of a busy citizen, because its culture harmonised the faith of the Gospel with secular learning and civilisation. That concept of Christian education is still relevant today.

CATHOLIC SCHOOLS IN ENGLAND

Whether or not one approves of diversity in the provision of education, Catholic schools in England educate about ten percent of the current pupil population and, as such, are an important component of the state education system. Given the acceptance of the dual system by mainstream political opinion, albeit in some instances slightly reluctantly, they are likely to remain so in the foreseeable future.[1] The cost of their provision, maintenance and improvement represents a significant financial commitment by the Church. The current insured replacement value of Catholic schools in England and Wales, amounts to approximately £6.5 billion excluding the value of the land on which they stand. In addition, Catholics contribute about £20 million a year towards the upkeep of those schools. This is over and above their acceptance through general and local taxation of their fair share of the cost of providing and maintaining all other state supported schools, many in areas where there is no Catholic provision for their own children.

From 1945-1959 the Catholic population had to find 50% of the cost of providing a school building from its own resources over and above its contribution towards the provision of schools for non-catholic children. In 1959 the grant increased to 75%; to 80% in 1967; 85% in 1975 and to its current 90% in 2002. Despite the increasing level of grant, which some of the sector's detractors suggest is some sort of unfair subsidy, providers of Voluntary Aided schools, such as the Catholic Church are, in fact, net contributors to the national education system. Voluntary aided schools cost the state less to provide and to maintain than Community schools yet, in some parts of the country, for example the Archdiocese of Birmingham, the current Catholic population is still paying off commercial loans that were necessary for building schools commissioned in the 1950s and '60s. That enormous financial commitment involved begs the question as to why the English bishops have made the provision and development of schools such a priority.

In a recently published booklet designed to help school governors, staff and clergy have a common understanding of the key theological reasons behind the Church's teaching about Catholic education and the provision of schools, the Director of Schools of the Archdiocese of Birmingham emphatically reminds his intended audience that they are mechanisms for advancing an essentially religious enterprise,[2] and its opening paragraph reaffirms orthodox Catholic teaching:

> *The Church believes that Jesus Christ is "the way, the truth and the life".[3]*
> *Those who profess this faith believe that in Christ the truth about Almighty*
> *God and the truth about humanity are revealed.[4] The unfolding of this*
> *truth constitutes the Church's teaching and its proclamation constitutes the*
> *mission of the Church, making Christ known to all peoples.*
>
> (Stock, M., Christ at the Centre, 2005, p. 3)

THEOLOGICAL AND PHILOSOPHICAL UNDERPINNINGS

Proponents of Catholic education argue that their schools have a distinctive educational philosophy and purpose based on a religious understanding of the nature of humanity and upon their function supporting the role of the Catholic Church in society. The basic principles were set out in the encyclical *Divini Illius Magistri,* written by Pius Xl in 1929. It was a defence of the Church's responsibility for Catholic youth in the face of increasing pressure on them to embrace the militarism and amorality of Fascist movements in Western Europe. At the same time in Eastern Europe young people were being prepared for a soviet style secular future.

Though the encyclical was, primarily, a message for Italians it also set out the essential principles of a Catholic education for the faithful of all nations. In particular, it described Catholic thinking on the nature of the Church's mission, its understanding of the nature and dignity of the human person, and its teaching about the agents of education, that is, the relationship between parents, the Church and the State. In particular, it argued that education is part of the central mission of the Church[5] which cannot be separated from its wider evangelical mission to humanity.[6] That mission, it argued, was one specified by Jesus Christ himself, the essential purpose of which was to teach what people should do and how they should act in their mortal lives in order that they might achieve the purposes for which God created them.[7]

In respect of education, the Church's understanding was made clear. Parents held prime responsibility for their children's growth and human development. From that premise it argued that any form of compulsory education determined by the state must only be carried out with their free co-operation. It was recognised, however, that parents shared their responsibilities with the state, which had a legitimate concern for the welfare of its citizens.[8] Nevertheless, given the social circumstances at the time, Pius XI was wary of any claim by the state to have control over the education and nurturing of children and young people. The ideas contained in the encyclical were adapted by the English bishops in a manifesto of principles as one element of their on-going dialogue with politicians over the role of Catholic schools in the developing state system.[9] They declared:

1. It is no part of the normal function of the State to teach.

2. The State is entitled to see that citizens receive due education sufficient to enable them to discharge the duties of citizenship in its various degrees.

3. The State ought, therefore, to encourage every form of sound educational endeavour, and may take means to safeguard the efficiency of education.

4. To parents whose economic means are insufficient to pay for the education of their children, it is the duty of the State to furnish the necessary means, providing them from the common funds arising out of taxation of the whole community. But in so doing the State must not interfere with perental (sic) responsibility, nor hamper the reasonable liberty of parents in their choice of a school for their children. Above all, where the people are not all of one creed, there must be no differentiation on the ground of religion.

5. Where there is need of greater school accommodation the State may, in default of other agencies, intervene to supply it; but it may

do so only "in default of, and in substitution for, and to the extent of, the responsibility of the parents" of the children who need this accommodation.

6. The teacher is always acting *in loco parentis*, never *in loco civitatis*, though the State to safeguard its citizenship may take reasonable care to see that teachers are efficient.

7. Thus a teacher never is and never can be a civil servant, and should never regard himself or allow himself to be so regarded, (sic) Whatever authority he may possess to teach and control children, and to claim their respect and obedience, comes to him from God through the parents, and not through the State, except in so far as the State is acting on behalf of the parents.

(Declaration on Education, Low Week, 1929)

THE SECOND VATICAN COUNCIL AND EDUCATION

The main purpose of the Second Vatican Ecumenical Council (1962-65), called by the then Pope, John XXIII, was to highlight the Church's apostolic and pastoral mission, and re-present Christian doctrine in such a way as to make it more accessible, not just to the faithful but to the world generally. Its declarations and directives were intended to renew Catholic thought, action and practices.[10] In respect of education, while the underlying principles formulated by Pius XI in 1929 were been retained in subsequent years, the emphases given to them in Church documents altered to some degree in response to changing social conditions. *Divini Illius Magistri* was a defensive document, primarily addressed to the Catholic faithful. The educationally orientated conciliar and post-conciliar documents[11] of the Second Vatican Council were outward looking, addressed to the world as well as to the Church.

The Second Vatican Council's Declaration on Christian Education *(Gravissimum educationis)* re-affirmed the primacy of parents and the family. While it retained a suspicion of the state's secularising instincts this was no longer a main feature. However, the Church clearly remained anxious to delineate the boundaries of legitimate state involvement in education. In doing so, it has argued, more recently, that the correct relationship between state and any school, not just Catholic schools, is based not so much on institutional relations as on the right of each person to receive a suitable education of their choice. It argues further for this 'right' on the basis of the principle of subsidiarity,[12] according to which the state's duty to protect and defend the liberty of its citizens and to guarantee distributive justice should "ensure that public subsidies are so allocated that parents are truly free to select schools for their children in accordance with their conscience".[13] It is worth noting, perhaps, that the human rights recognised and asserted in the secular declarations of the United Nations assume that any state monopoly of education is not conducive to good government.

While the general tenor of the Second Vatican Council clearly acknowledged secular needs, the principal aims of the Church are still couched in religious terms.

> *"Christ did not bequeath to the Church a mission in the political, economic or social order: the purpose he assigned to it was a religious one"*
>
> (Gaudium et spes, 1965, §42)

While co-operation with the state was now expected as the norm in educational matters, it is important to recognise and to hold onto the idea that, for the Catholic Church, education is primarily a religious activity and only subsequently does it serve social and economic purposes. This emphasis is in contrast to the understanding of most Western governments who during the last century have, arguably, made the economic function of education their over-riding priority. Consequently, the distinctiveness of Catholic education derives from the specific characteristics of Catholicism itself. The Declaration on Christian Education describes the Church's involvement in education as follows:

> *"For her part Holy Mother Church, in order to fulfil the mandate she received from her divine founder to announce the mystery of salvation to all men and to renew all things in Christ, is under an obligation to promote the welfare of the whole life of man, including his life in this world insofar as it is related to his heavenly vocation; she has therefore a part to play in the development and extension of education"*
>
> (Gravissimum educationis, 1965, Preface)

> *"That as a baptised person is gradually introduced into a knowledge of the mystery of salvation, he may daily grow more conscious of the gift of faith which he has received; that he may learn to adore God the Father in spirit and in truth especially through liturgical worship; that he may be trained to conduct his personal life in righteousness and in the sanctity of truth, according to his new standard of manhood, i.e. the new creation given through baptism"*
>
> (Gravissimum educationis, 1965, §2)

For Catholics, the revealed teaching of God through scripture speaks of the purpose of existence in terms of the development of the person to the fullest extent of human nature. It speaks of life with God on earth and in eternity. The scriptures describe the human race (created by God the Father, redeemed by his Son and sharing in the life of God through his Spirit); what they are to become ("be perfect as your Father in heaven is perfect", Matthew. 5. 48); and the means by which they are to achieve it ("love God and your neighbour as yourself", Luke. 10. 27).

The Catholic understanding of the human potential for perfection requires some explanation in respect of the purpose of education as it is understood by the Church. The word 'perfect' in Matthew's Gospel (Matthew. 5. 48), *teleios* in Greek, imposes upon Christians the obligation of going beyond a traditional, Pharisaic-like interpretation of the commandments. Something more than adherence to laws seems to be implied; it is a moral completeness derived from a personal and experiential knowledge of God. Consistent with this view of God, the nature and purpose of human existence and a belief in an after-life, the Church argues:

> "... true education is directed towards the formation of the human person in view of his final end and the good of society to which he belongs, and in the duties which, as an adult, he will have to share."
>
> (Gravissimum educationis, 1965, §1)

For the Church, 'formation', the idea of full human development in the light of God's intended purpose, includes religious education. As such, it has been recognised as a basic human right in the Universal Declaration of Human Rights (United Nations, 1948, Article 18) and in the subsequent Declaration of the Rights of the Child (United Nations, 1959, Principle 2). Such rights are consistent with the theology of the Second Vatican Council and affirmed in the Declaration on Religious Freedom (*Dignitatis humanae*) which claims:

> "Every family, in that it is a society with its own basic rights, has the right freely to organise its own religious life in the home under the control of the parents. These have the right to decide in accordance with their own religious beliefs the form of religious upbringing ... which is to be given to their children. The civil authority must therefore recognise the right of parents to choose with genuine freedom schools or other means of education ..."
>
> (Dignitatis humanae, 1965, §5)

The principles enunciated in the conciliar and post conciliar documents have been encoded in the revised Canon Law for the Latin Rite[14] and re-asserted at the close of the old millennium.[15] Consequently, individual Catholic schools exist as religious and educational organisations, but also as part of a world wide religious movement claiming a universality of purpose. In the same way that Origen claimed his school provided a synthesis of faith and culture in second century Alexandria, the integration of faith, culture and reason has remained central to the Church's world-wide educative mission, providing schools that are intended to be "a place of integral education of the human person through a clear educational project of which Christ is the foundation; its ecclesial identity; its mission of education as a work of love [and] its service to society …".[16] However, it must be remembered that such declarations are intended for universal application and, by their nature, differing local circumstances will affect the ways in which those ends are pursued.[17]

WHO ARE CATHOLIC SCHOOLS FOR?

The existence of a Catholic sector within the state system of maintained schools in England has its origins in the decision of the newly restored Catholic hierarchy to make the provision of Catholic elementary schools their highest priority.[18] The purpose was to ensure the development and transmission of Catholic faith and culture for the then predominantly poor and working class Catholic community.[19]

Community is a complex concept, but it is apparent that membership of a discernible group is what gives individuals a prime source of individual identity and worth. Religious faith can be one of the main and more potent elements in the formation of a community, and its shared experiences a source of strength and solidarity. It can be argued, therefore, that religious groups or communities are fundamentally cultural organisations in as much as they are concerned primarily with the propagation and promulgation of particular values relating to an understanding of the nature and purpose of humanity. Their purpose is achieved, at least in part, in the process of personal interaction of their adherents. Consequently, their educational priorities, both for and in schools, rest on a complex set of moral and social preferences and beliefs about what is good for individuals and society as a whole.

The complexity of relationships between community, culture and school is, perhaps, exemplified in the English circumstances. First, England is only one of four interlocked national groups within the United Kingdom. Further, it comprises a number of distinct communities, of which Catholics, who may belong to one of several different ethnic groups, are but one. English citizens can, therefore, hold multiple identities, and Catholics in England can trace their roots in, at least, three differing directions.

There are those whose Catholic ancestry lies in pre-Reformation times.[20] Their personal consciousness will have been formed by memories of savage persecution, prejudice and exclusion. Some, especially if they have had the necessary financial resources, have used the network of Catholic independent schools, some of which look back beyond reformation England, for the education of their children.

There are a significant group of men and women who have converted from the established national Church and brought with them their own educational and cultural legacy. While it may be the case that some turn to the state or even to Anglican foundations for their education, they are likely to embrace the educational opportunities provided by Catholic primary and secondary schools. Historically, some have regarded Catholic education so highly established they have established their own Catholic schools, as in the case of Cardinal Newman and his Oratorian community.

The third major group comprise those whose Catholic roots lie outside England. Of those who can claim membership of one of the many immigrant groups, the Irish have, since the middle of the nineteenth century, dominated the inner city population and the large dioceses of the Midlands and the Northwest of England. Since the Second World War they have also formed a significant proportion of the catholic population of the southern dioceses. In more recent years as populations have, generally, become more mobile, there has been sizeable Catholic immigration into England from many parts of the world.[21]

In educational matters, the Church has adapted and evolved its response in an attempt to meet their contemporary needs through schools provided by dioceses. The essential thrust of those efforts since 1850 has been to provide a mechanism through which the, mainly, working class, immigrant Catholic communities were able to successfully integrate themselves into mainstream society.[22] In particular, they enabled the mainly poor,[23] deprived and uneducated Irish community of nineteenth century origins, to acquire valuable skills, achieve economic success, and eventually obtain a degree of social and political significance in the twentieth century. While for many the integration of the poor working class Irish communities into mainstream English society is seen as wholly desirable, some have argued that, in return for state aid and support for its schools, the Catholic hierarchy have contributed to the suppression of Irish culture and the incorporation of succeeding generations into the dominant Protestant cultural ethic,[24] so that by the second or third generation only a surname may be the clue to their original allegiances - even their original religious adherence.[25]

It is the case that the Catholic Church in England established its schools, in the first instance, for the direct and sole benefit of the Catholic community.[26] This remains the primary, but not the only, purpose of Catholic schools. The Church does not want to stand apart from the society in which it exists (however much some might wish that it did) and recognises that its schools are integral to the existing economy, culture and society as a whole. Though an expression of the reality of a particular Church, they fulfil a public service contributing to the common good, providing an education clearly rooted and guided by world-view of the Catholic faith. As such, though they are provided primarily for baptised Catholics, they are by no means exclusively reserved for them, and, where the state and circumstances allow,[27] they are open to all those who appreciate and wish to share their essentially religious purposes.

Their existence, whether within the state maintained sector or not, guarantees cultural and educational pluralism and the freedom for parents to ensure their children receive the sort of education they wish them to have. Consequently, the very act of providing an alternative to state schools in circumstances where the rights of parents are respected and educational diversity is valued, is a significant contributory factor towards developing and preserving social cohesion in pluralistic societies.

SUMMARY
This chapter started by referring to the document 'Christ at the Centre' prepared by the Director of Schools for the Archdiocese of Birmingham. That same document provides a neat summary of the arguments made in this chapter. I am grateful to Fr. Stock for permission to reproduce his conclusions in slightly modified form below.[28]

Catholic schools exist as an **arm of the Church** and its religious mission, trying to place Christ and the teaching of the Catholic Church at the centre of people's lives, rooting spiritual development, learning and teaching, the formation of culture and society in the historic person of Jesus of Nazareth, Christ, the Son of God.[29] Catholic schools, therefore, are more than just institutions for equipping pupils with knowledge and skills necessary for the workplace and responsible citizenship. They are intended to be communities, where spiritual, cultural and personal worlds are harmonised to form the basis of the values, motivation, aspirations and the moral imperatives that inform individual choices and actions.[30]

The Church provides Catholic schools to **assist parents** to fulfil their parental role, arguing that, as it is parents who have given life to their children, they always retain prime responsibility for the education and religious formation of their children.[31]

They **serve the local Church community**, providing a partnership between the home and the parish by integrating those two components of Catholic education. Pope John-Paul II described the process as follows:

> *"The parish community is a place for religious and spiritual education. School is a place for cultural education. The two dimensions must be integrated, because the same values inspire them: they are the values of Christian families who, in a society dominated by relativism and threatened by existential emptiness, intend to offer their children an education based on the unchangeable values of the Gospel."*
>
> (Pope John Paul II, Address to Teachers and Students of the Catholic Villa Flaminia Institute, Rome, 23rd February 1997, §2)

Although Catholic schools are established first and foremost to facilitate the right of Catholic parents to choose a Catholic education for their child, they **provide a general service by contributing to the common good**[32] of society and its culture. They strive to be a public benefit, helping develop highly educated, skilled and cultured individuals who recognise and understand their civic obligations. The Church argues further that they:

> *"... fulfil a public role, for their presence guarantees cultural and educational pluralism and, above all, the freedom and right of families to see that their children receive the sort of education they wish for them."*
>
> (The Catholic School on the Threshold of the Third Millennium, 1997, §16)

NOTES

1   The two main political parties in the UK actively support the concept of parental choice (as far as is practicable) in where and how their children are educated and in doing so speak supportively of Catholic schools. In a speech to the Catholic Association of Teachers, Schools and Colleges on 2nd February 2005, Phil Willis MP, the Liberal Democrat Shadow Secretary of State for Education, made clear that any perceived antipathy to Catholic schools and 'faith schools' in general by the third main party in UK politics were "myths". He emphasised *"We have no proposals whatsoever to close Church schools or to prevent the establishment of others"; that "the partnership between church and state has served us [the country] well"; that it would be "unacceptable to deny Muslims or other faiths the same opportunities as Catholic ..."; and made it clear that "the Liberal democrats do not want to stifle choice or diversity ...".* It is interesting that he felt it necessary to deny that which, clearly, many felt was Liberal Democrat policy. The House of Commons Education and Skills Committee Report on the Schools White Paper *Higher Standards, Better Schools for All* (2006) also accepted that it is not possible or desirable to reverse the trend towards choice and diversity of school provision - see §§107; 108; 168. On the other hand, during the passage of the Education and Inspection Bill in October and November 2006, there were attempts both by backbench members and government ministers to introduce clauses requiring Catholic schools to give priority in admissions to Catholic schools of quotas of non-Catholic pupils. Though the relevant amendments were subsequently withdrawn and/or defeated in the respective Houses, the Hansard debates on education from 2004 onwards clearly illustrate a growing opposition to Catholic and other religiously based schools from secularists and atheists within the legislature.

2   See Stock. M. (2005) *Christ at the Centre: a summary of why the Church provides Catholic schools*, Birmingham, Archdiocese of Birmingham Diocesan Schools Commission

3   The Gospel of St. John, 14:6.

4   *Gaudium et spes*, [Pastoral Constitution of the Church in the Modern World], 7th December 1965, §22, in: A. Flannery (1981) (ed) *The Conciliar and Post Conciliar Documents*, Leominster, Fowler Wright.

5   Pope Pius XI (1929) *Divini Illius Magistri* [The Christian Education of Youth], §16-18, Encyclical, Rome, 31st December, http://www.vatican.va/roman_curia/congregations/documents.

6   ibid *Divini Illius Magistri*, [The Christian Education of Youth], §§25-26

7   ibid *Divini Illius Magistri*, [The Christian Education of Youth], §7

8   ibid *Divini Illius Magistri*, [The Christian Education of Youth], §§12-18; 29-50. Within the English context, the bishops had long acknowledged the legitimate interests of the state in the education of children. For example, *"... it is the duty of the State or civil authority to provide for the good order and well-being of the community and, as these depend principally on proper education ... it is the duty of the State ... to assist parents in the discharge of the aforesaid duty, or compel them to fulfil it if they neglect to do so"*, Bourne, F. (1906), *The Catholic Attitude on the Education Question*, p. 5. See also, "... it cannot be denied that the State is justified in providing for the education of its people. It has a right to protect itself from the dangers arising from ignorance and vice ... to protect children from the neglect and sin of parents, and to guard their rights to receive an education which shall fit them for human society and for civil life", Bourne, F. (1929), *The Catholic Attitude on the Education Question*, p. 7. For details see bibliography.

9   In the 'Acta' (i.e. meeting records) of the Low Week Annual Meeting of the Bishops of England and Wales, Wednesday 10th April, 1929, under the heading Education Policy the following is noted: *"It*

was decided to reaffirm the Bishops' previous declaration on Education policy, and to embody in a manifesto a set of principles prepared by His Eminence [Cardinal Bourne, Cardinal Archbishop of Westminster] *for the Albert Hall Meeting of 25th May; further to add a question to be submitted to each candidate at the General Election."* The bishops' *Declaration on Education* was issued on their behalf through the Catholic Parents Association by the Hon. Sec: Mrs. A. M. Patmore, 66 St. Albans Road, Ilford, Essex.

10 Pope John-Paul II (1992) *Fidei depositum* [Deposit of Faith], in: *Catechism of the Catholic Church* (1994), London, Geoffrey Chapman, pp. 2-6.

11 *Gravissimum educationis* [Declaration on Christian Education] (1965); *The Catholic School* (1977); *Lay Catholics in Schools: Witnesses to Faith* (1982); *The Religious Dimension of Education in a Catholic School* (1988); *The Catholic School on the Threshold of the Third Millennium* (1997). For full details of these references see bibliography.

12 The principle was first developed in the encyclical *Quadragesimo Anno* (1931) – see §§79-80. It postulates that all social bodies exist for the sake of the individual, so that whatever functions individuals can discharge effectively should not be taken over by society.

13 *Gravissimum educationis* [Declaration on Christian Education] (1965), §6, in: A. Flannery (1981) (ed) *The Conciliar and Post Conciliar Documents*, Leominster, Fowler Wright; reiterated in: Congregation for Catholic Education, *The Catholic Church on the Threshold of the Third Millennium*, Rome 28th December, 1997, §17

14 Canon Law – the laws governing the activities of the Church - was re-codified in 1983 and among other things defines the parameters within which Catholic schools, as instruments of the Church, have to work. Canons 793-795 refer to the Catholic education generally and the role of parents; canons 796-806 to Catholic schools. The issue of parental responsibility dominates four out of the first six canons; clearly a priority in Catholic educational thinking. The school's role is described as *"the principal means of helping parents to fulfil their role in education"*. The role of parents is strengthened by the clear requirement that the school should co-operate closely with them, through such vehicles as parents' associations and parents' meetings (Can. 796). The relationship of the Catholic school to the bishop is the essence of the last six canons. He has to see that such schools are built (Can. 800; 802), give permission for them to be built (Can. 801), authorise them to bear the title Catholic (Can. 803), supervise them (Can. 804; 806), and to appoint - and if necessary see to the removal of - teachers of religion (Can. 805).

15 *The Catholic School on the Threshold of the Third Millennium* was published in 1997. In a world it regards as being beset with materialism and pluralism in values, it reasserts the ecclesial identity of the Catholic school, as a genuine instrument of the Church (§11) necessarily working with parish and diocese in their pastoral work (§12). It re-affirms the Church's commitment to the poor and underprivileged (§13) and its desire to work in dialogue and collaboration with public authorities (§§16-17). The word community is stressed as a theological as well as a sociological term (§§18-19) and the need to both co-operate with and support parents is also emphasised (§20).

16 See Congregation for Catholic Education (1997) *The Catholic School on the Threshold of the Third Millennium*, Rome, 28th December, §4.

17 In England the normal pattern of Catholic education in the decades since the Second Vatican Council (1964-67) has remained one of its schools serving the faith community. However, changing social circumstances in England in the past three decades, coupled with the new legislative framework for education, have impacted upon the Catholic community and its schools as they have developed in recent years. Consequently, there has been debate about the way in which Catholic schools should

respond to the changes (Arthur, 1995; Grace, 1995, pp. 159-178; Hyper, 1996). Differing models of Catholic school have been developed (Chadwick 1994; McLaughlin et al, 1996) sometimes with diocesan approval but also, on occasions, contrary to the views and wishes of the Ordinary, albeit claiming the documents of the Council as justification (Caines, 1994; Hastings, 1996; Murray, 1996). For full details of these references see bibliography.

18 Province of Westminster, 17th July 1852, in: R. E. Guy, (1886) *The Synods in English: being the texts of the four synods of Westminster*, London, St. Gregory's Press.

19 The historical background of the Catholic community and its development over the years since 1850 have been outlined in more detail in Chapter 1.

20 See summary in chapter 1. For much greater detail about the spread and location of the major recusant communities, see, for example, Bossey, J. (1975) *The English Catholic Community 1570-1850*, London, Darton, Longman & Todd, pp. 404-431.

21 For a list of the main Catholic immigrant groups in England and Wales see Chapter 1, endnote 6

22 Accounts of their early experiences of, and impact upon, society at the time show remarkable parallels to those of ethnic minorities in contemporary Britain. See, for example, collections of local history essays in R. Swift & S. Gilley (eds) 1885; 1989; 1999). For full details see bibliography.

23 It is important to recognise that though Irish immigrants were predominantly Catholic and poor, there was a notable middle-class Irish element in nineteenth century Britain and also significant numbers of Protestant Irish immigrants. See, for example, essays by Miskell, L.; Herson, J.; Belcham, J. and others in: R. Swift & S. Gilley (eds) (1999) *The Irish in Victorian Britain: the Local Dimension*, Dublin, Four Courts Press.

24 See, for example, Hickman M. J. (1999) Alternative histographies of the Irish in Britain: a critique of the segregation/assimilation model, in: R. Swift & S. Gilley (1999) (eds) *The Irish in Victorian Britain: the Local Dimension*, Dublin, Four Courts Press. See also, Hickman M. J. (2000) Catholicism and the Nation State in Nineteenth Century Britain, in: M. Eaton, J. Longmore & A. Naylor (eds) (2000) *Commitment to Diversity*, London, Cassell.

25 A recent (unpublished) analysis of the ethnic background of pupils attending Catholic Secondary Schools in Birmingham found remarkably few pupils designated as being Irish (WIRI) in their schools PLASC (Pupil Level Annual School Census) data returns, despite research by Birmingham City Council in 1996 (*The Economic Needs of the Irish Community in Birmingham*) showing the Irish born population (N.B. not including second generation Irish) to represent about 4% of the city total, the plethora of Irish names on Catholic secondary school registers, and the huge annual St. Patrick's Day parades in the city.

26 This remains the primary, but not the only, purpose of Catholic schools.

27 Following the implementation of the Education Act 1944, the task facing the Catholic bishops was to provide sufficient places for Catholic pupil population. At that time demand for places exceeded supply, and not simply in the Catholic sector. However, in order to do so the bishops had to prove that there was sufficient initial, and sustained long-term, demand for places from Catholic pupils before they could obtain permission to open a new, or expand an existing, Catholic school. Those provisions remain in place today.

As the pupil population began to decline during the 1970s many schools had surplus capacity. Where Catholic schools had surplus places they would (usually) admit any non-Catholic pupils who applied. In the 1980 Education Act, in an attempt to enhance for parental choice, the Conservative government laid a duty on admissions authorities to enable parents to express a preference as to the school they wished their child(ren) to attend and set down conditions under which schools had to comply with the stated preference. Section 6(3) of the Act allowed the governors of voluntary aided (or special agreement) schools and the local education authority to come to an agreement about their admissions which could, if it was so desired by both parties, keep some empty places in case Catholic parents moved into the area, and/or to limit the number of non-Catholics admitted in order to preserve the Catholic character of the school. This provision remained on statute until the government, with the full support and agreement of the Catholic hierarchy, repealed what was by then section 91 of the Education Act 1998, in the Education Act 2002.

28 For a fuller summary of the four main reasons why the Church provides schools see Stock, M. (2005) *Christ at the Centre: a summary of why the Church provides Catholic Schools*, Birmingham, Archdiocese of Birmingham Diocesan Schools Commission, pp. 3-4.

29 In the second series of fifteen talks on Christianity given on the BBC in 1942, C. S. Lewis argued *"I'm trying here to prevent you from saying the really silly thing that people often say about him: 'I'm ready to accept Jesus as a great moral teacher, but I don't accept his claim to be God.' That's the one thing you mustn't say. A man who was merely a man and said the sort of things Jesus said wouldn't be a great moral teacher. He'd either be a lunatic — on a level with the man who says he's a poached egg — or the Devil of Hell. Of course you can take the line of saying He didn't say these things, but His followers invented them. But that's only shifting the difficulty. They were Jews too: the last people who would invent such a thing, the people who had never said anything of the sort about Moses or Elijah. That theory only saddles you with twelve inexplicable lunatics instead of one. We can't get out of it that way. You must make your choice. Either this man was, and is, the Son of God: or else a madman: or something worse. You can shut Him up for a fool: you can spit at him and kill him as a demon: or you can fall at His feet and call Him Lord and God. But don't come to Him with any patronizing nonsense about His being a great human teacher. He hasn't left that open to you. He didn't intend to.* See Hooper, W. (1996) *C. S. Lewis: A Companion and Guide*, London, HarperCollins, p. 308.

A more scholarly and extensive exposition of the same conclusion about the divinity of Jesus can be found in Redford, J. (2004) *Bad, Mad or God? Proving the Divinity of Christ from St. John's Gospel*, London, St. Pauls Publishing.

30 This concept is explored in *Gravissimum educationis*, [Declaration on Catholic Education] (1965), particularly §§ 4, 5, & 8, in: A. Flannery (ed) (1981) *The Conciliar and Post Conciliar Documents*, Leominster, Fowler Wright.

31 See *Gravissimum educationis* [Declaration on Christian Education] (1965), §3 in: A. Flannery (ed) (1981) *The Conciliar and Post Conciliar Documents*, Leominster, Fowler Wright. The principle is also spelt out in the 1983 Code of Canon Law, Can. 796, §1, "*Christ's faithful are to consider schools as of great importance, since they are the principal means of helping parents to fulfil their role in education.*"

32 This concept is regarded by the Catholic Church as having universal application and is defined as the sum total of social conditions which allow people, as groups or as individuals, to reach their fulfilment more fully and easily. There are three essential elements within the concept: i) respect for the individual and the natural freedoms that are indispensable for their personal growth; ii) social well-being and development of the group, and; iii) peace and justice. For a fuller explanation, see *Catechism of the Catholic Church*, (1994) London, Geoffrey Chapman, §§1905-1912.

Chapter 5

THE NATURE AND PURPOSES OF CATHOLIC EDUCATION

CONTEXT

Following the rapid development of the education system in post-war Britain, mainstream Sociology of Education textbooks[1] used in the expanding Teacher Training Colleges in the 1960s and 1970s introduced prospective teachers to notions about the function of education in society. They often had long sections explaining and exploring the socialising role of schools in the life of young children. The following is, perhaps, a typical example of the general understanding at that time of the purposes of schools and the education they provided.

> *"Education is the organised part of the process through which each successive generation learns the accumulated knowledge of a society. This cultural transmission is necessary so that people can fit into the existing pattern of life and associate with others in a predictable, efficient and humane way. ... The process of education in the process of converting children into useful, responsible adults means it is never concerned solely with knowledge as a preparation for occupation. Inevitably it has to ensure that each generation shares a common set of values, the same idea of right and wrong. ... Schools are agencies of socialisation operating alongside the family, religion, the social services and the local community."*
>
> (Shipman, M. D., 1968, p. 3)

In addition to schools' socialising role, such textbooks also highlighted the political, economic and selective functions of a state maintained or controlled school system.[2] Missing from many such descriptions was any discussion or analysis of the inherently value laden character of education. However, the process of educating involves human interaction and the school's environment and activities are, consequently, rooted in an understanding, explicit or otherwise, of the fundamental nature of humanity. While the omission might be very understandable in a relatively homogeneous society (such as England in the 1950s, or Japan today), it becomes more problematical in politically, socially, culturally and ethnically diverse societies. The greater the diversity, it could be argued, the more complex the educational enterprise.

The word education has its etymological roots both in the Latin *educere* (to lead out) and *educare* (to form). The first emphasises, among other things, the freedom and autonomy of learners to determine their own understanding, values and beliefs, the second the idea of teachers moulding the personality of pupils to appreciate truth, goodness and the relative value of different world views. Many people believe, therefore, that all schools must, inevitably and unavoidably, have an ideological character. They argue, for example, that just as Spartan education tried to develop effective soldiers (in comparison to the Athenian desire for good democrats) and, for most of the 20th century, Russian schools sought to develop ideological committed communists, so, in England today, while so called faith schools will promote their specific religious values, beliefs and practices, Community and other types of secular schools will initiate pupils into the prevailing political, social and economic doctrines of the time, such as political liberalism, socialism or free-market capitalism. The degree to which the process may be unwitting or deliberately planned will vary, but every educational system must, necessarily, be rooted in a concept of what the particular society, or community, believes an educated person should be.[3] From that understanding, its schools will seek to provide an environment and curriculum responding to the particular world-view and aim towards helping develop a certain type of person with particular attitudes and values consistent with its vision of the human condition and its corresponding 'good life'.

If it is the case that all societies inculcate the customs and beliefs they wish to maintain, educational debate should not be concerned with the question of whether it is appropriate for schools to influence their pupils in this way but exactly what knowledge, values, attitudes and practices should form the content of that inculcation.[4]

HUMAN LIFE - A CATHOLIC PERSPECTIVE

The Church's view of its educative role starts from two basic premises about human existence upon which it builds its particular view of humanity and the purpose of human existence. They are a belief in the existence of a transcendental God[5] and a conviction that an historical person, Jesus of Nazareth, is the Son of God through whom humanity is redeemed.[6] Those beliefs form the basis of the Church's understanding of the unique relationship each individual has with God before birth, during life and after death, and, consequently, its understanding of the purpose of human existence. It asserts:

"Man is by nature and vocation a religious being. Coming from God, going toward God, man lives a fully human life only if he freely lives by his bond with God."

(Catechism of the Catholic Church, 1994, §44)

"When he [mankind] works not only does he transform matter and society, but he fulfils himself. He learns, he develops his faculties, and he emerges from and transcends himself. Rightly understood, this kind of growth is more precious than any kind of wealth that can be amassed. It is what man is, rather than what he has, that counts. ... Technical progress may supply the material for human advance but it is powerless to actualise it. Here then is the norm for human activity - to harmonise with the authentic interests of the human race, in accordance with God's will and design, and to enable men as individuals and as members of society to pursue and fulfil their total vocation."

(Gaudium et spes, 1965, §35)

A Catholic understanding of the dignity of the human person is also rooted in those beliefs. The Church argues that all human life is concerned with a search for God. This fundamental impulse can be ignored, forgotten or denied but never eliminated because it is inherent to the human condition.[7] In the context of education, it is expressed as follows:

"In today's pluralistic world, the Catholic educator must consciously inspire his or her activity with the Christian concept of the person ... It is a concept that includes a defence of human rights but also attributes to the human person the dignity of a child of God; it attributes the fullest liberty, ... the most exalted destiny, ... establishes solidarity through mutual love and an ecclesial community ... calls for the fullest development of all that is human, [and] proposes Christ, Incarnate Son of God and perfect man as both model and means ... ."

(Lay Catholics in Schools: Witnesses to Faith, 1982, §18)

The previous chapter described, briefly, the framework within which the Catholic Church sees its world-wide role in providing schools. The conciliar and post-conciliar documents of the Second Vatican Council relating to education are more concerned with the nature and purposes of the education provided in those institutions. They reflect a move away from the position adopted by the Church in the first part of the 20th century in which Catholic schools were seen as a bulwark against perceived evils in society at that time. The change in emphasis makes it clear that Catholic education has a role within the secular world and is, in a sense and in part, for the world's benefit. In those documents the Church refers to 'education' as a process of formation. In doing so it implies its belief in a particular given human nature towards which people are naturally orientated but have the free will to reject. From that view of the nature of education comes a belief, therefore, that children should be guided or trained to understand and appreciate their God given nature and act in accordance with it, in a context whereby any response to the benefits it offers is freely given by the individuals concerned. Children must not be coerced.[8]

THE DISTINCTIVENESS OF CATHOLIC EDUCATION

Given its religious perspective on life itself, the Church asserts that a holistic or complete education must have a religious context. It is inevitable, therefore, that Catholic schools in England should claim (and seek) to differ from the prevailing secular model in the character and style of education they offer. Because they are civic institutions, their pedagogical methods and characteristics would be much the same as those in any maintained school. However, if they remain true to the primary purpose of Catholic education in England and aim to be Christian communities, their educational goals should be rooted in Christ, his teachings as recorded in the Gospels, and be concerned with transmitting the essential doctrines, devotions and corporate religious vision of Catholicism.[9] Consequently, while they should, under most circumstances, conform to the generally accepted school programmes of the day, they must necessarily seek to implement them within an overall religious perspective of human life and purpose. This, the Church claims, affects the nature of the curriculum though not necessarily its content, the relationship between teacher and taught and the internal school processes.[10]

In claiming its schools are based on a philosophy in which faith, culture and contemporary life are brought together in harmony, it describes their fundamental and general purpose as being:

> "a place of integral formation by means of a systematic and critical assimilation of culture...a privileged place in which, through a living encounter with a cultural inheritance, integral formation occurs."
>
> (The Catholic School, 1977, §26)

Their special function is to develop a culture which:

> "... enables young people ... to grow ... in that new life which has been given them in baptism ... (and) so orients the whole of human culture to the message of salvation that the knowledge which pupils acquire of the world, of life and of men is illuminated by faith."
>
> (Gravissimum educationis [Declaration on Christian Education], 1965, §8)

It is expected that the school culture will be rooted in the person and teaching of Christ, since the Church claims that:

"in Christ, the Perfect Man, all human values find their fulfilment and unity."

(The Catholic School, 1977, §35)

"it is and has been, from her beginning, the belief of the Church that she has an obligation to provide an education for her children by which their whole lives may be inspired by the spirit of Christ."

(Gravissimum educationis [Declaration on Christian Education], 1965, §3)

The task of providing such an education involves the school in developing appropriate forms of catechesis for pupils. By catechesis, the Church means a systematic transmission of Christ's teaching and the doctrines of the Church with a view to initiating individuals into a full Christian life. It is built on a certain number of elements; (1) the initial proclamation of the Gospel to arouse faith (evangelisation); (2) examination of the reasons for belief (apologetics); (3) experience of Christian living, including celebration of the sacraments; (4) integration into the ecclesial community and (5) apostolic and missionary witness.[11] In practice, since for some Catholic pupils initial evangelisation may not have taken place, catechesis may involve not only nourishing and teaching their faith but also with arousing it. However, its specific aim is to develop an existing faith. To do so, the Church argues, it should:

- *be systematic and designed to reach a precise goal;*
- *deal with essentials, not transform itself into theological research;*
- *be sufficiently complete, that is, more than just bible study;*
- *open to all the other factors of Christian life since it is intrinsically linked with the whole liturgical and sacramental activity.*

(Catechesi tradendae [Catechesis in our time], 1979, §21)

The Church suggests there are four identifiable groups of Catholic students at different stages of intellectual maturation whom it seeks to catechise in school. As they mature, different methodological or pedagogical approaches will be appropriate. For example, when children first go to school it is likely that catechesis will be didactic in character and directed by teachers and other adults mainly towards giving witness in the faith. While retaining their witness, teachers will use other pedagogical methods when teaching adolescents and those entering adulthood, to help them assume responsibility for their own lives. For despite claims by its critics to the contrary, in fact the Church argues that a religious education is something offered, not imposed.[12]

That dual role, of supporting Catholic parents in transmitting Catholic culture and working for the common good of the secular society in which they operate, creates tensions between secular and religious values both within and for education.[13] Despite the assertion by many that all schools cannot help but inculcate prevailing ideologies in children, others believe that pupils should be taught to evaluate beliefs and practices rationally, and to accept only those that can withstand criticism. Whether this is a practical proposition either in schools or general life is disputed. Pope John Paul II commented:

> "... there are in the life of a human being many more truths that are simply believed than truths which are acquired by way of personal verification. Who, for instance, could assess critically the countless scientific findings upon which modern life is based? Who could personally examine the flow of information which comes day after day from all parts of the world and which is generally accepted as true? Who in the end could forge anew the paths of experience and thought which have yielded the treasures of human wisdom and religion? This means that the human being – one who seeks truth – is also the one who lives by belief."
>
> (Fides et Ratio [Faith and Reason], 1998, §31)

Nevertheless, those who place a pre-eminent value on rationality or human autonomy argue that uncritical ideological inculcation is indoctrination, a charge often levelled at Catholic schools. Some go further, claiming that an education which has its roots in a belief in the existence of a transcendent God that cannot be proved (in the scientific sense) must be, by definition, indoctrination, a sub-branch of teaching, and therefore not really an appropriate educative role for a school.[14] On the other hand, scientific rationalism also entails assumptions incapable of scientific proof and is no less ideological than religious or other socio/political doctrines that can, and might be, fostered in secular schools, for example, humanistic individualism or extreme relativism.

In its own defence, the Church asserts that a pedagogy of faith is not simply a question of transmitting human knowledge, but of communicating God's revelation in its entirety. It argues that a theological dimension is essential for interpreting and solving present day problems in society. Therefore, the

Catholic character and quality of religious instruction and the ways in which it is integrated into all aspects of the education provided by the school is essential to its purpose (and the underlying basis for the reason why Catholic parents should prefer it for their children). Whether or not that is the case, it is recognised that children will have different levels of understanding of their faith and commitment to it.[15] In addition, there may well be pupils attending the school whose parents adhere to a different faith or come from an entirely secular or atheistic background. Consequently, it is expected that while Catholic teachers will teach and act in conformity with their own religious convictions and in accordance with the identity of the school:

> *"... they must have at the same time the greatest respect for those students who are not Catholics. They should be open at all times to authentic dialogue, convinced that in these circumstances the best testimony that they can give of their own faith is a warm and sincere appreciation for anyone who is honestly seeking according to his or her own conscience."*
> (Lay Catholics in Schools: Witnesses to Faith, 1982, §42)

Moreover:

> *"In Catholic schools, teaching of religion must help students to arrive at a personal position in religious matters that is consistent and respectful of the positions of others, so contributing to their growth and to a more complete understanding of reality."*
> (Consecrated Persons and their Mission in Schools, 2002, §54)

In its understanding of the catechetical role of its schools, the Catholic Church also has a very clear view about purposes that it regards as inimical to education in general, which are in contrast to the economic benefits currently dominating planning and thinking in many areas of the contemporary English educational system.

> *"Education is not given for the purpose of gaining power but as an aid towards a fuller understanding of, and communion with man, events and things. Knowledge is not to be considered as a means of material prosperity and success, but as a call to serve and to be responsible for others."*
> (The Catholic School, 1977, §56)

EXPRESSING CATHOLIC VALUES
A Catholic school is more than an educative institution with distinctive religious characteristics: it is a key part of the Church, and an essential element in the Church's mission. Cardinal Hume has argued that to meet

its purpose, the Catholic school should have a single vision, an integrated concept of what makes a fully authentic and mature human being, and the school's educational community should be, as far as is possible, a genuine community of faith. The educative process should not be confined simply to the curriculum, nor to the academic, technical, artistic and sporting achievements of the school. School should be a place in which there is the intention not only of exploring the mystery that God is, but also of demonstrating the Gospel in action.[16]

If Cardinal Hume's views are to be realised in practice, the role of teachers, both as individuals and as a community, is vital. In a Catholic school they are more than just employees. By accepting posts in the school they minister to those in their care, to the best of their ability, in the name of the Church and of the Gospel. They are the human agents charged with the development of the Church's understanding of fully mature human beings and the prime movers in demonstrating the Gospel in action to their pupils. From the witness and example of the teachers and, particularly, the leadership of the school, children should experience learning and living within a Catholic atmosphere, in which they can express their own faith, particularly through their participation in the liturgical and sacramental life of their schools. In doing so they will be helping to make them:

> *"meeting places for those who wish to express Christian values"* ... *[and]* *"committed to the task of forming men and women who will make the civilisation of love [the Christian ideal for society] a reality."*
>
> (Pope Paul VI, 1974; 1976)

The Church's expectation of teachers in its schools has been spelt out in various post-conciliar documents, papal statements and incorporated, in practical terms, in guidance to governors of Catholic schools concerning any staff appointments that they make and also in the contracts of employment they are expected to use.[17] The following extracts give clear indications of its understanding of the role of a teacher in helping governors of a Catholic school fulfil their responsibility to preserve and develop its Catholic character.[18]

> *"By their witness and their behaviour teachers are of the first importance to impart a distinctive character to Catholic schools."*
>
> (The Catholic School, 1977, §78)

> *"The Church looks upon you [teachers] as co-workers with an important measure of shared responsibility ... To you it is given to create the future*

and give it direction by offering to your students a set of values with which to assess their newly discovered knowledge. ... [The changing times] demand that educators be open to new cultural influences and interpret them for young pupils in the light of Christian faith. You are called to bring professional competence and a high standard of excellence to your teaching ... But your responsibilities make demands on you that go far beyond the need for professional skills and competence ... Through you, as through a clear window on a sunny day, students must come to see and know the richness and joy of a life lived in accordance with Christ's teaching, in response to his challenging demands. To teach means not only to impart what we know, but also to reveal who we are by living what we believe. It is this latter lesson which tends to last the longest."
(Pope John Paul II, Address to Catholic Educators, Sept. 12th, 1984, §§1-3)

"Conduct is always much more important than speech ... The more completely an educator can give concrete witness to the model of the ideal person ... the more this ideal will be believed and imitated. ... The life of the Catholic educator must be marked by the exercise of a personal vocation in the Church, not simply by the exercise of a profession."
(Lay Catholics in Schools: Witness to Faith, 1982, §§32; 37)

"Catholic teachers who freely accept posts in schools, which have a distinctive character, are obliged to respect that character and give their active support to it under the direction of those responsible."
(The Catholic School, 1977, §80)

In England, Catholic school governors have the powers under civil law to ensure that those whom they choose to appoint to posts within the school can and will contribute positively to the development and growth of what is essentially an ecclesial community. The principle statutes that apply are defined in the School Standards and Framework Act 1998, particularly Section 60(5)(a) and (b) and 60(6), the Education Act 2002 and the Education and Inspection Act 2006, together with the regulations that are derived from them. Section 60 (5) applied to teachers; section 60 (6) to non-teaching staff. Their respective provisions will be explored more fully in chapter 6.

SUMMARY
This chapter provides a brief review of the essentially religious character of Catholic education. It is rooted in a belief in God and in the historical person of Jesus of Nazareth, from which it derives a specific understanding and perspective of the meaning and purpose of human existence. This

religious perspective inevitably influences the way in which its schools function. Whilst they are accountable to society for the way in which they help the young develop into good citizens, they are also accountable to the Church community for seeking to achieve that goal within the context of the values and attitudes enshrined in Catholic doctrine.

NOTES

1   For example, see Ottaway, A. K. C. (1953) *Education and Society: An Introduction to the Sociology of Education*, London, Routledge & Kegan Paul; Lester Smith, W. O. (1957) *Education*, Harmondsworth, Penguin; Musgrave, P. W. (1965) *The Sociology of Education*, London, Methuen; Shipman, M. D. (1968) *Sociology of the School*, London, Longman; Banks, O. (1968) *The Sociology of Education*, London, Batsford; Swift, D. F. (1969) *The Sociology of Education: Introductory Analytical Perspectives*, London, Routledge & Kegan Paul; King R. (1969) *Education*, London, Longman.

2   In summary, these were described as maintaining and developing the assumptions underpinning a country's political system and ensuring its home-grown future politicians; developing an appropriate pool of capabilities within the labour force; and promoting the economic well-being both of individuals and the state. An accessible and extended account of the economic functions of schools in the immediate post-war decades can be found in Musgrave, P. M. (1972) *The Sociology of Education*, London, Methuen (Second Edition – University Paperbacks, Chapter 17, 312-349).

3   While this may indeed be the (unintended) effect of the form of education experienced by pupils in secular schools in England, recent evidence from regional soundings about the current state of primary education undertaken by researchers from Cambridge University suggest that some parents saw schools were providing, or should be providing, an antidote to the pervading and corrosive influence of consumerism and individualism of current society. A few headteachers stressed the need for schools to be counter-cultural, providing an education that did not reflect social trends but helped children towards a sense of critical independence. See Alexander R. & Hargreaves, L. (2007) *Community Soundings: The Primary Review, regional witness sessions, Cambridge*, University of Cambridge Faculty of Education.

4   See Alexander, H. A. (2005) Education in Ideology, *Journal of Moral Education*, 34. 1. 1-18.

5   Not everyone accepts the argument of theists that God exists. However, this does not imply that the theists' position is, of itself, in any way irrational. Philosophical grounds for such a belief rest mainly on ontological arguments that point to the necessary existence of a supreme being, upon cosmological arguments rooted in experience of caused things, and versions of teleological arguments based on features of apparent design in the world including the demands of morality, the existence of beauty and human rationality. Other rational grounds include religious experience, revelation through scripture, the claims of the historic person of Christ and propositions such as Pascal's wager. (That is it makes sense in as much as, if one believes and commits oneself to a life of faith in God and it turns out to be true, then one gains enormously, while if it is false one has lost nothing).

6   In this context *redemption* implies a liberation from a state of bondage caused by sin to the freedom that is brought by God's forgiveness and the promise of eternal life with Him. While the process of redemption is central to Christian faith, it has not been explicitly defined. See Fiorenza, F. S. (1990) Redemption, in J. A. Komonchak, M. Collins & D. Lane (eds) (1990) *The New Dictionary of Theology*, Dublin, Gill & Macmillan, pp. 836-851. However, the concept is pivotal in the Church's understanding of the nature of God and Jesus and on which the Church builds its particular view of humanity and the purpose of human existence.

7   See Catechism of the Catholic Church, (1994) London, Geoffrey Chapman, §§355-368.

8   See Dignitatis humanae [Declaration on Religious Liberty] (1965), §10, in: A. Flannery (ed) (1981) *Vatican Council II – The Conciliar and Post Conciliar Documents*, Leominster, Fowler Wright.

9   See Haldane J. (1996) Catholic Education and Catholic Identity, in: T. H. McLaughlin, J. O'Keefe, & B. O'Keeffe (eds) (1996) *The Contemporary Catholic School: Context, Identity and Diversity*, London, Falmer Press. Haldane's analysis, however useful, does not imply that there is one universally accepted, single, overriding model of Catholic school, see, for example, Gallagher, J. (1996) and Hastings, P. (1996) both in: T. H. McLaughlin, J. O'Keefe, & B. O'Keeffe (eds) (1996) *The Contemporary Catholic School: Context, Identity and Diversity*, London, Falmer Press. See also, Sullivan, J. (2000) *Catholic Schools in Contention*, Dublin, Lindiafarne, particularly chp. 1.

10 See Sacred Congregation for Catholic Education (1988) *The Religious Dimension of Education in a Catholic School*, London, Catholic Truth Society, §§67; 68.

11 See Catechesi tradendae [Catechesis in our time] (1979), §18, in: A. Flannery (ed) (1982) *Vatican Council II – More Post Conciliar Documents*, New York, Costello Publishing Company.

12 See Dignitatis humanae, [Declaration on Religious Liberty] (1965), §3, in: A. Flannery (ed) (1981) *Vatican Council II – The Conciliar and Post Conciliar Documents*, Leominster, Fowler Wright; Sacred Congregation for Catholic Education (1982) *Lay Catholics in Schools: Witnesses to Faith*, London, Catholic Truth Society, §42.

13 See Grace, G. (2002) *Catholic Schools: Mission, Markets and Morality*, London, RoutledgeFalmer, particularly chapter 8.

14 For discussions of the nature of indoctrination and its relationship with the type of education provided in Catholic schools, see, for example, various chapters in: Snook, I. A. (ed) (1972) *Concepts of Indoctrination*, London, Routledge & Kegan Paul; See also Mitchell, B. (1900) *How to Play Theological Ping-Pong: Collected Essays on Faith and Reason*, London, Hodder & Stoughton, chp. 6, pp. 88-97; Barrow R. & Woods, R. (1975) *An Introduction to Philosophy of Education*, London, Methuen, chapter 5, pp. 63-78; Hirst, P. H. (1981) Education, Catechesis and the Church School, *British Journal of Religious Education*, 3. 3. 85-101; Leahy, M. (1990) Indoctrination, Evangelisation, Catechesis and Religious Education, *British Journal of Religious Education*, 12. 3. 137-144; [N.B. There is a good critique of Hirst's 1981 paper in: Thiessen, E. J. (1993) Two concepts or two phases of liberal education, in: L. J. Francis and D. Lankshear (eds) (1993) *Christian Perspectives on Church Schools*, Leominster, Gracewing].

15 See Francis, L. J. (2002) Catholic Schools and Catholic Values: a study of moral and religious values among 13-15 year old pupils attending non-denominational and Catholic schools in England and Wales, *International Journal of Education and Religion*, 3. 69-84. Francis argued that pupils in Catholic schools can be categorised into four groups; active, sliding, and lapsed Catholics and non-Catholics. The non-Catholic group can, of course, be subdivided into those who adhere to a religious faith (likely with the same level of commitment as Francis ascribes to Catholics) and those who claim no religious adherence.

16 Hume, B. (1988), *Towards a Civilisation of Love*, London, Hodder & Stoughton, pp. 103-117.

17 For a general explanation of such expectations see the post-conciliar documents prepared by the Sacred Congregation for Catholic Education, *The Catholic School* (1977); *Lay Catholics in Schools: Witnesses to Faith* (1982) *The Religious Dimension of Education in a Catholic School* (1988). For full details see bibliography.

Specific guidance is usually provided by the relevant Diocesan Director of Schools to school governors to help them understand the essentially religious character of their schools when they appoint staff and, therefore, the legal context within which they must make their judgements and decisions during the appointment process.

Model contracts of employment for use in Catholic Schools in England and Wales are prepared by the Catholic Education Service (CES). They specify the religious character of the school and the consequent expectations placed on teachers and other staff – for details of the terminology used in the various types of CES contracts, see, *http//www.cesew.org.uk/publications/contracts&appointments*.

18 Education Act 2002, Section 21(4); SI 2007/0957 School Governance (Constitution) Regulations 2007, Regulation 8.

Chapter 6
THE LEGAL RIGHTS AND RESPONSIBILITIES OF PARENTS

THE FAMILY AND THE STATE: CATHOLIC SOCIAL TEACHING

In order to appreciate the case being made for Catholic schools it is necessary to understand the Church's position concerning the nature of human life within society. This first section, therefore, draws heavily on the *Compendium of the Social Doctrine of the Church*,[1] published by the Pontifical Council for Justice and Peace in 2004. It describes the Church's moral teaching about the relationship between individual citizens and the society in which they live.

The Church starts from the position that since individual human beings pre-exist any form of collectivist state organisation and are a necessary precondition for the formation of any political entity or structure, the state exists for their benefit, not the individual for the state. It contends, nevertheless, that we are essentially social beings and that community life is a defining characteristic of the human condition. That does not mean, of course, that community life is necessarily harmonious or uniform and the Church accepts and acknowledges social pluralism, which it regards as both an inevitable and healthy condition.

The basic principles on which the Church's social doctrine is built are found in the concepts of the intrinsic God given **dignity of the human person** (in which, it argues, the roots of all human rights are found); **the common good; subsidiarity** and **solidarity**. It is important to understand that those four principles represent an interconnected moral unity precisely because, from the Church's perspective, they refer to the ultimate and organisational foundations of life in a just society. Further, the Church regards human rights as deriving primarily from God the creator, not any state, international body or legislature. Their articulation and implementation is, however, contingent upon state power and, the Church argues, it is one of the prime functions of the state to affirm and protect those rights that flow from respecting the demands of human dignity. Directly connected to the expectation that such rights will be secured are the necessary and corresponding duties falling on the individuals so protected.

Two of the above principles are particularly pertinent to the purposes of this chapter. The **common good** can be defined as the sum total of conditions which allow people, either as groups or as individuals, to reach their fulfilment more fully and more easily. It is 'common' because, the Church asserts, individuals cannot find true fulfilment alone; they exist with and for others. From this it follows that people should be concerned with the general welfare of all, not simply their own personal or group interests. It is not just a matter for individuals, however, but also a responsibility of the state to conduct its legislative activities in such a way as to harmonise differing sectional interests, to provide justice for all members of society including any minority groups.

The second concept is that of **subsidiarity**.[2] It derives from the principle that all social bodies exist for the sake of the individual, so that whatever functions individuals can effectively discharge should not be taken over by society, and what small organisations, societies or associations can do, a larger political entity, such as the state, should not appropriate to itself. Adapted for political purposes, it becomes the principle whereby power and decision making responsibilities are devolved to the lowest practical level and, therefore, requires the state to refrain from taking upon itself those activities that can be (and perhaps are already being) effectively accomplished by a lower-order organisation. This concept is inherent to the Church's understanding of the importance of the family vis-à-vis the state. It argues that the family is a freely created community of persons, the first human society and the natural community in which human social nature is experienced and developed. It argues further:

> "A society built on a family scale is the best guarantee against drifting off course into individualism or collectivism, because within the family the person is always at the centre of attention as an end and never as a means."
> (Compendium of the Social Doctrine of the Church, 2004, §213)

Consequently, it asserts the priority of the family over the state and society in general, arguing that, in their relationship with families, all should abide by the subsidiarity principle.

THE STATE AND PARENTAL RIGHTS: INTERNATIONAL LEGAL PERSPECTIVES

Much of the Church's teaching outlined above is reflected within the existing legal framework of the United Kingdom that has, in recent years, been heavily influenced by various international declarations and conventions. For example, in relation to the primacy of the family, the United Nations Universal Declaration of Human Rights states that:

> *"The family is the natural and fundamental group unit of society and is entitled to protection by society and the state"*

Article 16(3)

and also that:

> *"Parents have the prior right to choose the kind of education that shall be given to their children."*

Article 26(3)

While it is the case that current Human Rights legislation in the UK is rooted in the Universal Declaration, it must be borne in mind that the Declaration and the various subsequent UN Conventions that are derived from it have not all been formally incorporated into our legal system. Many of their provisions are, therefore, largely aspirational and do not necessarily, of themselves, have direct legal force in England, though may well influence legal judgements and attitudes. The International Convention on Civil and Political Rights is one such convention which appears to have influenced the way in which recent governments have developed policies suitable for a pluralistic, multi-ethnic and multicultural society. Article 27 states:

> *"In those states in which ethnic, religious or linguistic minorities exist, persons belonging to such minorities shall not be denied the right, in community with other members of their own group, to enjoy their own culture, to profess and practise their own religion, or to use their own language."*

It has been argued that minorities to whom the Convention applies are afforded the benefits of a degree of special protection and any individual seeking the protection of Article 27 can do so solely on the basis of their membership of an identifiable group.[3] The Convention's rights apply whether or not a minority group is recognised by the state and are protected in this way to ensure the survival and continued development of the cultural, religious and social identity of the minority concerned. The test of the state's compliance with Article 27 will be primarily through meeting objective criteria, e.g. minority schools and, possibly, the means by which members of the minority group can obtain access to them.[4]

The International Convention on the Rights of the Child grew out of the Declaration of Human Rights, was adopted by the United Nations General

Assembly in 1989 and ratified by the UK government in 1991. It sets out the fundamental rights and freedoms of all people under the age of 18 (the UN definition of the end of childhood unless, under national legislation, the age of majority is earlier) and, while not conferring legally enforceable rights, it does impose minimum obligations on signatory nations. The following Articles are particularly relevant when considering the respective rights and duties that states and parents have for children:

> *"States Parties shall respect and ensure the rights set forth in the present Convention to each child within their jurisdiction without discrimination of any kind, irrespective of the child's or his or her parent's or legal guardian's race, colour, sex, language, religion, political or other opinion, national, ethnic or social origin, property, disability, birth or other status."*
>
> Article 2 (1)

> *"(1) States Parties shall respect the right of the child to freedom of thought, conscience and religion.*
>
> *(2) States Parties shall respect the rights and duties of parents ... to provide direction to the child in the exercise of his or her right in a manner consistent with the evolving capabilities of the child.*
>
> *(3) Freedom to manifest one's religion or beliefs may be subject only to such limitations as are prescribed by law and are necessary to protect public safety, order, health or morals, or the fundamental rights and freedoms of others."*
>
> Article 14

> *"States Parties shall use their best efforts to ensure recognition of the principle that both parents ... have the primary responsibility for the upbringing and development of the child ... ."*
>
> Article 18 (1)

PARENTAL RESPONSIBILITY AND EDUCATION: CHURCH TEACHING

Consistent with its emphasis on the dignity of the person, the Church argues that the parents have the prime and irreplaceable role in the upbringing and education of its children. It states that:

> *"the rights and duties of parents to educate their children is essential since it is connected with the transmission of human life; it is original and primary with regard to the educational role of others on account of the uniqueness of*

*the loving relationship between parents and children; and it is irreplaceable
and inalienable, and therefore incapable of being entirely delegated to others
or usurped by others."*

(Compendium of the Social Doctrine of the Church, 2004, § 239)

Despite its insistence on the primacy of parents, the Church recognises and
acknowledges that the wider society has a legitimate interest in children's
education, though its extent should be limited to what the Church, referring
back to the concept of subsidiarity, describes as "the special competence
and contribution proper to itself."[5] How the Church sees this operating
within England and Wales is outlined later in this chapter.

PARENTAL RESPONSIBILITY AND EDUCATION: LEGISLATIVE FRAMEWORK[6]

Members of the Council of Europe signed the European Convention on
Human Rights on 4th November 1950. The UK government ratified it in
1951. It came into force in 1953 but it was not until 1966 that individuals
within the UK could take a case to the European Court of Human Rights.
The introduction of the Human Rights Act in 1998 enabled British people
to seek redress against the state in our own courts. For the purposes of
this chapter, the relevant sections of the Convention are Articles 9, 14 and
Article 2 of the First Protocol.

Article 9 gives qualified rights to religious minorities. It provides protection
against persecution and requires the state to respect the religious beliefs of its
citizens, subject to certain controls. Article 14 is concerned, in a general way,
with preventing unfair discrimination in relation to other Convention Rights.

*1. Everyone has the right to freedom of thought, conscience and religion
… to manifest his religion or belief, in worship, teaching, practice and
observance.*

*2. … subject only to such limitations as are prescribed by law and are
necessary in a democratic society in the interests of public safety, for the
protection of public order, health or morals, or for the protection of the
rights and freedoms of others.*

Article 9

*"The enjoyment of the rights and freedoms set forth in this Convention
shall be secured without discrimination on any grounds such as sex, race,
colour, language. Religion, political or other opinion, nation or social origin
associated with a national minority, property, birth or other status."*

Article 14

The right to education is the subject of Article 2 of the First Protocol of the Convention.

> *"No person shall be denied the right to education. In the exercise of any functions which it assumes in relation to education and to teaching, the state shall respect the right of parents to ensure such education and teaching in conformity with their own religious and philosophical convictions."*
>
> First Protocol - Article 2

This Article, however, has been subject to reservations and caveats by a number of countries and, as far as the UK is concerned, the Article must be read subject to the reservation secured at the time the Protocol was signed. Accordingly this provides that the principle in the second sentence applies:

> *"only so far as it is compatible with the provision of efficient instruction and training and the avoidance of unreasonable public expenditure."*

As such, it is consistent with the longstanding provisions set out, firstly, in the Education Act 1944, Section 76 and subsequently included in the Education Act 1996, Section 9. However, the requirement that the "state shall respect the rights of parents ..." is legally much stronger than the phrase used in sections 9 and 509(4)(b) of the Education Act 1996; namely requiring local authorities merely to "... have regard to ...".

The provisions outlined above contained in the ratified International Conventions seem to support, and be supported by, the established position of parents in UK law. Though education in England and Wales is compulsory, it has always been, and remains the case, that parents have the right and main responsibility for determining the form of education that their children will receive. This does, of course, have practical limitations. In legal terms, the wishes of the parents cannot be taken as determinative. However, the essential principles are clearly set out in the Education Act 1996. Parents have the primary responsibility for ensuring that their children receive an effective education and, while the vast majority delegate that responsibility to a state maintained school, they are not required to do so. They can educate their children elsewhere. Where they do want to take advantage of the state maintained educational provision, they are able, under current admissions arrangements to express a preference as to the type of school they wish for their children and have a reasonable expectation, within legal caveats, that their preference will be accommodated.

"The parent of every child of compulsory school age shall cause him to receive efficient full-time education suitable –

(a) to his age, ability and aptitude, and

(b) to any special educational needs he may have,

either by regular attendance at school or otherwise".

Education Act 1996, Section 7

(previously s.36 of the Education Act 1944)

"In exercising or performing all their respective powers and duties under the Education Acts, the Secretary of State, local education authorities and the funding authorities shall have regard to the general principle that pupils are to be educated in accordance with the wishes of their parents, so far as that is compatible with the provision of efficient instruction and training and the avoidance of unreasonable public expenditure."

Education Act 1996, Section 9

The legal (as opposed to moral) question of what might constitute a suitable education, and how best this might be provided, also rests primarily with parents. The following judgements given in English courts about the type of education that children should receive, given before incorporation of Human Rights legislation into UK law, seem to be consistent with that legislation and with the moral position articulated by the Church. The first by Viscount Jowett, Lord Chancellor in Baxter v Baxter [1947] All E.R. 886, affirmed the right of parents to bring up their children within their existing religio/cultural framework when he said:

"In any view of Christian marriage, the essence of the matter as it seems to me, is that children, if there be any, should be born into a family, as that word is understood in Christendom generally; and in the case of a marriage between spouses of a particular Faith that they should be brought up and nurtured in that Faith."

The following two judgements are not directly connected, but both address the interpretation of what might constitute a 'suitable' education, especially within the context of a diverse society. In a case brought at Worcester Crown Court in 1981 (Harrison & Harrison v Stevenson), the judge defined a 'suitable education' as one which was such as:

"1. to prepare the children for life in modern civilised society, and

2. to enable them to achieve their full potential."

This limited clarification was extended by the judgment in the case of R v Secretary of State for Education and Science, ex parte Talmud Torah

Machzikei Hadass School Trust (1985) (Times, 12 April 1985). Mr. Justice Woolf held that:

> *"education is 'suitable' if it primarily equips a child for life within the community of which he is a member, rather than the way of life in the country as a whole, as long as it does not foreclose the child's options in later years to adopt some other form of life if he wishes to do so".*

LEGITIMATE POWERS AND RESPONSIBILITIES OF THE STATE
ATTENDANCE AT SCHOOL

There are few today who would argue against the value of compulsory education both for individuals and the societies within which they live.[7] Indeed, under Article 2 of the First Protocol of the European Convention for the Protection of Human Rights, education is regarded as a universal right, with international pressure being brought to bear on those countries which, for a variety of reasons, do not have some form of provision for, at least, elementary education. It is a perfectly reasonable and moral position for the state, therefore, to use coercive legislation and make the education of children compulsory. This does not necessarily imply, of course, that children should be educated in a school[8] provided by the state or any other institution.

Legislation for England and Wales recognizes the primary role of parents but still places an obligation upon them; namely to have their children educated. They cannot legally deny their children a suitable education, though there is wide discretion for them to decide its nature and character. Should they decide to send their child to a state maintained school, parents commit an offence if the child fails to attend regularly at that school. Note that it is the parents who are accountable in law whether or not they are in any way complicit in the child's non-attendance. They may have a defence, however, if they live beyond walking distance from the school at which the child is registered and the local authority has not made suitable transport arrangements for the child.[9]

The current legislation concerning the provision of transport has its roots in the Education Act 1944. It would seem that section 55 (Provision of transport and other facilities) owes its origin to the existence and proposed development of the denominational sector while the powers of direction on the part of the Minister (Secretary of State) were deliberately included to secure access to such schools should parents live within a local authority that seemed reluctant to provide suitable arrangements. Such a political stance clearly accepted the primacy of parents in the education of their children. Given the way in which that understanding seems to have been accorded diminished significance in recent parliamentary debates,[10] it is perhaps useful here to quote at length extracts from a paper[11] prepared by Michael Power, the former Deputy Director, now retired, of the Catholic Education Service. In it he charts the passage of the 1943 Education Bill to enactment in 1944 and some of its subsequent amendments.

Pages 2-3

"...... *Clause 53 of the Education Bill 1943 read:*

"A local education authority may make such arrangements for the provision of transport and otherwise as they consider necessary or as the Minister may direct for the purpose of facilitating the attendance of pupils at schools or young people's colleges or at any course or class provided in pursuance of a scheme of further education in force for their area, and may pay any reasonable travelling expenses of such pupils."

The generality of the terms of the Clause does, however, disguise its true purport. Mr Butler and his colleagues had recognised at a much earlier stage that the "auxiliary" schools, the then generic term for controlled, aided and special agreement establishments, amended later in the House of Lords with the substitution of the word "Voluntary", in many instances would have natural catchment areas of much larger size than the county schools. The Clause featured in the Bill because of that recognition. In other words, its very existence was because of the proposed development of the Voluntary sector. This is made eminently clear in a speech Mr Butler made when moving one of a number of Government amendments to the Clause during the Committee consideration of the Bill:

".....nor could I make it any clearer that it is our desire that children belonging to a particular denomination should go to a school of that denomination. That is the whole object of that clause."

(Hansard, House of Commons, May 9th 1944, Col.1752)

And later, in response to a question, stated of the Clause:

"It is all for the purposes of enabling children to attend schools which are suited to the beliefs and desires of their parents. I can give a definite undertaking about that."

(Hansard, House of Commons, May 9th 1944, Col 1753)

... Again, Government intention in 1943 and 1944 appears unambiguous. The powers of the Minister and "direction" in transport matters feature in the Board

---

of Education's explanatory memorandum, Cmd..3492, December 1943 where these powers are described as being proposed to be put in place in order to:

"deal with any cases in which transport facilities are unreasonably withheld."

And later, when the Bill was being considered at Committee Stage in the House of Lords, a Government Minister, the Earl of Selborne observed:

"I would also draw your Lordships' attention that under Clause 53 the Government, for the first time, are taking power to direct authorities to provide transport where circumstances render it appropriate."

(Hansard, House of Lords, June 22nd, 1944, Col. 414).

[Two] amendments made to the original Clause during the passage of the Bill must be noted. Firstly, the words "may make such arrangements" were replaced by the words "<u>shall</u> make such arrangements". ...

Secondly, the phrase at the end of the original Clause, "and may pay any reasonable travelling expenses of such pupils" was deleted and in its stead was inserted:

"and any transport provided in pursuance of such arrangements shall be provided free of charge".

Pages 18-19

A number of amendments to S.55 were added to the original provisions between 1986 and 1993. One important amendment ... was eventually agreed in the House of Lords during the passage of what became the Education Act 1993. These are currently to be found at S.509, Education Act 1996. ...

At Second Reading of the Bill in the House of Lords, the Duke of Norfolk lent powerful support to a proposed amendment to S.55. This he pursued doughtily through the Committee Stage, as Hansard faithfully records.

Eventually Government conceded that a jointly agreed amendment would be acceptable. That which was ultimately agreed was a variation of the seventh version of an amendment which was tabled for debate or discussion with Department of Education officials.

The amendment extended the then Section 55(3) in adding to the requirements which all LEAs were "to have regard" before determining whether transport costs were to be met free of charge, the requirement to have regard to "any wish of his *(the pupil's)* parent for him to be provided with education at a school or institution in which the religious education provided is that of the religion or denomination to which his parent adheres."

During the debates, the Duke of Norfolk constantly reminded fellow Peers of the original intentions of the 1944 Government, and with some telling effect.

The amendment endeavoured to restore some of that "original intention" and in his speeches the Duke used a number of Hansard quotations from Commons debates, some of which appear in Part 1 of this paper.

The Duke also made the point that the Churches were not seeking to increase the size of the current "transport bill", but to preserve then existing provisions.

Shortly after moving the amendment, which was subsequently accepted by Government, the Lord Harvington intervened briefly:

> "My Lords, I am afraid that I cannot resist the temptation of being able to stand here tonight and say that I attended every sitting in another place when the 1944 Act was being considered and heard Rab Butler say the words which my noble friend the Duke of Norfolk has just quoted. What he has said was the Government's intention then..."
>
> (Hansard, Col 113, HL 21 June 1993)

(Lord Harvington had previously sat in the Commons as the MP for St. Pancras North from 1937 to 1945, then Wing Commander Grant-Ferris...)

The amendment was included in Schedule 19, paragraph 15 of the 1998 Act."

EDUCATION OTHER THAN IN SCHOOL

Under the provisions of section 7 of the Education Act 1996 parents may decide to educate their children at home. However, if it appears a child of compulsory school age is not receiving a suitable education, either by regular attendance at a school or by some other appropriate means, local authorities have a duty to take action.[12] Case law has established that, where a child is receiving education at home, the authority may ask the parents for information to help it assess whether it is suitable.[13] If, after considering all the information provided, it still appears that the child is not receiving suitable education, the local authority may look to serve the parents with a school attendance order. However, the onus would be on the authority to show conclusively that the child was not receiving a suitable education. The test, should the matter come to court, is whether on the balance of probabilities a reasonable person would conclude that a suitable education is being provided.[14]

PARENTAL AND CHILDREN'S RIGHTS

While Article 2 of the First Protocol places an obligation on the state, in the exercise of any functions which it assumes in relation to education and teaching, to respect the right of parents to ensure such education and teaching in conformity with their own religious and philosophical convictions, no mention is made of any rights accruing to the child. Their religious and philosophical convictions carry only subsidiary weight (if any).

Some have argued that this is an inappropriate state of affairs and that greater consideration should be given to the rights of children.[15] The idea that children enjoy rights is not a new one but there are difficulties when decisions are made, especially if the child's wishes conflict with those of the parents. The immaturity and inherent powerlessness, particularly of young children, means that their rights are only ever enforceable as obligations on adults who can, legitimately, only be either their parents (or guardians) or the state. In Western democracies it would require unusual circumstances for the state to usurp the normal functions of parents,[16] though in cases of, for example, real or alleged child neglect or abuse it may well do so, irrespective of the expressed wishes of the child. On the other hand, it is argued that older and more mature children should, at least, have their views taken into account when decisions are made on their behalf. Of course, when they attain adulthood, they can legally make their own decisions entirely independently of the views of their parents if they so wish.

When developing a legal framework of parental and children's rights in education the prime concern of the post-war international agencies was to protect children from indoctrination by fascists and by other undesirable political extremists. This applies particularly in state schools.[17] One way of achieving freedom from possible state indoctrination was to give parents rights over their children so that those rights would prevail not only over the children's rights but also over the wishes of (possibly malevolent) governments. Certainly, the United Nations seems to regard the protection of children from state indoctrination as more important than protecting them from (possible) parental indoctrination.[18] Consequently, Article 18(4) of the Convention on Human Rights requires states to:

> "... have respect[19] for the liberty of parents and, when applicable, legal guardians, to ensure the religious and moral education of their children in conformity with their own convictions."

and, using the same phraseology, Article 13 of the International Covenant on Economic, Social and Cultural Rights, requires the state to:

> "have respect for the liberty of parents and, when applicable, legal guardians, to choose for their children schools other than those established by the

public authorities, which conform to such minimum standards as may be laid down or approved by the State and to ensure the religious and moral education of their children in conformity with their own convictions."

Given that phraseology, it is clear that the rights of children in this area are (generally) subordinated to those of their parents. The various associated relevant declarations, and the consequent human rights cases, have failed to resolve the question of what rights children may have under international law if they come to disagree with the religious or philosophical views of their parents. The dilemma is that, if parents must be given the right to intervene on behalf of their children, in order to assert and protect their children's rights, then the children themselves cannot be given a right to litigate separately and/or in disagreement with their own protecting parents. However, it has been argued that children of an appropriate age and maturity should have their own views respected and taken into account.[20] In England, some have argued the principle of "Gillick competence" transfers easily to the Article 9 sphere of the freedom of thought, conscience and religion and to the right to education in Article 2 of the First Protocol.[21] While this may be the case above the age of compulsory education, it is hard to see any application before that age while the law still places the duty solely upon parents to ensure their children are educated.[22]

SUMMARY

While recognising that in modern Western democracies the education of the young is of legitimate interest to both parents and the state, this chapter tries to explain and defend the case for the primacy of parents for the education of their children both on moral and legal grounds. Further, it tries to show that the state has a moral obligation to use the available public finances in such a way as to enable rather than restrict the exercise of those rights.

The moral position advocated by the Catholic Church has been defined in its social teaching over many years. The underlying concepts of that teaching have, by and large, been accepted and incorporated into the various international Declarations and Conventions on Human Rights and into the UK legislative framework. While it is the case under such legislation that there is no legal obligation upon governments to provide or support any particular type of school (including Catholic schools)[23], it seems that there is a measure of legislative support for the continuance of such state maintained schools as are already in existence. In such circumstances, it appears that human rights legislation defends the rights of parents, placing them above the rights of states, in determining the nature and character of the education that children receive. In England, consequently, the Church would argue that for those Catholic parents who wish their children to receive an education within a Catholic environment, it is incumbent on the state both to do all that is reasonable to facilitate the parents' wishes to send their children to a Catholic school and to desist from any actions that would make it more difficult for them to exercise that parental responsibility.

NOTES

1   Pontifical Council for Justice & Peace (2004) *Compendium of the Social Doctrine of the Church*, London Burns & Oates - see particularly §§ 144-245.

2   See the encyclical by Pope Pius XI *Quadregesimo Anno* (1931) §§ 79-80

3   Whitbourn, S. (2003) *Education and the Human Rights Act 1998*, Slough, National Foundation for Educational Research.

4   For further explanation of minority rights under the Convention see – Smith, R. K. M. (2003) *International Human Rights*, Oxford, Oxford University Press.

5   Pontifical Council for Justice & Peace (2004) *Compendium of the Social Doctrine of the Church*, London, Burns & Oates, §240.

6   A comprehensive explanation of the legal duties of parents as defined by the Education Act 1944, and before the onslaught of legislation beginning in 1980, can be found in Taylor, G. & Saunders, J. B. (1976) *The Law of Education*, London, Butterworths, pp. 34-39.

7   The de-schooling ideas developed in the late 1960s and early 1970s have found little favour with Western democratic governments. See, for example, 'The Futility of Schooling' and 'School the Sacred Cow', both in: Illich, I. (1971) *Celebration of Awareness*, Harmondsworth, Penguin; also, Goodman, P. (1972) *Compulsory Miseducation*, Harmondsworth, Penguin.

8   The Education Act 1944, section 114, defined a 'school' as an institution at which full-time education is provided for more than five pupils of compulsory school age. That definition was incorporated in the Education Act 1996 in section 463. Section 172 of the Education Act 2002 added to that definition: *(1) "Independent school" means any school at which full-time education is provided for (a) five or more pupils of compulsory school age, or (b) at least one pupil of that age for whom a statement is maintained under section 324, or who is looked after by a local authority, … and which is not a school maintained by a local authority or a special school so maintained.*

9   The parents may have a defence under the provisions of the Education Act 1996, Section 444 (4) where the child is of compulsory school age and is registered at a school but fails to attend regularly at that school if:

(a)   … the school at which the child is a registered pupil is not within walking distance of the child's home, and

(b) ... no suitable arrangements have been made by the local education authority for...

   (i)   his transport to and from school,

   (ii)   boarding accommodation..., or

   (iii)   enabling him to become a registered pupil at a school nearer to his home."

10 Clearly there are differences of opinion on this matter, though in the UK the majority still generally support the dual system of (mainly Church sponsored) religious and secular (State sponsored) schools. There were attempts made in the House of Commons on 6th February 2002 (by Mr Frank Dobson) and in the House of Lords on 17th and 30th October 2006 (by Lord Baker) to introduce - via amendments to the Education Bill 2002 and Education and Inspection Bill 2006 respectively – a quota system into the admissions processes of new Church or faith based schools for pupils who were not adherents to the particular faith with the intention of promoting social cohesion. In the case of Lord Baker, he argued that his amendment had, at its heart, *"the shape of our society"* and that it was *"principally about Muslim schools"*. (Hansard 30th October, Columns 106-107). Both proposals had their supporters, though in each case the amendments were defeated. Given that regulations require Church or faith-based schools to show there is a sufficient and sustainable demand from adherents to the particular faith to justify a school before one can be opened, the effect of a quota system of non-adherents would be to deny parents who are practising adherents the possibility of having their children educated in a school that could secure religious and moral education in accordance with their religious convictions. In the House of Commons in 2004, Dr. Evan Harris tried to introduce a Bill prohibiting parents exercising that 'right'. These recent examples illustrate how, in today's society, the perceived good of social engineering is given priority over parental rights by a significant minority in the legislature.

11 Power, M. (2001) *Home to School Transport: A Discussion Paper*, unpublished internal document, London, Catholic Education Service.

12 Education Act 1996, sections 437-443.

13 In Phillips v Brown, Lord Donaldson said: *"Of course such a request is not the same as a notice under s 37 (1) of the Education Act 1944 [now s 437 (1) of the Education Act 1996] and the parents will be under no duty to comply. However it would be sensible for them to do so. If parents give no information or adopt the course ... of merely stating that they are discharging their duty without giving any details of how they are doing so, the LEA will have to consider and decide whether it 'appears' to it that the parents are in breach of s 36"* [now s 7 of the Education Act 1996].

14 Note that the test about "suitability" is not the high level used in criminal courts of "beyond all reasonable doubt".

15 See Parker-Jenkins, M. (2005) *The legal framework for faith-based schools and the rights of the child*; also Mason, M. (2005) *Religion and Schools – a fresh way forward? A rights-based approach to diversity in schools*, both in: R. Gardner, J. Cairns & D. Lawton, (eds) (2005) *Faith Schools: Consensus or Conflict*, London, RoutledgeFalmer. There is a good review of the arguments in Parker-Jenkins, M. et al., (2005) *In Good Faith: Schools, Religion and Public Funding*, Aldershot, Ashgate, Chapter 8.

16 See Fortin, J. (2003) *Children's Rights and the Developing Law*, London, Lexis Nexis, 2nd edition. She discusses the essential immaturity of children, how it prevents their free exercise of many rights and how the existence of children's rights may damage the family unit as a whole. In an interesting analogy she compares the family unit to a small state and the relationship of the family-state with the nation as a form of international relations. In International Law, the nation-state may not usually invade the sovereignty of another state; in her analogy, the family-state.

17 In *Kjelsden and others v Denmark* 1 EHRR 711 (1976) the European Court of Human Rights said, *"The state in fulfilling the functions assumed by it in regard to education and teaching, must take care that information or knowledge included in the curriculum is conveyed in an objective, critical and pluralistic manner. The state is forbidden to pursue an aim of indoctrination which might be considered as not respecting parents' religious and philosophical convictions. That is the limit that must not be exceeded."*

18 For further discussion of the background to this dilemma, see, Van Bueren, G. (1994) *The International Law on the Rights of the Child,* Boston and London, Martinus Nijhoff Dordrecht.

19 In this Convention, and in the extract from the Covenant on Economic, Social and Cultural Rights set out in the subsequent paragraph, the word 'respect' means more than just take into account. But it does not provide the parent with the right of veto or a mandatory power over a public authority. It requires that the parents' conviction(s) must be considered, given due weight, and valued, but not necessarily followed if there are valid reasons for not doing so. Thus it seems 'due weight' must be given if a valid conviction is raised, but that need is not be taken as either a veto or a factor which compels the authority to do something if valid circumstances outweigh the conviction. Where a decision does not support the parental conviction(s), it is open to the parents to challenge the reasons given by the public authority for its actions in not doing so.

20 In an American case, *Wisconsin v Jonas Yoder,* a dissenting minority in the US Supreme Court held that, if an Amish child wished to stay in High School beyond the age of 14 or 15 (when Amish parents traditionally withdraw their children from school to concentrate on learning the agrarian skills which are appropriate to Amish parents' particular religious and philosophical convictions) and if the Amish child is sufficiently mature to have that desire respected, then the state would be able to override the parents' objections, even though those objections be rooted in the parents' firmly-held religious beliefs. However, the majority of the US Supreme Court took the opposite view.

21 See Hancox, N. (2005) *The Selective Funding of Faith Schools: A Legitimate Exercise of State Power?* Un-published LL.M thesis, University of East Anglia. He argues that, though the Human Rights Act is clear in giving parents control of any religious or philosophical bias in their children's education, the judgement in the case of *Gillick v West Norfolk and Wisbech AHA* may well apply to the field of education (although it has not yet been tested in the Courts). The case addressed the question of how the developing maturity of adolescents can be reflected in their legal powers to make decisions. There comes a time in every growing child's life when he or she reaches maturity and can take on the rights and responsibilities of adulthood. What the House of Lords said in *Gillick* is that the age of maturity is not the same as the legal age of majority and that for some purposes (particularly the personal health issues in *Gillick*) a child is competent to make her own decisions and that her parents need not be involved. Hancox suggests that many 16 and 17 year olds could be regarded as having 'Gillick competence' when it comes to choosing whether they want to attend a Church or faith school at sixth-form level — and if so, choosing which faith they want to follow at school even if it is contrary to the wishes of their parents.

22 Nevertheless, exactly such a proposal was recommended by the Joint Parliamentary Committee on Human Rights in its report on the Education and Skills Bill (Nineteenth Report, 13th May 2008, paragraph 1.45) in relation to pupils participation in Religious Education lessons and Religious worship.

23 The Belgium Linguistics Case [(1979-80) 1 EHRR 252] tested principles arising from the combination of Article 14 and Article 2 of the First Protocol of the Human Rights Act. Although this case was not about the provision of Religious based schools (parents complained that, under

Belgian law, their French-speaking children were unable to be educated in the French language since they lived in a Dutch-speaking part of Belgium where the schooling was conducted in Dutch) the judgement has particular relevance for the existing 'dual system' of education in England. The ECtHR held that the first sentence of Article 2 does not require that states establish an educational system or subsidise a particular type or level of educational system: *'The Convention lays down no specific obligations concerning the extent of these means and the manner of their organisation or subsidisation.'* Instead, the obligation on the state was to guarantee individuals the *'right of access to educational institutions existing at the time'* and that the State should regulate education which *'may vary in time and place according to the needs and resources of the community and of individuals'*.

Chapter 7

THE LEGAL CONTEXT FOR CATHOLIC SCHOOLS IN ENGLAND

INTRODUCTION

The educational system of any country cannot be considered in a vacuum. It is, inevitably, closely bound up with developing social and cultural conditions, and needs to be understood in relation to them and the legal parameters within which they are determined.

As outlined in the previous chapter, while there is a statutory responsibility placed upon parents to ensure their children are educated, there is no corresponding responsibility for that education to take place in school; either one maintained by the state or in a private institution. In part, this reflects the historical development of the current state system of education from its church dominated voluntary and philanthropic beginnings and explains the initial reluctance of the state to interfere in what was, and still is, essentially a matter for parents.[1] Nevertheless, though parents are not obliged to send their children to school in order to comply with the civil law, the vast majority of them do so.

This chapter considers the legal basis for Catholic schools in England and Wales. However, it is not intended to be an exhaustive and definitive legal guide but will describe, in general terms, the significant provisions in civil and church law that are essential to the preservation of the distinctive character and purposes of Catholic schools, enabling them to exist and function, both as an integral part of the national educational system and as mechanism to fulfil the salvific mission of the Catholic Church.

HISTORICAL CONTEXT

It could be argued that a starting point for the development of education in England and Wales can be dated from around the middle of the eighteenth century.[2] It was not until the middle of the nineteenth century, however, that the state began to enact specific educational legislation for the general child population of England and Wales,[3] as it became increasingly clear to government that voluntary efforts would not meet the national need.

Prior to that political imperative, the main impetus for mass education was humanitarian or religious in character, and was realised mainly, but not entirely, in charity schools established by Church of England parishes.

By about 1760, charity schools, both religious and secular, were educating some 30,000 children. In addition to those provided by the Church of England, there were also nonconformist and Catholic charity schools. However, these latter groups did not have any central co-ordinating bodies to stimulate and channel their activities in the way the Society for the Promoting of Christian Knowledge (SPCK) promoted the educative work of the Church of England.

Thus, when government did finally legislate in the later part of the nineteenth century, it was against the background of an existing system of voluntary Church and secular schools;[4] if the ad hoc provision of charity schools of the period can be properly termed a 'system'. In February 1870, the Liberal government introduced a Bill, which W. E. Forster, in charge of the Education Department at that time, argued would "complete the present voluntary system, to fill the gaps, sparing the public money where it can be done without, ...". The subsequent Education Act 1870 did not create a new system of education, or one that was completely compulsory or free. It left open the possibility for voluntary schools and, by providing newly created school boards which were to overcome deficiencies of provision where voluntary efforts did not succeed, established what is now termed the dual system of education. Paradoxically, one of the effects of school boards was to stimulate voluntary efforts. Between 1870 and 1876 over a million and a half new school places were provided; two-thirds by the various Churches.[5] Although school boards were abolished by the Education Act of 1902, the dual system of state and voluntary schools was retained.

THE ORIGINS AND DEVELOPMENT OF THE CATHOLIC SCHOOL SECTOR

The development of what we recognise as the Catholic system of education today can be traced back to the restoration of the Catholic hierarchy in England in 1850, as the anti-Catholic legislation that had developed since the Reformation was dismantled. England at that time was, in effect, a missionary area for the Catholic faith. The first act of the bishops as a collective body was to make the provision of Catholic elementary schools their highest priority.[6] The purpose was to ensure the development and transmission of Catholic faith and culture for the predominantly poor and working class Catholic community and, in doing so, contribute to the common good of society.

The Church claims its schools provide an education that is appropriate for any civic institution, but taught within a specifically religious cultural context that permeates all aspects of their day-to-day activities.[7] The Catholic bishops' current commitment is set out in, what they regard as, five key areas of the distinctive character of their schools, including the search for excellence and education of all, with a particular duty to care for the poor and disadvantaged.[8] Their concern for the poor and under privileged is not new but has formed a central element of its educative mission in England and Wales for over 150 years.[9] Then it was expressed in the drive to build elementary schools before churches. Now it is reflected in their espousal of voluntary aided and comprehensive status for diocesan schools together with a rejection of pupil selection by ability or aptitude. It is worth noting that the seven existing Catholic selective grammar schools are not diocesan schools but belong to religious orders.

The twenty-two dioceses in England and Wales are charities having essentially religious purposes. Their deeds of trust will make clear that their various activities are concerned with the advancement or maintenance of the Catholic religion.[10] Consequently, they are not educational charities *per se*, though their religious purposes are advanced through the provision of schools under the control of their respective bishops, but maintained by the state. As such, they are bound both by civil and canon (church) law relating to school ownership, use of school buildings, the employment of staff, their activities and the curriculum they teach.

The civil law comprises primary legislation (Acts of Parliament including Charity law), regulations (Statutory Instruments) and guidance (Circulars, Statutory and Non-Statutory Guidance). Under civil law the governing body carries the full duties and responsibilities of the employer and, as such, is bound by relevant employment law as well as educational law. Canon law is one of the major world legal systems. It comprises the norms and regulations underpinning the structure of a universal church. It describes the powers of the diocesan bishop and other diocesan structures, but its essential purpose is to define and protect the rights of individuals, with respect to the rights of others and the ecclesial community as a whole.

The current Code of Canon Law[11] is constructed to be in conformity with the decrees of the Second Vatican Council and recognises the principle of subsidiarity, leaving as much latitude as possible for the local bishop.[12] The relevant sections for education are in Title III (Catholic Education) of Book III (The Teaching Office of the Church). Canons 793 to 795 inc., are concerned with education generally, while canons 796 to 806 inc. refer specifically to Catholic schools.

SCHOOL AND DIOCESAN RELATIONSHIPS

The 1983 Code of Canon Law reserves for the local Ordinary (i.e. the diocesan bishop, or vicar acting in his name) the responsibility for controlling Catholic schools and diocesan education policy[13]. He fulfils that responsibility in respect of schools mainly through the foundation governors he appoints, together with the Diocesan Schools Commission[14] and the Diocesan Department of Religious Education. Diocesan schools, and the land that they are built upon, are owned by the diocese.[15] Both are held in trust by diocesan trustees appointed by the bishop. The trustees' role under the civil law applying to charities is to safeguard the interests of the Catholic community within the diocese as a whole and to serve diocesan needs under the terms of the appropriate diocesan trust deed.

Being primarily religious rather than educational charities, Catholic schools are provided by the Church to meet the legitimate rights of baptised Catholic parents[16] who wish to have their children educated in accordance with their own religious convictions. In this way, they are one arm of the evangelistic activity of the Church. Their aim is to be communities of faith within the wider Catholic body and to promote the Gospel of Jesus Christ, by their teaching, their worship and their communal relationships, both within the school and with the wider community. The prime purpose and ethos of the school is designed to enable the pupils to grow in every way to Christian maturity, rooted in a religious understanding of the nature and purpose of life as taught through the Magisterium of the Church. Consequently, for schools to be truly Catholic they must be conducted in accordance with the 1983 Code of Canon law, the teachings of the Catholic Church[17] and the diocesan trust deed[18].

It is the case that there may be other Catholic schools within the diocesan boundary, mainly owned by religious orders which have their own trustees, but no school can be legitimately regarded as having a Catholic religious character without the express approval and agreement of the diocesan bishop.[19] Since the bishop is responsible for all religious activities within his diocese, he has the right under canon law to determine what should be taught in religious education lessons, to agree the appointment of those responsible for religious education and to inspect all aspects of religious education in Catholic schools within the diocese. While the diocese has ownership of the school buildings, it is the governing body that runs the institution. However, the provisions of civil and canon law complement each other in such a way as to ensure that, in all essential matters, the bishop can have confidence that he retains control of the school and can secure its Catholic character through his ability to appoint and remove an overall majority of the governing body[20]. Those members, termed foundation governors, have an absolute duty to secure the school's Catholic character under the provisions of both civil and canon law.

RELATIONSHIP WITH THE MAINTAINING AUTHORITY

Successive Acts of Parliament since 1870[21] have recognised and confirmed the dual system of education in this country, i.e. the provision of schools both by the state, through local authorities, and by voluntary organisations (usually, but not always, churches). The concept embodied in legislation is of separate but collaborating bodies. This means that, for the Catholic sector, the dioceses that provide Catholic schools are coordinate with, not subordinate to, local authorities, whose responsibilities and powers in relation to voluntary schools are clearly delineated.[22] In relation to individual Catholic voluntary aided schools, case law has established that local education authorities have only those powers specified in legislation. Any powers not mentioned in statute as being the responsibility of any particular body remain with the individual governing body of the school.[23]

As well as these negative circumstances that separate the responsibilities and competencies of the governing body of an aided school vis-à-vis the maintaining authority, the state provides specific positive powers to governors to enable them to carry out their legal responsibilities. Legislation ensures that the governing body makes all staff appointments, determines pupil admissions, the nature of religious education and collective worship, and the content of sex education programmes. It also controls the use of the premises and decides term and holiday dates. All these responsibilities must be carried out within the context of the Instrument of Government which sets out a formal statement about what the school is, how it must be conducted and the composition of the governing body.

STATUTORY RESPONSIBILITIES OF THE GOVERNING BODY

Acting as a corporate body, all governors of any maintained Catholic school, whatever their status or appointing body, have a duty under civil law to conduct the school with a view to:

"a) promoting high standards of academic achievement,"

and, in doing so, they must comply with:

"b) the instrument of government, and any trust deed relating to the school."

(Education Act 2002, section 21(2))

Both the instrument of government and trust deed will contain a clause defining the school's essentially religious ethos, character and purpose. While the exact wording will differ in the various diocesan trust deeds, the 'ethos' statement that is required as part of the Instrument of Government of all maintained schools, will read as follows in all diocesan Catholic schools:

"The school was founded by and is part of the Catholic Church. The school is to be conducted as a Catholic School in accordance with the canon law and teachings of the Roman Catholic Church, and in accordance with the Trust Deed of the diocese of .... and in particular:

(a) religious education is to be in accordance with the teachings, doctrines, discipline and general and particular norms of the Catholic Church;

(b) religious worship is to be in accordance with the rites, practices, discipline and liturgical norms of the Catholic Church;

and at all times the school is to serve as a witness to the Catholic faith in Our Lord Jesus Christ."

So while the responsibility to safeguard the school's Catholic character school falls upon all governors, both individually and corporately, foundation governors have additional responsibilities. They are called to serve in a specific Church ministry. They have a responsibility to assist the bishop in carrying out the provisions of the trust deed relating to schools, in such a manner as is consistent with any determinations made by the bishop and trustees that are (lawfully) included in any commissioning letter sent to them on their appointment.

Their duties under civil law are similar and non-discretionary. It is not a matter of trying their best to meet the requirements laid upon them. They have an absolute responsibility in as much as they are appointed:

"(a) ... for the purpose of securing[24] that the [religious] character of the school ... is preserved and developed, and -

(b) ... for the purpose of securing that the school is conducted in accordance with ... the provisions of any trust deed relating to the school."

(School Governance (Constitution) Regulations 2007, Regulation 8)

EMPLOYMENT AND PERSONNEL POLICIES

In most instances, the governing body, as a whole, fulfils its statutory functions through the staff that it employs. It carries the full duties and responsibilities of an employer and, as such, is bound by relevant employment law as well as specific regulations relating to education. It is also bound by ecclesiastical laws[25] in so far as they do not conflict with civil legislation.

The principal education statutes relating to the employment of staff in Catholic maintained schools are found in the School Standards and Framework Act 1998, the Education Act 2002 and the Education and Inspection Act 2006. The specific rights of Catholic school governors were first set out in the Education Act 1998, section 60. Those provisions were not, in fact, new but simply made explicit that which has been implicit in all education legislation since 1944. At that time, non-teaching staff, it was reasonably assumed, would have no educative impact upon children and so the legitimate demands that could be made on teaching staff (in order to secure that children were educated in accordance with the religious convictions of their parents) did not apply. For teachers, the legislation broadly confirmed the following rights.

When employing teaching staff and determining their remuneration or promotion, the governing body may take into account candidates' religious opinions, affiliation, practice and their willingness to teach Religious Education and give preference to Catholics.

Any conduct by a teacher that is incompatible with the precepts, or with upholding the tenets of the Catholic Church may be taken into account by the governing body in connection with possible termination of their employment.

In recognition of the increasing use of non-teaching staff in teaching or quasi-teaching capacities, the Education and Inspection Act 2006, section 37, amended section 60(6) of the 1998 Education Act, extended the provisions in respect of teachers to non-teaching staff (in England only, not Wales).

The Human Rights Act 1998 and the provisions of European Council Directive 2000/78/EC established a general framework for equal treatment in employment and occupation. The Employment Equality (Religion or Belief) Regulations 2003 and the Employment Equality (Sexual Orientation) Regulations 2003 that derive from these statutes made it unlawful to discriminate against an employee or potential employee on the grounds of their religion or belief or their sexual orientation. On the face of it, these provisions seem to run counter to those of section 60 of the Education Act 1998. However, exemptions[26] included in both sets of regulations ensure any clash is avoided. The first is where, having regard to the nature of the employment or the context in which it is carried out, there is a genuine and determining occupational requirement and it is proportionate to apply that requirement in the particular case, for example, of a religious organisation. The second exemption applies where an employer has an ethos that is based on religion or belief. This second exemption is somewhat broader in that the employer need not demonstrate that being of a particular religion or belief is a 'determining occupational requirement'.

Schools, such as those in the Catholic sector, which have explicit religious purposes[27], fall into those exemption categories and, consequently, the provisions of section 60(5) of the 1998 Education Act applicable to all teaching staff are unaffected.[28] Nevertheless, if a school wished to **exclude** non-Catholics from any non-teaching post (as opposed to giving preference to a Catholic candidate), it is almost certain that the governing body would have to show there was a genuine occupational requirement in order to do so, as for example, with the post of chaplain. Some have argued that, despite the extension of powers provided by section 37, it may not be morally or legally appropriate to give **preference** to a Catholic applicant for a non-teaching post in the school such as a cleaner. On the other hand, the governing body could (probably) do so when advertising for a classroom assistant (dependent upon the specific tasks involved in the post). However, any dispute arising from possible conflict between these two pieces of legislation in England has yet to be tested in court.

Regulations are made by the appropriate Secretary of State. They derive from powers specified in primary legislation and, in nearly all cases, take the form of Statutory Instruments. Use of the word '*shall*' within a particular regulation places an absolute duty upon a governing body. The use of '*may*' generally confers full discretion on whether or not to act in a particular way. *'Must have regard to'* signifies a duty to take into account, carefully consider and give due weight to a particular issue, but does not remove a governing body's powers of discretion in the matter and is not a requirement to comply.

The School Staffing (England) Regulations 2003 derive from the provisions of the Education Act 2002, section 36 and came into force on 1st September 2003. They are designed to provide flexibility for governing bodies to conduct staffing matters as they regard as appropriate, consistent with good governance and in compliance with other relevant binding legislation. Consequently, many of the regulations provide the governing body with discretionary powers. For Catholic schools, dioceses will expect that such discretion be used to ensure consistency with the statutory duty to preserve and maintain the Catholic character of the school.

Guidance is provided by the Secretary of State to explain and clarify the provisions set out in Regulations. It can be either statutory or non-statutory. In statutory guidance the use of the word *'must'* in the Guidance refers to a statutory duty; the word *'should'* indicates the Secretary of State's recommended course of action to which consideration must be given, but need not necessarily be followed if there is good reason not to do so. Governing bodies are required also to have regard to non-statutory guidance. Again, where discretion is available, the governing body of a Catholic school can and should use its powers in such a way as to ensure its employment policies are consistent with the school's fundamental purpose and any legitimate directions from the school's trustees, so fulfilling its statutory duty to maintain and develop the religious character of the school.

Circulars are communications from the Secretary of State which may be advisory, or explanatory or serve other purposes, including giving decisions and approvals for action that do not require parliamentary involvement, as would be the case with primary legislation or regulation through a statutory instrument. However, they may still impose legally binding duties depending upon the phraseology employed in the particular circular.

A Memorandum on the Appointment of Teachers provides guidelines from the Bishops of England and Wales. In many dioceses the Memorandum will form part of the bishop's directive to the governing body on appointments in Catholic schools. Where that is the case, its provisions would be binding in canon law[29] and, therefore, form part of the diocesan trust. Following them would enable the governing body to fulfil its statutory duty to conduct the school in accordance with the instrument of government and trust deed.[30] Furthermore, most dioceses will have established and published their expectations of teachers who freely choose to work in their schools. For example, in the Archdiocese of Birmingham, they have been defined in a document issued by the Diocesan Schools Commission on behalf of the trustees. In brief, all teachers are expected to be loyal to the aims and essential purposes of the school and make a positive contribution to its Catholic character to the best of their abilities and knowledge.[31]

In addition, the model Catholic Education Service contract of employment for a headteacher, teacher or other employee, which dioceses expect to be used by their schools, will include a clause emphasising the ecclesial and religious character of the school and the corresponding duties of the employees. For example:

> "... The teacher hereby agrees: ... to have regard to the Roman Catholic character of the School and not do anything in any way detrimental or prejudicial to the interests of the same; ... ."
> Catholic Education Service, Model Teacher Contract, Clause 4, iii, (a)

Once appointed, all staff should be helped to understand and meet the obligations of their contract and the details of their job descriptions, through the process of induction, their performance management,[32] other on-going training (INSET) and continuing professional development (CPD).

ADMISSIONS

In all voluntary aided schools the governing body is the admissions authority and has the legal responsibility for making all decisions on admissions issues. However, it may delegate the responsibility to a committee. In respect of Catholic schools, in the same way as for staffing matters, the governors are required to ensure their admissions arrangements and oversubscription criteria are consistent with their statutory duty to preserve and maintain the Catholic character of the school. In practice, supported by both civil and canon law, this will mean giving priority in admissions to baptised Catholics.

Those responsibilities, and the level of governor control over admissions that allows them to successfully carry them out, remain intact following the provisions of the Education Act 2002 that first required local authorities to develop schemes for co-ordinating admissions arrangements for all maintained schools in their area. Such schemes are, essentially, no more than an administrative process intended to make school admissions easier, more transparent and less stressful both for parents and for admissions authorities resulting from multiple applications to different schools.

Nothing in the new arrangements or subsequent related legislation takes away the governing body's powers or responsibilities for admissions. Governors still decide who will and will not be admitted in accordance with their admissions policy and over-subscription criteria. However, it does mean that the local authority will be involved in some of the administrative work involved. In essence, the new arrangements must enable governing bodies to administer their admissions policy (assuming it meets the legal requirements). Governing bodies are not required to adapt their admissions policy to fit the local authority's co-ordinating arrangements. Nevertheless, government's increasing intervention in the process since 1980, albeit to ensure a more equitable and consumer orientated system of allocating places, can be regarded as an erosion of governors' rights to control admissions, and many argue that the thrust of recent legislation is not supporting the efforts of Catholic communities to provide a Catholic education for the children of practising and committed Catholic parents. Certainly, some of the provisions of the Education Act 2006, though generally supported by the bishops, have proved most controversial.[33]

CURRICULUM AND INSPECTION

From the earliest period of state involvement in education, one pre-condition for receiving financial support has been the right of the state to see, through various forms of inspection and regulation of the content, extent and teaching of the curriculum, that public money is being spent in a way that it regards as appropriate.[34] The balance between local and central control over the content of the curriculum has varied over the generations and, if too directive, has the potential to be a source of conflict between Church and state. Section 23 of the Education Act 1944 placed control of both the secular and religious curriculum in aided schools with the governing body, so enabling Catholic schools to provide a curriculum for them built around Catholic values. Until the mid-1980s successive governments maintained a 'hands-off' policy in respect of the curriculum but, following the intervention in the on-going debate about education by the then Prime

Minister James Callaghan in 1976,[35] the trend has been towards much greater central state control of both the content and methodology of what is taught in state maintained schools (with the striking exception of Academies).[36] This trend appears to have resulted (perhaps inevitably) in a curriculum infused with politicised secular values.[37] The first legislative step in that process was contained in the Education Act of 1986, section 19 of which required the governors of Catholic schools to have regard to the curriculum provided in local authority schools. Just two years later, the Education Reform Act 1988 defined the curriculum[38] that was to be taught in all mainstream maintained schools while the Education Act 1992 established a process of school inspection by a non-ministerial government department, the Office for Standards in Education (OfSTED), that would, among other things, ensure schools complied with the new centrally determined curriculum.[39]

Part of OfSTED's purpose was to break up what was seen by some as a cosy relationship within the educational establishment between schools, local authorities and Her Majesty's Inspectorate. Among other things, it selects tenders for inspections of schools, colleges and other educational institutions, issues contracts, provides quality control and assurance of the inspection process, collects, collates and analyses data arising from inspections and prepares public reports in the light of the findings. Though Catholic schools are required to teach the National Curriculum, responsibility for the content of the religious curriculum remains with the governors, and through them, the Church, so enabling Catholic schools to fulfil their religious mission. Inspection of such denominational religious education and worship is outside OfSTED's remit.[40]

While OfSTED has responsibility for inspecting and reporting on what is termed the secular curriculum, under the provisions of the Education Act 2005, section 5, together with its associated regulations,[41] government has recognised its lack of competence for all matters to do with both Religious Education and Worship in Catholic schools. Under the provisions of Section 48 of the Education Act 2005 and canons 804(1) and 806(1) of the 1983 Code of Canon Law for the Latin Rite, the diocese retains those responsibil-ities.[42] While this separation of powers and responsibilities seems relatively straight-forward, philosophical differences in understanding the distinction made between religious and secular education, has led to a somewhat messy compromise in relation to sex education. The governing bodies of both primary and secondary Catholic schools can determine whether to include sex education in the curriculum. Those that do so will (usually) follow a diocesan approved syllabus[43] which would be taught within the Religious Education curriculum inspected under section 48 by the diocese, or as part of the pupils' Personal Health and Social Education programme inspected by both OfSTED (under section 5) and the diocese (under section 48). However, there are aspects of sex education that all schools are required to teach as part of the science element of the National Curriculum that falls solely within the remit of OfSTED inspections.

LAND AND BUILDINGS

Although governors control the use of the school buildings, they remain in the ownership of the diocese. Any significant alteration to them, therefore, would require the permission of the trustees, though this division of responsibilities between owner and occupier is not always observed in practice. However, it is the case that the trustees own the premises and, for example, retain the powers to require the governors to quit them if, in the view of the trustees, they are being used it in such a way that it is inconsistent with the purposes of the trust.[44]

SUMMARY

The scope of this chapter does not allow for an exhaustive explanation of the legislative context within which Catholic sector schools in England, in collaboration with the state, are able to carry out their religious mission. It has focused upon the essential elements that secure the minimum level of autonomy necessary for them to function as Catholic institutions within a secular state.

The Church has long recognised the desirability of such partnerships while insisting, consistent with the principle of subsidiarity, that each party acknowledges and respects its own areas of competence. While not written with any particular educational system specifically in mind, it can be argued that the Church's 'Declaration on Christian Education', made in 1965, affirms the priority of parents in the education of their children, and is reflected in the legislative framework of the English dual system.

"It is the duty of the state to ensure that all its citizens have access to an adequate education and are prepared for the proper exercise of their civic rights and duties. ... [It] should safeguard the rights of children to

an adequate education ... be vigilant about the ability of teachers and the standard of teaching ... watch over the health of the pupils and in general promote the work of schools in its entirety. In this, however, the principle of subsidiarity must be borne in mind and therefore there must be no monopoly of schools [by the state] which would be prejudicial to the natural rights the human person ... and the pluralism which exists in many societies."
(Gravissimum educationis [Declaration on Christian Education], §6)

The development success of the partnership in England has both advantages, and drawbacks. The Church's current reliance on the state, whether directly through grants towards the costs of building and maintaining its schools, or through the use of the many services provided by local authorities, may lead some politicians to assume that Catholic schools exist for the state's socio-political purposes rather than their religious mission. Consequently, the minimum legal rights described above are an essential element of the necessary autonomy that Catholic schools require if they are to provide the appropriate support that Catholic parents' need to help them educate their children in a manner consistent with their religious convictions. Whether the current legislative framework provides an appropriate balance between the legitimate interests of parents and the state remains a matter of debate.

NOTES

1   This position is explored in detail in chapter 5 and is variously reflected in the provisions of Universal Declaration of Human Rights, Article 26 (2) (3); European Convention on Human Rights, Article 14, Article 2 of the First Protocol to the Convention; Education Act 1996, section 9.

2   See Barnard, H. C. (1961) *A History of English Education from 1760 (Second Edition)*, London, University of London Press; Curtis, S. J. (1967) *History of Education in Great Britain (Seventh Edition)*, London, University Tutorial Press.

3   The first government grant – a sum of £20,000 - towards helping private groups meet the cost of providing schools was made in 1833.

4   The *National Society for Promoting the Education of the Poor in the Principles of the Established Church* was formed in 1811. The Free Churches formed the *British and Foreign School Society* in 1808, with the equivalent Catholic organisation, the *Catholic Poor School Committee*, being established much later, in 1847.

5   See Hughes, P. (1950) *The English Catholics in 1850*; Beales, A. F. C. (1950) *The Struggle for the Schools*; Gwynn, D. (1950) *Growth of the Catholic Community*; all in: G. A. Beck (ed) (1950) *The English Catholics 1850-1950*, London, Burns Oates. See also *The Case for Catholic Schools*, (1955) London, Catholic Education Council, pp. 72-79.

6   Province of Westminster, 17th July 1852, in: R. E. Guy (1886) *The Synods in English: being the texts of the four synods of Westminster*, London, St. Gregory's Press.

7   Sacred Congregation for Catholic Education (1988) *The Religious Dimension of Education in a Catholic School,* London, Catholic Truth Society.

8   Summarised in its position paper *The Common Good in Education* (1997) London, Catholic Education Service.

9   Marshall, T. W. M. (1850) General Report on Roman Catholic Schools (1849), in: *The Catholic School*, 2. 1. p. 40, London, Catholic Poor School Committee.

10 See, for example, that of the Archdiocese of Birmingham - *Birmingham Roman Catholic Diocesan Trustees Registered 3rd July 1931*.

11 Sheehy, G., et al. (1995) *1983 Code of Canon Law for the Latin Rite*, The Canon Law Society of Great Britain and Ireland, London, Geoffrey Chapman.

12 Komonchak, J. A., et al. (1987) *The New Dictionary of Theology*, Dublin, Gill and Macmillan.

13 Canons 800-806.

14 A body set up by the bishop through which schools are commissioned. Only a diocese, acting under the authority of its bishop (or a religious order acting with the specific permission of a bishop) can commission, establish or provide a school that can be truly regarded as being Catholic.

15 The legal necessity for the diocese to own the land on which a school is built was set out by the then Minister of Education (Miss. Ellen Wilkinson) when moving the Second Reading of the Bill which became the Education Act 1955. In respect of Schedule 3, she explained that since charity law did not allow trustees to expend charitable funds erecting buildings on land they did not own, the question of ownership was vital or trustees would be prevented by law from providing the schools which was one of the main purposes of the proposed Act. Thus, since 1944, where a Local Authority provides land for a denominational school it must convey title to the land to the diocesan trustees.

16 The right to a religious education has been enshrined in the United Nations Universal Declaration of Human Rights (1948, Article 18) and Declaration of the Rights of the Child (1959, Principle 2) and, subsequently, into our civil law by the Human Rights Act 1998 (Article 14; 1st Protocol, Article 2).

17 Ethos statement in the Instrument of Government for governing bodies reconstituted under the Education Act 2002, section 20.

18 See, for example, that of the Archdiocese of Birmingham - Birmingham Roman Catholic Diocesan Trustees Registered 3rd July 1931.

19 Canon 803 (1) - *"A Catholic school is understood to be one which is under the control of the competent ecclesiastical authority ..."* ; Canon 803 (3) - *"No school, even if it is in fact Catholic, may bear the title 'Catholic school' except by the consent of the competent ecclesiastical authority."* See also, the Explanatory Notes provided in the various Statutory Instruments, *Designation of Schools Having a Religious Character (England) Order*, issued by the Secretary of State under s. 69(3) of the Education Act 1998.

20 Statutory Instrument 2007/0957, *School Governance (Constitution)(England) Regulations 2007*, Regulation 18(1)(d); (2)(b).

21 Education Acts of 1902, 1944, 1988, 1998, 2002, 2006.

22 That does not mean, however, that dioceses have the same powers, or overall strategic role, within the maintained sector as do local authorities.

23 See Judgement by Lord Haldane in *Gillow v Durham Local Education Authority, 1913*; known as the 'Gillow Principle'.

24 The duty to secure is non-discretionary. Schedule 9 (2) of the Education Act 1998 amended the previous conditional duty contained in section 78(2) of the Education Act 1996 by removing the bracketed phrase *"(as far as is possible)"*. Under the provisions of the Education Act 2002 those duties were retained but transferred from the face of the Act to the School Governance (Constitution) Regulations 2003, Regulation 8.

25 Canons 803(2); 804; 805 relate to staffing in Catholic schools.

26 The exemptions are set out in Regulation 7 in the Statutory Instrument, SI 2003/1660, *The Employment Equality (Religion or Belief) Regulations 2003.*

27 Diocesan trust deeds will (in most cases) contain clauses to the effect that they are charities for the purpose of the advancement of religion, the specific activities of which are under the absolute discretion of the diocesan Ordinary (i.e. bishop).

28 Regulation 39(a) of SI 2003/1660, *The Employment Equality (Religion or Belief) Regulations 2003*, states that they are *"without prejudice to sections 58-60 of the School Standards and Framework Act 1998"* (and any subsequent amendments thereof unless future primary legislation determines otherwise).

29 Canon 806 (1) – *"The diocesan bishop ... has the right to issue directives concerning the general regulation of Catholic schools ... ."*

30 Education Act 2002, section 21(4).

31 In a similar fashion and using very similar phraseology to the Archdiocese of Birmingham, the Schools Commission of the Diocese of Middlesbrough has defined, on behalf of the diocesan trustees, their expectations of teachers in its *Diocesan Handbook for Governors*. The Handbook is issued to its schools as guidance to inform, and be used by, the governing body in its recruitment processes (as well as in other matters).

32 See the Statutory Instrument 2006/2661, *The Education (School Teacher Performance Management) (England) Regulations 2006*, made by the Secretary of State for Education and Skills under the powers conferred on him by sections, 21, 131 and 210 of the Education Act 2002.

33 Section 44 of the 2006 Act places a prohibition on any form of interview by the school of prospective parents or pupils. Some governing bodies, especially where there are insufficient places to meet the demand from parents of baptised Catholic pupils, argue that the prohibition prevents them offering the limited places they have to those whom they feel will most benefit from, and are most deserving of, a Catholic education, i.e. those committed to the regular practice of the Catholic faith. While recognising that it may be the case that some parents decide to have their children baptised solely to secure a place in a Catholic school though they have no commitment themselves, others argue that (a) it is not for governors to judge the relative worth of a child's faith journey; (b) an interview process will, by inevitably favouring articulate parents/children, become a form of social selection not in keeping with the Church's commitment to the poor.

34 A comprehensive examination of the development of government involvement in the curriculum and inspection of schools is not appropriate here. For an historical outline of the curriculum and inspection regime for the elementary education introduced by the 1870, 1902 and subsequent Education

Acts before 1944, see Barnard, H. C. (1961) *A History of English Education From 1760 (Second Edition)*, London, University of London Press, chapters XIX ff; Curtis, S. J. (1967) *History of Education in Great Britain (Seventh Edition)*, London, University Tutorial Press, Chapters VIII-XI..

35 At a foundation laying stone ceremony at Ruskin College, Oxford on 18th October 1976, James Callaghan spoke of the need for a national debate about education. He argued that the *"purpose of education"* should not remain solely a matter for the professionals but become the subject of general discussion because of concerns about *"the methods and aims of informal [methods] of instruction [prevalent at the time] the strong case for a core curriculum of basic knowledge, the role of the inspectorate in relation to national standards, the need to improve relations between industry and education. ... [and the] problem [that] is the examination system."* For a full text of the speech see, *http://education.guardian.co.uk/print/o,,4277858-109002,00.html.*

36 The Education Act 2002 established a new category of independent state maintained schools; Academies. Their foundation rests upon a formal funding agreement between the sponsor and the government made under the provisions of Section 65 of the Act, ensuring some measure of state control over such matters as their pupil intake. Section 76 gives them exemption from the National Curriculum though, under the provisions of Section 78 they have to provide a broad and balanced curriculum which "promotes the spiritual, moral, cultural and physical development of pupils ... and prepares them for the opportunities, responsibilities and experiences of later life". They are also subject to the common OfSTED inspection regime.

37 See the account of the gradual erosion by the state of the Catholic school governing body's autonomy in curriculum matters in: Arthur, J. (1995) *The Ebbing Tide*, Leominster, Gracewing, pp. 173-186. See also the various claims made in: Whelan, R. (ed) (2007) *The Corruption of the Curriculum*, London, Institute for the Study of Civil Society, that the school curriculum no longer aims to impart knowledge and encourage academic exploration but to achieve particular socio-political goals.

38 The school curriculum comprises religious education (subject to the appropriate conscience clauses), the National Curriculum of core and foundation subjects, and other subjects outside the National Curriculum.

39 Provisions of both Acts of Parliament have been subsequently amended, re-enacted and extended central control of the curriculum through both primary legislation and the work of the Qualifications and Curriculum Authority established by government under the provisions of the Education Act 1997, sections 21-26 (as amended by the Education Act 2002). Current provisions in the Education and Inspections Act 2006 and its associated Regulations and Guidance retains the general tendency towards centralising control of curriculum content evident in earlier legislation (in part by determining, through QCA, which school examinations will be approved and, therefore, funded) with the inspection regime having a similar direct influence upon pedagogical methodology. For a full explanation of the role and powers of QCA in relation to government see, *Memorandum of Understanding between the DfES and the QCA*, http://www.qca.gov.uk/qca_4947.aspx, (accessed 9th July 2007).

40 The 2005 Education Act limits what OfSTED inspections under section 5 can inspect in schools with a religious character. It must not extend to -

(a)   denominational education, or
(b)   the content of collective worship which falls to be inspected under section 48.

However, some elements of the secular curriculum may be taught through the Religious Education lessons, for example, elements of the newly introduced social cohesion curriculum. In such circumstances, it is likely that OfSTED inspectors would observe and comment. In a briefing prepared by Adrian Gray HMI, and issued in 2007, inspectors were advised (among other matters) that:

- it is acceptable for section 5 inspectors to visit all lessons, including religious education, and assemblies, even if a section 48 inspection is taking place at the same time. It may be helpful to explain to the headteacher your reasons for doing this, e.g. following a particular inspection trail, seeking out good practice etc. However some schools may hold specifically denominational activities such as prayer meetings which fall outside OfSTED's remit;

- avoid commenting on specifically denominational content of assemblies or RE lessons, but it is acceptable to comment on educational issues such as the contribution of assemblies to pupils' personal development or the quality of teaching in all lessons, including RE.

41 Statutory Instrument SI 2005/2038, *Education (School Inspection)(England) Regulations 2005*.

42 Her Majesty's Chief Inspector has acknowledged that the powers to investigate parental complaints under the provisions contained in the Education & Inspections Act 2006, Section 160, do not extend to any matters that fall to be inspected under Section 48, including those relating to the school's Catholic character or the content of any religious syllabus and teaching. [Private correspondence dated 10th April 2007 from HMI Miriam Rosen, Director for Education, (writing on behalf of HMCI, Christine Gilbert) to the author following an unanswered query put to her at the Diocesan Commissioners Conference, Newcastle, March, 2007 as to the exercise of HMCI powers of investigation.]

43 Such as, for example, the sex education programme 'All That I Am' developed jointly by the Archdiocese of Birmingham Department of Religious Education and the Department of Health Teenage Pregnancy Unit.

44 This does not mean that the school will necessarily close. It may be that it continues in existence as a school (though not necessarily a Catholic school) by transferring to another site within the Local Authority at the Authority's expense.

Chapter 8

CONTRIBUTING TO THE COMMON GOOD: OUTCOMES OF CATHOLIC EDUCATION

INTRODUCTION

There is a view expressed in a number of Western style democracies that the state should not seek to promote any particular vision of the good life, whether secular or religious, but simply provide a neutral theatre[1] where different versions can co-exist peacefully. Further, that it should not interfere in, or seek to undermine, individual or group activities that do it no harm. For many, this analysis is deficient because it does not take into account the social character of human existence and the importance of the constituent elements that enable communities to work effectively for mutual benefit of their members. They argue that its emphasis on secular individualism militates against attempts to promote the concept and actuality of the common good.[2] In respect of education, custom and international law take a communal view, recognising that while parents are the prime educators of their children the state also has a legitimate interest in the matter, but should take full cognizance of, and give the fullest respect to, those parental rights. Discussion about education should not, therefore, become a battle-ground about the primacy of parents or the state in the matter of child rearing, but the development of a mutually supportive relationship between the two in order that all might benefit.

The Catholic Church's view of the essentially religious character and purpose of the education it seeks to provide in its schools is outlined in chapter six. Even so, the Church fully accepts that both parents and the (secular) state have a legitimate interest in the education of children. Any evaluation of its schools, therefore, should be concerned with both their effectiveness in helping parents in their task of transmitting Catholic faith and culture to their children and in teaching the skills and attitudes common to all state maintained educational institutions. The Church argues that its schools make a positive contribution to society, and as a matter of equity, parents who want their children educated within the religious environment they seek to provide, should receive the same support from the state as those who have different, perhaps non-religious, aspirations for their children.

If its argument is to prevail, however, it must show that the claimed benefits are evidentially based. On the other hand, critics of the inclusion of Catholic schools within the maintained system must provide evidence that they are harmful to individuals or the state, if they are to justify their opposition on anything other than ideological grounds.

RELIGION IN A SECULAR SOCIETY – BENEFIT OR HARM?

Leaders of the main religious communities and denominations within the UK argue that their religion has a positive societal as well as individual value though, for many critics, they may not be self-evident. While this chapter is concerned, primarily, with the impact of Catholic sector schools in England, that they are regarded by the Church as one arm of its salvific mission requires some investigation of their religious context.[3] Whatever the reality may be, this wider perspective should shed light upon the more localised effects of religious based schooling. It may be the case that the weight of empirical research, as opposed to theoretical assertions, shows that religious belief and practice actually subverts, or damages, legitimate activities of the state, for example, by creating human and social deprivation, social unrest (actual or potential), division, intolerance and other social ills. On the other hand, the evidence may show it provides positive social benefits.

Despite the undoubted decline in religious practice in Britain in recent decades, especially among the younger generations,[4] it remains the case that the overwhelming proportion of the population of England and Wales describe themselves as having some religious affiliation[5]. There is evidence that young members of this group tend to hold differing personal and social opinions compared to those claiming no such affiliation[6] and that religion is an important element of their self identity which, in turn, affects their attitudes and actions in a number of areas of social and public significance.[7] Many of these may be controversial, for example, attitudes towards sexual promiscuity, marriage, the family and to abortion, but the fact of they are controversial does not, of course, mean such views must be harmful to the state, or be excluded from public discourse simply because they are rooted in a religious perspective of humanity.

In recent times there has been a large and growing literature dealing with the impact of religion upon individuals and society. The cumulative evidence strongly suggests that many (though not all) forms of religion may be particularly beneficial in a variety of ways.[8] Only a very small minority of published reports find negative associations. Given that general situation, let us consider some specific characteristics. One essential trait of a functioning pluralistic democratic society is that of tolerance towards others holding differing political or social attitudes. Evidence concerning the attitudes of religious adherents is mixed. While religious belief has been found to be associated with high levels of intolerance towards others, there is also evidence that those who have an intrinsic (as opposed to extrinsic) religious orientation are less prejudiced in their behaviour and attitudes.[9] Effective functioning societies also depend for their own well being, in large measure, upon the stability of their constituent family structures. The importance of committed and coherent family groupings in nurturing a strong sense of self worth and well-being is well established,[10] and is a characteristic of many religious communities. For example, it has been argued that:

> "One of the most evident contributions of traditional religion to society has been the idea of the sanctity and integrity of the family, in more recent times, the nuclear family. This idea is, symbolically and concretely, expressed in the commitment of marriage vows and in the moral condemnation of divorce. Clearly, different religions and different Christian denominations have differing attitudes to divorce and family break-up. My references are to the more traditional denominations (of Christianity and of Judaism). It is members of these denominations who are most interested in educating their children within religious schools. The highly secularized denominations are little different in their social beliefs from non-church members."
>
> (Holmes, M., 1992, Chp. 6, p. 105)

Where communities are effective in encouraging strong and mutually sup-portive and permanent family ties, it does seem that children tend to accrue beneficial social traits.[11] Paradoxically, the evidence suggests that the more confident and secure children are in their own identity, the more open they are likely to be towards others and other cultures. They are less likely to have anti-social and personal behavioural problems, to drop out of school, develop drug dependencies, suffer from depression and other social ills, to be sexually promiscuous, to become involved in crime and have difficulty in establishing and maintaining permanent supportive adult relationships.[12] Religious practice also seems to be associated with positive attitudes towards school and school discipline,[13] and also with higher levels of volun-teerism and involvement in communal activities.[14] None of this means that religion *per se* produces good social habits. It may simply be that those who value religious activities tend to have attitudes that encourage positive social behaviour rather than there being some direct causal relationship with religious faith. In contrast there are those who argue that religion inevitably generates and perpetuates intolerance and social unrest.[15] In support of the contention they often cite the chronic lack of social cohesion evident in Northern Ireland, as evidence of the inherent harm caused by religious affiliation to differing Christian denominations.[16] However, while the existing high level of inter-community intolerance is an inescapable fact, no direct causal link with religion *per se*, or with the school system, has been established and many would argue that the conflict, though rooted in religious upheavals of the 16th century, is characterised by political and economic motives rather than having any essentially religious aims[17].

> *"Religion, per se, plays an insignificant role in the stereotypes of Northern Ireland. Power is the crucial factor."*
>
> (O'Donnell, E. E., 1977, p. 155)

> *"Northern Ireland is ... a special case, having roots of embittered division which go back three centuries."*
>
> (Holmes, M., 1992, p. 105)

> *"The Conflict was never exclusively about religion. Politics was at least as influential a factor. ... settler against native; Anglo-Scot against Irish; Unionist against Nationalist ... and in a society where resources (of land, wealth and food) have traditionally been limited ... competition was particularly ferocious. ... It is unduly simplistic to speak of the Northern Ireland Conflict as religious or even chiefly as religious. ... The use of the title Protestant or Catholic simply acknowledges their formal membership of a particular community rather than connotes commitment to Christian discipleship and behaviour."*
>
> (Barnes, L. P., 2005, p. 132)

> *"[The last thirty years of Northern Ireland's 'Troubles'] was about questions of sovereignty or economic and political power ... We are horribly wrong in imagining that Northern Ireland is some atavistic throwback to the religious wars of the sixteenth or seventeenth centuries."*
>
> (Burleigh, M., 2006, p. 379, 413)

In addition, it is a matter of record that the Christian Churches and their official representatives have done much to help mitigate and, it would seem, facilitate the ending of political violence in Northern Ireland that has raged over the past thirty years.[18] In the English context, it can be argued further that, despite much public anti-Catholic sentiment and discrimination,[19] the Catholic Church has been responsible for ensuring successive waves of Irish immigrants were successfully integrated into the existing home communities, so preventing any replication of the political turmoil found in the North of Ireland. For example, it is claimed:

> *"[The Irish in England] were a very visible minority, identified as unwelcome immigrants and subject to discriminatory practices. In the critical period 1830-70 … [they] were differentiated as an immigrant labour force, a social problem and a political threat. The Catholic Church became the agency of this process [of incorporation to create a single nation-state] as regards the Irish Catholic working class in Britain. … The long-term aim of the Catholic authorities was not just to produce good Catholics but also … a body of loyal respectable working class Catholics … The prime objective of Catholic elementary schools … was designed not only to arrest lapsation [in religious practice] but also to weaken Irish national identity."*
>
> (Hickman, M. J., 1999, pp. 246; 249)

> *"In Britain, the aim [of the Catholic Hierarchy] in educating Irish working class children was incorporation and denationalisation."*
>
> (Hickman, M. J., 2000, p. 64)

If one element of the Church's strategy in England was indeed to promote the incorporation of Irish immigrants as Hickman has argued, it appears that it may have had some long-term success. While the Irish community has retained much of its cultural identity,[20] its integration and assimilation has been notably successful.[21] For example, there is little evidence of second and third generation members of the Irish Catholic community seeking to assert their ethnic background in an aggressive and anti-social manner, despite a paucity of attention to Irish matters given by state institutions or within local authority schools.[22]

RELIGIOUS EFFECTIVENESS OF CATHOLIC SCHOOLS

Little empirical research has been undertaken in the UK into the religious effectiveness of Catholic schools. This is somewhat surprising given the Church's commitment to its schools and their declared purposes. Of those studies which have been done, many have used over-simplistic research designs often overlooking important criteria, since school effects are only one of many influencing factors. In addition it must be recognised that schools themselves differ in many ways. However, even though there has been a general decline in religious practice in recent years, a review of the available evidence leads to a number of general but firm conclusions indicating positive religious effects from Catholic schooling.[23]

> "The cumulative effect of studies in the United States, the United Kingdom, and Australia shows that, while parents have the strongest influence on their children's religiousness, the school also has an independent influence which arises from the school climate. It is not the result of formal education but is due to the attitudes that are fostered and the effectiveness of pastoral care."
>
> (Hyde, K., 1990, p. 333)

There are consistent reports from studies in Britain, the USA and Australia showing greater levels of religious behaviour by school pupils claiming adherence to Catholicism than pupils of other Christian denominations. While not conclusively proving the case, it can be argued that the existence of an independent school effect on the religiousness of pupils is highly probable. Studies in Australia[24], the quality of which are such that they are generally regarded as definitive, confirm that the major religious influence on students is parental (as one would expect) but, importantly, also demonstrate that a Catholic school can have an independent influence depending upon school climate. It seems that pupils need to experience a religious environment in school in order to be open to the Christian message that it seeks to impart. The school's procedures in its day-to-day administration, the style of life it values and what it celebrates or rewards are important elements in creating a positive climate, as well as student morale, their attitude to the principal and their own adolescent freedom. An effective religious based school is one that reinforces and supports a good religious atmosphere at home. That may not be particularly remarkable, but the evidence also shows that religiously effective schools will have a positive influence on students whose home life contains little or no religious activity. Schools having an impoverished religious culture, on the other hand, have little positive religious influence on such pupils.

A major project concerning the religious influence of primary schools in England was undertaken in a series of studies over a period of some ten years.[25] It found that the religious objectives of Catholic education seemed to be achieved because Catholic sector schools, even allowing for the influence of church attendance and parental attitude to religion, contributed greatly to favourable attitudes to religion among their pupils, much more so than that of other types of school. Nevertheless, it must be realised that the unmistakable religious influence which some Catholic schools exert is dependent upon the actual religious culture they are able to generate and sustain through their overall life, values, attitudes and practices; the label 'Catholic' on its own is not sufficient. While the quality of religious education lessons is, of course, most important, the major factor in those schools that are effective seems to be their success in becoming purposeful, prayerful and active religious communities.[26] As Bishop Konstant puts it, albeit in a slightly different context:

> "A Catholic school must in some way be a community of faith in which worship is appropriate, possible and wholly acceptable. If it were not catechesis and evangelisation would be impossible."
>
> (Konstant, D., 1997, p. 38)

CATHOLIC SCHOOLS AND SOCIAL COHESION IN ENGLAND

In its formal response to the Office of the Deputy Prime Minister (ODPM) Select Committee's Report on Social Cohesion in 1994, the government noted that it preferred to use the term community cohesion rather than social cohesion. It defined a cohesive community as one where:

> "There is a common vision and a sense of belonging for all communities: the diversity of people's different backgrounds and circumstances are appreciated and positively valued; those from different backgrounds have similar life opportunities; and strong positive relationships are being developed between peoples from different backgrounds in the workplace, in schools and within neighbourhoods."
>
> (ODPM Report to the House of Commons, July 2004)

Although the government emphasises 'a sense of belonging' and 'positively valuing diversity' in its definition, there are those who argue that the very existence of schools provided by, and for, a particular community must be damaging to the cohesion that government seeks. The claim is that schools that have admissions policies that give priority to children of a particular (faith) group, in this case baptised Catholics, will most probably (or even necessarily) develop in their pupils insular, intolerant and/or prejudicial attitudes towards others. The assumption underpinning the argument is that any separation of children on religious criteria must, necessarily, entrench ignorance of other world-views which, in turn, generates social disharmony. While it is the case that there have been instances of social unrest emanating from some minority ethnic/racial groups in England in recent years, identifying faith schools as a major cause cannot be supported in logic, nor is it supported by the available empirical evidence,[27] a situation accepted by senior politicians from all three main parties.

"The attack on faith schools from those who speak as if Muslim schools have caused riots in places where no such schools exist;[28] or as if Catholic schools were tearing Scotland apart; or as if parish schools could bring sectarian conflict to the English shires ... testifies to a prejudice ... ."

(Letwin, O., 2003, p. 4)

"The Government does not hold them [faith schools] responsible for ethnic or social segregation. Divisions within our communities are caused by a range of complex factors. In many cities there are schools which are not faith schools that have a predominance of pupils from a particular ethnic background because that is their local school ... ."

(ODPM Report to the House of Commons, July 2004)

"... the growth of Islamophobia, the rise in anti-Semitism and the all too frequent ghettoisation of immigrant groups in our urban areas should concern us all. Though to blame these occurrences on Church schools is clearly absurd."

(Willis. P., 2005)

There is also some misunderstanding about the pupil population of Catholic schools in England. Critics often confuse faith with ethnicity and/or culture, assuming the two are synonymous. However, because Catholic schools are part of a universal church, and the main criterion for entry to them is Catholic baptism, they tend, in fact, to have a much wider social and ethnic pupil mix than many other schools in England whose intake is more likely to be determined by the proximity of pupils' homes.

"People make the mistake of believing that most racial segregation in schools arises from faith schools. This is wholly incorrect. ... Catholic schools tend to be more diverse than most, in the true sense of the word. ... when we look at ethnic mix of schools, Catholic schools tend to be far more mixed than local authority schools. A healthy mix might be a school with a proportion of ethnic minority pupils[excluding Irish] somewhere between 55 and 40% - where these children neither predominate, nor are they isolated. Among state schools, about a quarter (25.6%) fall into this group. But among Catholic schools, a third (32.5%) would fit this description."

(Phillips, T., 2005)

On the other hand, no-one denies that schools, religious or otherwise, are theoretically capable of helping generate a sense of separateness or alienation in their pupils and so undermining social cohesion. However, there is no evidence that the existence or practices of Catholic schools in England since the introduction of compulsory universal education have, of themselves, fermented or promoted discord. Further, given more than half a century of 'good behaviour' it is reasonable to conclude that, in so far as it is possible to generalise, Catholic sector schools have not encouraged any form of social vandalism but, on the contrary, have promoted tolerance, good citizenship and active involvement in public life. Indeed it can be argued that, precisely because of their religious character, they are well placed to improve societal harmony through the social curriculum and the moral attitudes they seek to impart.

> "Positive knowledge and reasoning cannot ...provide an answer to the question, 'But should it be done?' Moral reasoning, on the other hand, ... provides a solid basis for moral community in a way which positivist reasoning cannot. And that is crucial to the task of generating a shared mind and spirit between people. ... A society which [is] unable to determine shared moral principles and values... will lack cohesion. More importantly, it will be denying itself precisely the means of producing a degree of moral cohesion which is essential for shared projects and ambitions for social living. Clearly the first place [where moral reasoning can begin] is the family and the setting in which a child first grows. The school is a crucial place of 'moral communion' ...[and] the task of a school in putting forward its vision of 'moral communion' is essential to its success as a contributor to education. Every school should be able to give a reasoned account of its moral perspectives, so that all can be drawn into this proper and crucial joint project: the school as a moral communion. Then it becomes a place in which students are properly prepared for the contribution they shall make to our society and its cohesiveness. ... It is rather futile to demand that schools teach 'citizenship' if there is neither agreement over the moral values that contribute to that citizenship, nor acceptance of the use of reason to lead us to universal values which form the basis of our common good. Catholic schools are clearly well placed to do this. Our understanding of reason is not so limited. Our moral communion is well spelt out. It is, indeed, a major factor in what is described, and esteemed, as our Catholic ethos. Moral reasoning explores the truth that every human being is essentially, communitarian, being born into a complex of relationships and finding fulfilment only within relationships. Shared moral reasoning as a basis for social cohesion is the alternative to radical individualism which has led us, so far, on a path that is clearly becoming a dead-end."
>
> (Nichols, V., 2006, pp. 3-4)

It is what schools teach and what their pupils learn that is crucial; not the school's religious or secular status.

POSSIBLE BENEFICIAL SCHOOL EFFECTS - PUPIL ATTITUDES AND BEHAVIOUR

Evidence from inspections by the government's Office for Standards in Schools (OfSTED) over a number of years shows that Catholic schools are, generally, highly successful in meeting the state's legitimate aims for a socially caring, cohesive, coherent and liberal democratic society. OfSTED, and other researchers, consistently report that Catholic school pupils' sense of community, their relationships with their fellows and with staff is better than in non-Catholic schools; and the schools are better at helping their pupils develop a sense of social responsibility.[29]

> "On the whole, despite some ambivalence about feeling at home in a Catholic school, the majority of [non-Catholic ethnic minority] pupils felt that the schools they were in were creating an atmosphere of mutual respect, supporting them personally and preparing them to go out into a world where they might not have an easy time."
>
> (O'Keefe, B. & Zipfel, R., 2003, p. 26)

> "[Referring to OfSTED inspection data] Academic results are very important for schools and their pupils. But so too are values, character, social and mutual responsibility, duty and compassion – all the ingredients which, together with curriculum and teaching, go to make up the 'ethos' of a school. ... [Catholic] schools are strong on ethos; unashamed about propagating values as well as standards; and resolute in their mission to children and families of all backgrounds, including the least advantaged in our society."
>
> (Adonis, A., 2006 pp. 3-5)

> "In Catholic secondary schools [OfSTED Reports from the inspection cycle 2003-5 show that] ... pupils' attitudes, behaviour, relationships and self-confidence were far more often excellent or very good than in other schools. ... In terms of self-knowledge and spiritual awareness, a far higher proportion of Catholic schools achieved excellent or very good judgements. They were more often very successful in setting high expectations, stimulating a desire to learn, developing the responsibilities for living in a community and protecting pupils from bullying, racism or other harassment."
>
> (Catholic Education Service, 2006)

These observations are, of course, a general assessment across sectors and will not necessarily be true of every single school, nor can it be conclusively shown that the observed effects are a direct result of school processes and procedures. Nevertheless, the evidence suggests that Catholic schools contribute positive benefits to a pluralistic, multi-cultural society.[30] There is no inspection evidence that they threaten or undermine the legitimate interests of the state. On the contrary, positive social outcomes associated with Catholic schools have been reported from a number of independent sources.

> *"[In Northern Ireland] The openness scale showed significantly higher scores for Catholics than Protestants [in their respective schools], for girls but not for boys, and in each group scores increased with age. ... there was a positive relationship between [favourable] attitudes towards religion and openness [defined as a willingness to value members of other traditions ...]. The young people most favourably disposed towards religion were also the most open to members of other religious groups."*
>
> (Greer, J., 1993, p. 458)

> *"[In the United States of America] Those who attend Catholic schools are less prejudiced than Catholics who attend public schools and less prejudiced than all public school graduates. Moreover, they are also more likely to be pro-feminist. All of these statements are true even when social class and educational achievement are held constant."*
>
> (Greeley, A., 1998, p. 183)

> *"From the evidence available [post-Vatican II Catholic schooling] is entirely compatible with the principles of a liberal education and the principles of a democratic and socially caring society."*
>
> (Grace, G., 2003, p. 157)

> *"... [our findings show] that Catholic secondary schools bring to the urban environment communities in which belief in God is the norm. Pupils educated in this environment develop a greater sense of purpose in their own lives, hold a greater commitment to world development, and are as open in their attitudes to other groups as young people educated in non-denominational schools. According to this account Catholic schools contribute greatly to the common good and add hope to the urban environment. Urban planners may need to recognise and to value the distinctive contribution made to urban living by the continuing involvement of the Catholic Church within the state-maintained sector of education."*
>
> (Francis, L. J. & Robbins, M., 2005, p. 122; 211)

Despite the sort of evidence cited above, many point, in particular, to Northern Ireland to illustrate the counter argument that faith based schools can generate and/or entrench sectarian attitudes, encourage closed attitudes and develop intolerance between differing communities. The issue at stake

"... concerns the extent to which the segregated school systems [in Northern Ireland] have had a societal impact. This question has been posed in two contrasting forms: firstly, does religious division in education help to fuel social conflict?, and secondly, can education provide a vehicle towards an amelioration of social conflict? ... Few would argue that the segregated school systems produced the conflict while few would deny any contributory role ... On the other hand there has been relatively little research on the more abstract notions of 'school ethos' and the 'hidden curriculum' of schools."

(Gallagher, A. M., 1995, Chp. 10)

The solution, some critics of Catholic schools would argue, is for the state to have only common schools and, given that position, they would see Catholic schools as inherently anti-social. Again, however, informed comment from Northern Ireland does not support such a simplistic analysis and so undermines the proffered solution. The following, it can be argued, illustrates the situation more accurately.

"To make the educational system itself the scapegoat for all the ills of Northern Ireland would obscure problems whose origins are of a much more complex character."

(H. M. Government, 1973, p. 7)

"Segregated education in the province [of Northern Ireland] has not been a major cause of community conflict, but another by-product of the religious and political antagonisms of the past."

(Crone, R. & Malone, J., 1979, p. 2)

"When questions about the role of separate schools [in Northern Ireland] were initially posed in the 1970s it was very difficult to find any evidence to prove that damage was caused by separation."

(Dunn, S., 2000, p. 89)

In addition, research undertaken in the years since Gallagher's comments raise doubts about the supposed benefits of what, in the Northern Ireland context, could be regarded as integrated or joint faith institutions rather than purely secular schools. It has been argued that rather than being uniquely appropriate mechanisms for helping reduce religious discrimination and intolerance, the little evidence there is from Northern Ireland suggests otherwise.[31] The following is one example of such findings. There are others.[32]

"[An exploration of] teachers' methods of delivering an ethos of tolerance, respect and mutual understanding in one integrated secondary school in Northern Ireland ... [found] that most teachers make 'critical choices'

which both reflect and reinforce a 'culture of avoidance', whereby politically or religiously contentious issues are avoided rather than explored. Although teachers are well-intentioned in making these choices, it is shown that they have the potential to create the conditions that maintain or even harden psychological boundaries between Catholics and Protestants rather than dilute them."

(Donnelly, C., 2004, p. 3)

ACADEMIC ATTAINMENT

The available evidence suggests that, on the basis of government preferred measures, Catholic schools compare favourably with other schools in respect of their pupils' academic attainment across both the primary and secondary phases.[33] These findings are consistent with OfSTED inspection data indicating that, on average, Catholic schools achieve higher academic standards than those in other state maintained primary and secondary schools. Perhaps more significantly, it seems their relative superior academic productivity across both phases is more apparent the greater the level of pupil deprivation.[34] On the other hand, the findings from value added analyses designed to establish the extent of pupil progress that could be attributed to institutional rather than personal or social factors are mixed. Indications of higher academic effectiveness in Catholic compared to similar state provided schools[35] can be contrasted with studies that have found little or no difference.[36] Recent, more statistically sophisticated studies, using national data sets and multi-level analysis, also report contrary findings.[37] However, the area of dispute seemed to be centred around the extent of the observed differentials in favour of Catholic sector schools rather than reporting any findings of inferior performance.

To overcome many of the difficulties associated with measuring pupils' academic progress while taking into account factors know to affect their levels of attainment, government has developed a methodology to compare institutions termed Contextualised Value Added (CVA). It uses a multi-level statistical modelling technique based on the actual test and exam results of pupils in a given year group. It calculates the national average results attained by each category of pupil – a statistical prediction – and compares each individual's actual test or examination results against that prediction. A pupil's score is the difference (positive or negative) from this prediction. Adjustments are made to the predictions where a pupil has particular personal or background characteristics. The adjustment reflects the statistical effect of a particular characteristic on attainment in the light of other factors such as gender, socio-economic circumstances, ethnicity and other characteristics that impact on pupils' learning. The CVA findings for both primary and secondary schools in 2006 and 2007 show the Catholic school sector performs better than the national average.[38] This evidence of a possible positive 'Catholic School effect' in English schools seems consistent with similar findings in America[39] and Australia.[40]

Overall, the evidence of high attainment in the Catholic sector seems well established, particularly in the light of the most recent CVA findings from OfSTED, though causal reasons are not yet established. However, the fact of their high levels of achievement does not necessarily provide an overwhelming argument for state support. What is being suggested here is much less than that. Simply, that in respect of the educational standards achieved by pupils attending Catholic schools, the evidence shows they provide benefits to individuals and the state. There is no evidence that they do harm by depressing children's academic achievement and, on that basis, it would seem there is every reason for state to value the educational contribution they make.[41]

AN ECONOMIC AND SOCIAL CONTRIBUTION TO SOCIETY[42]

The Catholic sector provides schools for more than three quarters of a million pupils; approximately 18% of whom are not adherents to the Catholic faith but whose parents want them, for a variety of reasons, to be educated within a Catholic environment. Some nineteen thousand students, approximately half of whom are not baptised Catholics,[43] choose to continue their education beyond the compulsory school age in the sixteen Catholic sixth form colleges in England and Wales. In addition, over one thousand pupils are educated in non-maintained special schools provided and run by the Catholic sector. If those pupils were not educated within the voluntary sector, the state would have to provide the necessary buildings, together with their full ongoing maintenance costs, in order to meet their educational needs. While for some opposed in principle to the concept of state support for faith schools that might well be 'a price worth paying', it would be a high price indeed.

The Catholic community has made significant financial contribution to the state's educational need by providing these facilities. In some cases dioceses have taken on, and still retain, a considerable level of debt to do so.[44] The current insured replacement value just of the schools in England and Wales is approximately £6.5 billion, excluding the value of the land on which they are built. Further, the Catholic community contributes a net annual £12 million towards the maintenance of and improvements to its school buildings, in addition to its contribution through taxation to the state's general expenditure on education. Arguments that the Catholic sector represents a drain on the state's resources and, therefore, Catholic parents enjoy a financially privileged position, are not sustained by the available evidence.

SUMMARY

Arguing mainly from within an English context, this chapter has made a number of points. The most important has been to challenge the notion that there can be any form of education that is free from any specific values or ideology. While for some, the concept of a neutral environment in which children can be educated may be attractive, it is simply not possible to achieve. Further, those who condemn a particular school system solely on the basis of their own philosophical preferences are simply seeking to impose one ideology on children rather than another, which may or may not be in accordance with sincere and legitimate convictions held by their parents.

If it were the case that a Catholic education is positively harmful to English society, then such a political programme might be justified. The evidence, however, suggests that the Catholic faith and the activities of the Catholic Church, particularly through it schools, provide benefits to society. In general terms, commitment to the tenets of religious (Catholic) faith serve the cause of personal and social morality and civic responsibility.[45] Further, in the English context, it can be argued that religious adherence, and the existence of religious based schools, is not nearly as harmful to society as differences in language, geography, and socio-economic standing.

If religion and its practice is of value to English society, and the evidence seems to suggest that it may well be, then it makes sense for the state to support the religious upbringing of children, or at least not seek to undermine or neutralize it by means of compulsory attendance in secular (perhaps sometimes anti-religious) schools.

If it is the case that Catholic schools are particularly effective both academically and in developing positive social attitudes in their pupils, as the evidence from OfSTED data consistently seems to show, then it makes sense for the state to support such institutions.

This in no way denies the fact that religious institutions can have negative social effects, in the same way as secular ones can do. Nor is it claimed that every Catholic school will necessarily be effective in developing tolerant, self directed adults having a clear sense of moral responsibility and civic duty. The point being made is that, in the English context, there is no evidence that religious commitment is generally harmful, and most social indicators suggest the opposite. It can be demonstrated that the religious commitment of the Catholic community working through its schools generally benefits society and there is no evidence that Catholic schools cause harm. If one acknowledges, therefore, the essential conditions of a liberal democratic society summarised in the opening paragraph of this chapter, there can be no objective evidential based case for the state to seek to undermine or remove its existing support for the voluntary sector generally, and Catholic schools in particular.

NOTES

1   There are political philosophers who, while subscribing to these principles, would argue that it is not actually possible to provide an absolutely neutral framework, in the sense that the state itself must have some form of prevailing ideology or culture which cannot help but influence political thought and action in one direction or another. For example, the case for a secular state must rest on an assumption that there is no God, or that the concept of God should not form part of public life. This is demonstrably neither neutral nor inclusive of the vast majority of people living in the UK who claim they hold some form of Christian adherence. In the same way, states do not hold neutral world views. States, such as the UK, espouse democratic, liberal capitalistic values while others, say, communist China, take a different position. Consequently, given the practical impossibility of neutrality, any educational debate becomes one about forms and methods of inculturation that are acceptable rather than about mechanisms to ensure state neutrality in such matters.

2   A brief outline of this liberal/communitarian debate is included in chapter 2.

3   See Gravissimum educationis, [Declaration on Christian Education], (1965) §8, in: A. Flannery (ed) *Vatican Council II: the Conciliar and Post Conciliar Documents*, (1975) Leominster, Fowler Wright Books Ltd.

4   See, for example, analyses by Davie, G. (1994) *Religion in Britain since 1945*, Oxford, Blackwell; Gilbert, A. D. (1980) *The Making of Post-Christian Britain*, London, Longman; Brown, C. G. (2001) *The Death of Christian Britain*, London, Routledge; Bruce, S. (1995) *Religion in Modern Britain*, Oxford, Oxford University Press; Bruce, S. (2002) *God is Dead: secularisation in the west*, Oxford, Blackwell; Norman, E. (2002) *Secularisation*, London, Continuum.

5   Data from the Home Office taken from the 2001 National Census shows that over three-quarters of respondents reported some religious affiliation. The breakdown of the UK population by religion on April 1st 2001 was as follows:

Faith	%	Faith	%
Christian	71.6	Sikh	0.6
Buddhist	0.3	Other	0.3
Hindu	1.0	All Religions	76.8
Jewish	0.5	No Religion	15.5
Muslim	2.7	Not Stated	7.3

Data taken from http://www.homeoffice.gov.uk/comrace/faith, accessed 18th August 2005.

6   Francis, L. J. & Kay W. K. (1995) *Teenage Religion and Values*, Leominster, Gracewing; Francis, L. J. & Robbins, M. (2005) *Urban Hope and Spiritual Health*, Peterborough, Epworth. This phenomenon seems to be consistent with similar observations in Australia and Canada – see, for example, Bouma, G. D. (1992) *Religion: meaning, transcendence and community in Australia*, Melbourne, Longman Cheshire; Bibby, R. W. (1985) *Religious encasement in Canada: an argument for Protestant and Catholic entrenchment*, Social Compass, 16. 285-303.

7   See Francis, L. J. (2001) Religion & Values: A Quantitative Perspective, in: Francis L. J. ,Astley J. & Robbins, M. (eds) *The Fourth R for the Third Millennium*, Dublin, Lindisfarne Books; Francis L. J. (2005) *Faith and Psychology*, London, Darton, Longman & Todd Ltd.

8   In an extensive review of empirical studies relating to religion in childhood and adolescence it was noted that religiousness has been shown in many circumstances to have a positive association with acceptable and socially beneficial behaviour - see Hyde, K. (1992) *Religion in Childhood and Adolescence*, Birmingham, Alabama, Religious Education Press, pp. 278-292; 353. See also Layard, R. (2005) *Happiness: Lessons from a New Science*, London, Allen Lane; and studies specifically reporting positive effects of religion in adult populations, for example, Moberg, D. O. (1965) *Religiosity in Old Age*, Gerontologist, 5. 78-87; Frankel, B. G. & Hewitt, W. E. (1994) Religion and well-being among Canadian University Students: the role of faith groups on campus, *Journal for the Scientific Study of Religion,* 33. 1. 62-73; Koenig H. G. & Cohen H. J. (2001) *The Link Between Religion and Health: Psychoneuroimmunology and the Faith Factor*, Oxford, Oxford University Press; Weaver A. J., et al (2003) A Systematic Review of Research on Religion and Spirituality in the Journal of Traumatic Stress, 1990-1999, *Mental Health, Religion & Culture*, 6. 215-228; Francis, L. J. & Kaldor, P. (2002) The relationship between psychological well-being and Christian faith and practice in an Australian population sample, *Journal for the Scientific Study of Religion*, 41. 1. 179-184; Moreira-Almeida, A, Neto, F. L. & Koenig, H. G. (2006) Religiousness and mental health: a review, *Revista Brasileira de Psiquiatria*, 28. 3. [Note that the positive effects reported refer to general trends and cannot be ascribed to every individual. For example, there is no empirical evidence to show that all religious people are necessarily more (or less) moral, emotionally well adjusted and socially minded than similar non-religious people].

9   The term 'extrinsic religious orientation' refers to those adherents who make use of religion to meet their own need or personal benefit. Those concerned to lived religious lives for its own sake, e.g. who internalised religious doctrines, implemented them in their personal lives, sought to look outward to the needs of others and regularly attended church as having 'intrinsic orientation'. See Allport G. (1950) *The Individual and His religion: a psychological interpretation*, New York, Macmillan. For a comprehensive review of research into differential patterns of behaviour and attitudes of these two groups see Hyde, (1992) *Religion in Childhood and Adolescence*, Birmingham, Alabama, Religious Education Press, Appendix D, pp. 350-360. See also, Argyle, M. (1958) *Religious Behaviour*, London, Routledge & Kegan Paul; Allport G. W. (1954) The Nature of Prejudice, Cambridge, MA,

Addison-Wesley; Allport G. W. (1959) *Religion and Prejudice*, Crane Review, 2. 1-10; Allport G. W. (1960) *Personality and Social Encounter*, Beacon Press; Allport G. W. (1966) *Traits Revisited*, American Psychologist, 21. 1. 5-7; Allen R. O. & Spilka, B. (1967) *Committed and consensual religion: a specification of religious-prejudice relationships*, Journal for the Scientific Study of Religion, 6. 191-206.

10 For example, see Bowlby, J. (1953) *Child Care and the Growth of Love*, Harmondsworth, Penguin; Breckenridge, M. E. & Vincent, E. L. (1955) *Child Development*, London, W. B. Saunders Company; Hostler, P. (1959) *The Child's World*, Harmondsworth, Penguin; Winnicott, D. W. (1964) *The Child, the Family and the Outside World*, Harmondsworth, Penguin; Bowlby, J. (1988) Changing theories of childhood since Freud, in: E. Timms & N. Segal (eds) (1988) *Freud in Exile*, New Haven, Yale University Press; Kraemer, S. (1993) Domestic Organisation and Personal Identity, *Annual Review*, Windsor, St. George's House; Whitfield, R. (1995) Educating for Family Life: from advocacy to investment and action, *The Month*, December, pp. 465-469; Whitfield, R. (1996) Security of Attachment: a necessary objective in taking ourselves and our children seriously, *Annual Review*, Windsor, St. George's House.

11 The importance of the family in the development of social capital, which is, in turn, linked to high academic attainment and other desirable educational outcomes, is well documented. See for example, Coleman, J. S. (1988) Social capital and the creation of human capital, (1988) *American Journal of Sociology*, 94. 95-120; Fagan, P. (2001) *Family and faith: the roots of prosperity, stability and freedom,* Washington, DC, The Heritage Foundation; Croll, P. (2004) Families, social capital and educational outcomes, *British Journal of Educational Studies*, 52. 4. 390-416.

12 See, for example, Bibby, R. W. & Posterski, D. C. (1985) *The Emerging Generation*; King, A. J. C. et al. (1989) *Canada Youth and AIDS Study*; Morgan, P. (1999) *Farewell to the Family*; Frabutt, J. M. (2001) Parenting and Child development: Exploring the Links with Children's Social, Moral and Cognitive Competence, in: T. C. Hunt, E. A. Joseph & R. J. Nuzzi, *Handbook of Research on Catholic Education*, Westport, Connecticut, Greenwood Press; Dennis, N. & Erdos, G, (2000) *Families Without Fatherhood*; O'Neill, R. (2002), *Does Marriage Matter*; Social Justice Policy Group (2006) *Breakdown Britain*; Margo, J. et al. (2006) *Freedom's Orphans*, London, Institute for Public Policy Research.

13 Francis L. J. (1992) The influence of Religion, gender and social class on attitudes towards school among 11 year olds in England, *Journal of Experimental Education*, 60. 4. 339-348; Flynn, M. (1985) *The Effectiveness of Catholic Schools*, Sydney, St. Paul Publications; Flynn, M. (1993) Religious commitment and school achievement, *Catholic School Studies*, 62. 2. 21-27; Romi, S. (2002) Disruptive behaviour in religious and secular high schools, *Research in Education*, 71. 81-91.

14 Moberg, D. O. (1962) *The Church as a Social Institution*, New Jersey, Prentice-Hall; Moberg, D. O. (1965) Religiosity in Old Age, *Gerontologist*, 5. 78-87; Bernt, F. M. (1989) Being religious and being altruistic: a study of college service volunteers, *Personality and Individual Differences*, 10. 663-669; Wilson J. & Musick, M. (1997) Who cares? Towards an integrated theory of volunteer work, *American Sociological Review*, 62. 5. 694-713; Musick, M., Wilson J. & Bynum, W. B. (2000) Race and formal volunteering: the differential effects of class and religion, *Social Forces*, 74. 1. 1539-1570; Ozorak, E. W. (2003) Love of God and neighbour: religion and volunteer service among college students, *Review of Religious Research*, 44. 3. 285-299; Regnerus, M. D. (2003) Religion and positive adolescent outcomes: a review of research and theory, *Review of Religious Research*, 44. 4. 394-413; Reitsma, J., Scheepers, P. & te Grotenhuis, M. (2005) Dimensions of individual religiosity and volunteering in Europe, *Paper presented at the NCVO & VSSN 11th Researching the Voluntary Sector Conference*, University of Warwick.

15 The following media comment is, perhaps, typical of a more general prejudice that is unsupported by any empirical evidence. *"No single type of school founded on religion ... can contribute to the unification of society, even though it purports to instruct its members in toleration. Religions, being fundamentally irrational, are fundamentally intolerant of each other, and schools set up on the shoulders of religions inevitably propagate that intolerance into future generations."* See, Atkins, P. (2001) The Church school – good or evil: Against, *The Independent* - Education Supplement, p. 7, 1st March.

16 See, for example, comments made by Graham Allen MP (Labour member for Nottingham North) in the Hansard report of the House of Commons debate *Admission Policies of Faith Schools*, 14th February 2006; also the speech by Lord Taverne in the Hansard Report of the House of Lords debate *Faith Schools (Expansion) Bill*, 8th February 2006: British Humanist Association (2001) *Religious Schools: the case against*, London, British Humanist Association, p. 35; Dawkins, R. (2001) No faith in the absurd, *Times Educational Supplement*, p. 17, 23rd February.

17 For a fuller examination and demonstration of why the chronic unrest in Northern Ireland is not a religious conflict see McGarry, J. & O'Leary, B. (1995) *Explaining Northern Ireland: Broken Images*, Oxford, Blackwell, pp. 171-213; Holloway, D. (2005) *Understanding the Northern Ireland Conflict: A summary and overview of the conflict and its origins*, Belfast, Community Dialogue; also Burleigh, M. (2006) *Sacred Causes: Religion and Politics from the European Dictators to Al Qaeda*, London, Harper Collins, pp. 373-414.

18 Gallagher, E. & Worrall, S. (1982) *Christians in Ulster 1968-1980*, Oxford, Oxford University Press; Wells, R. A. (1999) *People behind the peace: community and reconciliation in Northern Ireland*, Grand Rapids, Eerdmans; Tanner, M. (2001) *Ireland's Holy Wars: the struggle for a nation's soul*, 1500-2000, New Haven, Yale University Press; Burleigh, M. (2006) *Sacred Causes: Religion and Politics from the European Dictators to Al Qaeda*, London, Harper Collins, p. 407.

19 See, for example, Greenslade, L. (1992) White skin, white masks: psychological distress among the Irish in Britain, in: P. O'Sullivan (ed) *The Irish in the New Communities, Volume 2*, Leicester, Leicester University Press; Hillard, P. (1993) *Suspect Community: People's experience of the Prevention of Terrorism Act in Britain*, London, Pluto Press; Williams, I., Dunne, M. & Mac an Ghaill, M. (1996) *Economic Needs of the Irish Community in Birmingham*, Birmingham, Birmingham City Council; Hickman, M. J. (1997) *Religion, Class and Identity: The State, the Catholic Church and the Education of the Irish in Britain*, Hampshire, Avebury; Hickman, M. J. & Walter, B. (1997) *Discrimination and the Irish Community in Britain*, London, Commission for Racial Equality,

20 For example, Irish clubs and associations in the major cities, Irish Studies courses in some English Universities, Irish dancing classes and competitions, public celebrations and wearing shamrock on St. Patrick's Day.

21 See Hornsby-Smith, M. P. & Dale, A. (1988) The assimilation of Irish immigrants in England, *British Journal of Sociology*, 39. 4. 519-543. Also, as part of a recent study of Catholic schools in the Archdiocese of Birmingham [see Morris, A. B. & Godfrey, R. (2006)] the ethnic backgrounds of some 5169 pupils in 34 Secondary schools located in thirteen different local authorities were taken from the schools PLASC returns to their respective LAs. [Though not reported in the published study] it was found that even in those areas of the diocese where families of Irish background are the majority grouping within the school's catchment area, remarkably few pupils indicated their ethnic background to be Irish, preferring the self-designation 'White British'.

22 Note the absence of any reference to the Irish community in Department of Education & Science Report of the Committee of Inquiry into the Education of Children from Ethnic Minority Groups

(1985) *Education for All* (Swann Report), London, HMSO. Despite being the Irish being the largest ethnic minority in England, it was not until 1997 that the Commission for Racial Equality examined Irish experiences (see Hickman, M. J. & Walter B, 1997, *ibid*). Even the Report of the Working Party on Catholic Education in a Multicultural Society (1984) *Learning from Diversity*, London, Catholic Media Office, relegates mention of the experience of Irish immigrants to appendix D. More recently, an authoritative map "… of the full spectrum of people who now make up British society" lists twenty-three different cultural and ethnic group but does not include the Irish. See, Woods, P., et al. (2006) *Cultural Diversity in Britain*, York, Joseph Rowntree Foundation, preface.

23 See Hyde, K. (1990) *Religion in Childhood and Adolescence: A Comprehensive Review of the Research*, Religious Education Press, Alabama, chapter 14.

24 See Leavey, M. C. (1972a; 1972b) and Flynn M. (1974; 1985). For full details see bibliography.

25 See Francis. L. J. (1979; 1980; 1983; 1984; 1987). For full details see bibliography.

26 There is some evidence of a positive association between pupils' examination scores at age 16 and high proportions of Catholic pupils on the school's roll. It is most evident with pupils who, within their particular schools, are academically weak. See Morris, A. B. & Godfrey, R. (2006) *A Statistical Survey of Attainment in Catholic Schools in England with Particular Reference to Secondary Schools Operating Under the Trust Deed of the Archdiocese of Birmingham*, Canterbury, National Institute for Christian Education Research.

27 It is perfectly possible to develop understanding of, and empathy with, others without direct contact; for example, how else could historical understanding develop? Nor does contact necessarily develop harmonious relationships. See discussion in Short, G. (2002) Faith Based Schools: a threat to social cohesion? *Journal of Philosophy of Education*, 36. 4. 559-572. See also, Short, G. (2003) Faith Schools and Social Cohesion: opening up the debate, *British Journal of Religious Education*, 25. 2. 129-141.

28 This is a reference to those who have argued, following the 'Cantle Report' into disturbances involving large numbers of people from different cultural backgrounds during the spring and early summer of 2001, that faith schools are a significant causal factor of social unrest.

29 Catholic Education Service (2006) *Quality and Performance: A Survey of Education in Catholic Schools*, London, CES. In the above document it is reported:

"Data drawn from Ofsted's national database of the findings of the inspection cycle from 2003-5 for all maintained schools show that the pupils in Catholic schools closely reflect the national school population in terms of levels of disadvantage and special educational needs (SEN), but they generally travel further to get to school. Catholic schools have a higher proportion of pupils from minority ethnic groups. They are much more successful than other maintained schools at creating an ethos where pupils learn effectively. Attendance is better and parents make a stronger contribution to their children's education. They are very effective in areas associated with pupils' personal development, attitudes and values, and particularly in cultivating self-knowledge and spiritual awareness. Parents are more likely to make a valuable contribution to their children's education than in other schools, particularly at secondary level. Attendance is better at all stages.

Ofsted reports identifying good practice in secondary schools in raising the academic achievements, and preventing the exclusion from school, of Black Caribbean pupils cite a disproportionate number of Catholic secondary schools as worthy of emulation. See OfSTED (2002) *Achievement of Black Caribbean Pupils: Good Practice in Secondary Schools*, HMI 448, London, OfSTED. Also, OfSTED (2008) *Reducing Exclusion of Black Pupils from Secondary Schools*, London, OfSTED. (Note that the reports do not specifically identify in the text these centres of excellent practice as being Catholic institutions. Comments made by HMI in private correspondence with the author suggests that it might be politically embarrassing to do so).

30 Data from OfSTED reporting similar findings can be found in a number of papers other than those referenced above that have been collated by the Catholic Education Service. For example, Key, T. (2006) *The Performance of Catholic Schools and Sixth Form Colleges*, Presentation, National Catholic Education Conference, May 18th; Morris, A. B. (1998), (2001). For full details see bibliography.

31 See Barnes, L. P. (2002) World religions in the Northern Ireland curriculum, *Journal of Beliefs and Values*, 23. 1. 19-32; Barnes L. P. (2005) Religion, education and conflict in Northern Ireland, *Journal of Beliefs and Values*, 26. 2. 123-138.

32 Donnelly, C. (1999) *Differences in Schools: a question of ethos*, paper presented at the British Education Research Association Annual Conference, University of Sussex, September 2nd–5th; Donnelly, C. (2004) Constructing the ethos of tolerance and respect in an integrated school: the role of teachers, *British Educational Research Journal*, 30. 2. 263-278; Barnes, L. P. & Kay, W. K. (2002) *Religious education in England and Wales: innovations and reflections*, Leicester, RTSF.

33 Hornsby-Smith, M. P. (1978); Nuttall, D. (1990); Sinnott, J. (1992); Thomas, S., et al. (1993); Kendall, L. & Ainsworth, L. (1997); Bishops' Conference (1999); Marks, J. (2001); Morris, A. B. (1998; 2001; 2005); Arthur, J. & Godfrey, R. (2005); Morris, A. B. & Godfrey, R. (2006)

34 Bishops' Conference, (1997, 1999); Morris, A. B. (2005); Morris A. B. & Godfrey, R. (2006)

35 Jesson, D., et al. (1992); Jesson, D. & Gray, J. (1993); Everrett, S. (1993); Morris, A. B. (1996); Marks, J. (2001). For full details see bibliography.

36 Kendall, L. (1996; 1997). For full details see bibliography.

37 Schagen, S., et al. (2002); Benton, T., et al. (2003); Morris, A. B. & Godfrey, R. (2006). For full details see bibliography.

38 For details of the government's Contextualised Value Added methodology see www.dcsf.gov.uk/performance tables/schools.

39 For details of the relative CVA performance of Catholic schools see Morris, A. B. (2008) *Academic Standards in Catholic Schools in England*, presentation at the 21st Congress of the German Corporation for Educational Science, Dresden, March 18th; Morris, A. B. (forthcoming) Contextualising Catholic School Performance in England

40 Data from the USA indicate that pupils attending Catholic elementary and secondary schools tend to obtain, on average, higher levels of academic achievement than those attending their state run counterparts and have better learning habits. In addition, they seem particularly effective with pupils from ethnic minorities and lower socio-economic groups. They tend to have lower drop-out rates and send more of their students to college (Coleman, J. S., et al. (1982); Greeley, A. (1982); Cibulka, J., et al. (1982); Hoffer, T., et al. (1985); Hill, P., et al. (1990); Bryk, A., et al. (1993); Teachman, J. D., et al. (1996); Reese, C. M., et al. (1997); Johnson, K. A. (1999); Hoffer, T. (2000); Jeynes, H. K. (2000; 2003). Generally, contemporary criticisms of the main body of research about Catholic schools in the USA did not attack the underlying claim that they were more successful in pursuing academic achievement than state schools. On the other hand, it is important to note that, despite the various American studies controlling for family background and other socio-economic factors known to influence levels of attainment, "*... there still exists no definitive data to conclude that Catholic schools, in and of themselves, are the major reason yielding these favourable outcomes for youth, particularly disadvantaged youth*" (Meegan, E. A., et al. 2002).

41 Evans, M. D. R. (2004) Do Catholic schools and independent schools enhance educational success?, *Australian Social Monitor*, 7. 3. 53-69; Kelley, J. (2004) Class, religion and education: who gains most from Catholic and independent schooling?, *Australian Social Monitor*, 7. 3. 69-80.

42 The government accepts that their adjusted performance measures tend to be better than the average and suggests as possible explanations "their strong values and unique ethos"; high levels of parental support; and "communities that value education". See, Treasury Minutes on the Nineteenth Report from the Committee of Public Accounts 2003-04, *Making a Difference: Performance of maintained secondary schools in England*, presented to Parliament by the Financial Secretary to the Treasury, June 2004 (Cm 6244), PAC Conclusion (vi) and §§21, 25, 27.

43 Much of the information in these paragraphs has been published previously. See, Catholic Education Service (2003) *Catholic Education: A CES Position Paper on Catholic Education in Schools and Sixth Form Colleges*, London, Catholic Education Service.

44 Catholic Education Service School Census data, 2002; 2003; 2004; 2005.

45 For example, the Archdiocese of Birmingham took on a debt of some £30 million in today's prices – together with a commitment to service the annual interest charges - in order to build, with the aid of government grants, the necessary number of primary and secondary school places that were required following the implementation of the Education Act 1944 and to meet the demands of the rising Catholic population. In the fourteen years between 1952 and 1966 some 84 new primary and 40 new secondary schools were built. Fifty years later that debt has nearly all been repaid. However, many of the schools built in the 1950s are coming to the end of their useful life and need to be replaced or refurbished. Consequently, despite the level of grant aid currently available, the debt is unlikely to be completely eliminated in the near future and may well begin to rise again.

46 This is the point made by St. Augustine of Hippo when he argues that Christianity makes people better citizens of the temporal (Roman) city. See, in particular, Books 2.19 and 19.17 in *Concerning the City of God Against the Pagans*, translated by Bettenson, H. (1972) London, Penguin Books. See also, Pope Pius XI (1929) *Divini Illius Magistri*, [The Christian Education of Youth] Rome, 31st December, §85.

Chapter 9

FIFTY YEARS ON – CONTEMPORARY CHALLENGES

INTRODUCTION

All institutions exist within specific social circumstances which, at different times and in different places, will influence and shape both the challenges they face, and their responses to them. Following the restoration of the Catholic hierarchy in 1850, the bishops' first collective decision was to begin the process of providing Catholic schools. Their reasons for so doing have been explored in chapter four. In brief, schools are an instrument of the Church's evangelistic missionary activity; assist parents in fulfilling their educative role; serve the needs of local church communities; and contribute to the well being of the wider society.[1] Those four guiding principles remain the raison d'être of today's Catholic sector schools. Diocesan planning of its educational provision has to be made against the background of the educational policies of the government of the day, and though particular circumstances may change over time, the essential conditions required to fulfil the bishops' educative purposes have remained constant. They need a supportive civil legislative framework in which they can secure their schools' ecclesial character and purpose and keep the associated costs within the limits of their financial resources.

In the immediate post-war years implementing the educational vision of the Education Act 1944 strained the nation's resources. When 'The Case for Catholic Schools' was written, the bishops' over-riding concern was financing the building programme necessary to meet post-war educational demand. While not denying there are still financial constraints today, it can be argued that the inherent costs of maintaining the voluntary aided status of its schools are no longer the pre-eminent problem facing the bishops. Consequently, this chapter focuses on other issues currently facing the Church and its schools. They include the development of a market approach towards the provision and content of education;[2] the comparative success of maintained Catholic schools; a declining pupil population; recruiting and training suitable staff; maintaining the capacity to respond effectively to the demands of a seemingly ever-increasing mass of legislation, the changing character of the Catholic community and, perhaps the most critical of all, the increasingly aggressive secularisation of culture with its tendency to privatise religion and exclude it from all aspects of public discourse concerned with the social, economic and political life of the country. The list is clearly not exhaustive but covers some of the more important challenges facing the Catholic sector (a more comprehensive summary is included as an appendix). They represent, of course, a personal view which should not be regarded as necessarily reflecting the perspectives, or totality of priorities, held by the English bishops, either individually or collectively, as they attempt to chart the on-going development of Catholic education and catechesis in their respective dioceses.

CONCEPTUAL CONFUSION

All forms of education are concerned with the transmission of culture, and educational priorities, both for and in schools, rest on a complex set of moral and social preferences and beliefs about what is good for individuals and society as a whole. In relatively homogeneous societies such frames of reference are not usually a matter for debate. However, difficulties and disputes may arise where there are significant groups and sub-groups within society who do not necessarily subscribe to its dominant ideology – in this case secular humanism – but view life from a different perspective. Secularism can be characterised as a belief system, attitude or style of life that denies or ignores the reality (or even the possibility of the existence) of God, excludes religion entirely from public affairs and regards nature as the only reality by which to order human activity. Needless to say, many parents do not accept this premise as a basis for their personal or public lives. Nor do they regard it as an acceptable framework for the education of their children.

Within any civic society, therefore, one major problem is to find a common language that helps various groups negotiate educational processes in such a way that accommodates legitimate but differing perspectives of the role, nature and content of education. This is a particular difficulty where elements of language and categories inherent in a religious tradition have been reinterpreted and absorbed into a secular culture. Common words seemingly providing common ground for discussion, but if their contextualised meanings are different, the resultant linguistic ambiguity creates the potential for mutual incomprehension. For example, 'vocational' usually means training for a manual occupation, not a (religious) calling to serve others; 'corporate' has none of the theological connotations implicit in the Pauline idea of body;[3] 'mission', as in 'mission statement', does not imply that the employees are missionaries; and when Church or OfSTED officers inspect the spiritual development of pupils, each will have very different things in mind.[4] Rehabilitating the theological characteristics of such common educational terminology can, if used with clarity and precision, illuminate the essentially religious character of Catholic education for both the Catholic and secular communities, especially where it is integrated into the language of school improvement and effectiveness.

In addition, many of the arguments utilised in the current debate about the place and role of the faith-based schools are conceptually vague or so multi-faceted that they tend to inhibit rather than facilitate fruitful dialogue. Labels such as race, ethnicity, religion and culture are often conflated or applied indiscriminately, while concepts such as community, social cohesion, inclusion, divisive and autonomy have so many shades of meaning that, without further clarification, they can hinder productive analysis and debate.

CATHOLICS AND CATHOLIC SCHOOLS IN A SECULAR SOCIETY

Catholic communities in England became integrated into society after a long period of historical persecution, repression and social segregation. Today, while active institutionalised persecution has long since been removed, evidence of what can be described as a form of covert institutional discrimination is becoming increasingly noticeable against the involvement or promotion of a (Catholic) religious perspective in public life.[5] It has even been suggested that many Catholics will be familiar with a form of religious prejudice that is akin to racism[6] manifest in an ideology that:

> "... relies heavily upon the secularising myth which reinterprets our history, casting all oppression, violence and tyranny at the doors of religious faith. It conveniently forgets that the great perpetrators of violence in the last century, for example, were the secular ideologies of Lenin, Hitler and Pol Pot, to say nothing of the effects of abortion and its six million victims in this country alone."

> (Nichols, V., 2005)

> "[It proposes] that our common enterprise can somehow be conducted in morally neutral terms ... that moral judgement is a private matter ... [and that] all we need is the clarification of what is lawful ... The process of secular democracy in our country at this time, while claiming to act

disinterestedly and in a morally neutral fashion is in fact engaged in an intense and at time aggressive reshaping of our moral framework. ... What government must realise is ...[that] it is simply unacceptable to suggest that the resources of the faith communities ... can work in cooperation with public authorities only if the faith communities accept not simply a legal framework but the moral standards [of] Government."

(Nichols. V., 2006b)

Despite the current antipathy towards manifestations of religious life and purpose and any discrimination, real or imaginary, intended or accidental, that may be experienced, Catholics, both individually and collectively, are now well established in material terms, are thriving and form a significant minority community within a pluralistic and multi-faith society. Any communal activities, however, take place within a cultural environment very different to that experienced by the bishops in the 1950s.

It is, perhaps, a measure of the turbulence and confusion of the current political climate that government displays such an ambivalent attitude towards religious based schools. On the one hand, it seems to welcome and support their existence and contribution to the educational system,[7] and to establish new categories of school having many of their structural elements (for example, a measure of autonomy from local authority control, self governance, control of admissions and responsibility for school land and assets), so providing the benefits of the existing Church school ethos[8] more widely than in the past. On the other hand, it has seemed reluctant to appreciate and support the socio-religious circumstances that have contributed to the successes it hopes can be emulated through other educational institutions.

"... this new secularist intolerance of religion has been accompanied by the state's increasing acceptance of anti-religious thinking. ... Yet this does not sit easily with what the state wants from religion. ... Catholic schools ... are among the most popular in British society. Most of them are over-subscribed, they work hard at integrating pupils and are among the most socially diverse. Where they can, they are happy to receive a significant number of people from other faiths – or from none. Whenever I meet politicians, of whichever persuasion, they invariable comment on how much admired our Catholic schools are. But I always say to them, "you cannot have the fruits without the roots". Catholic schools are rightly recognised as gems in our education system but we must bear in mind that they are underpinned by a community of faith lived by ordinary families. ... Remove

the faith which motivates those parents' choice of school and you remove
the heart from those very schools."

(Murphy-O'Connor, C., 2007)

In a similar fashion, it appears to recognise the positive contribution the
Catholic sector is making to promote social inclusion and cohesion yet at
the same time demands that the Church authorities must, when seeking
to open a new Catholic school, prove how it will promote these social
goods.[9] Even their status as religious charities will no longer be regarded
as prima facie evidence that they provide a general benefit to society under
the provisions of the Charity Law Act 2006.[10]

In the 19th and 20th centuries Catholic schools were an important
mechanism whereby an alien ethnic minority people (the Irish Catholics)
were successfully integrated into British society.[11] In the 21st century, their
ability to do so is, in legislative terms, presumed to be in doubt unless
proven otherwise, though there is no empirical evidence to support that
scepticism. Some argue that the demands being made of proposers of new
schools may well be aimed more at minority non-Christian faith groups
(particularly the Muslim community) than at the Catholic sector, though it
is not possible to confirm that belief by reference to official DfES or other
government documentation. Even if it is the case, the current climate in
which the bishops seek to secure the future of Catholic education seems
less benign than it has been for many years.

CATHOLIC CULTURE AND THE CATHOLIC COMMUNITY[12]

The term 'culture', used in a sociological or anthropological sense, refers to
the shared customs and understandings of a community that are acquired,
rather than inherited, and developed through several generations of
common, everyday, experiences both within families and the institutions
that form the focus of their lives. In the same context, 'community' means
more than a conglomerate of individuals living in a particular location.
Together, the two terms describe a frame of reference of a specific group
of people, having a shared value system and cultural attitudes by which,
collectively, they make sense of the world and their place in it.

Up until the 1940s, it could be argued, Catholics constituted a distinct subculture of the working class community. It had its own particular religious,
social and moral norms of behaviour, values and belief systems, though
levels of adherence and commitment to them may, of course, have varied,
and much if not all social activities could take place within the context

of parish organisations. Examples of religious behaviour would include attendance at Mass on Sundays and other religious festivals together with Friday abstinence from eating meat. Social and moral norms would include an expectation of sexual continence and life-long marriage. Social activities might involve the Parish Club, the Legion of Mary, Young Christian Workers and other similar religiously orientated associations. Two main contributory factors have been identified as encouraging the breakdown of this relatively poor, working class insularity. The first was a direct result of the new secondary schools introduced by the 1944 Education Act that replaced the previous parochially based all-age system of schooling. Catholic secondary schools drew their pupils from several parishes, often many miles apart, so weakening traditional community ties. On the other hand, the priority given by the bishops to a distinctive Catholic secondary education, provided in its own schools, helped preserve to some degree a sense of distinctiveness and a feeling of membership of an international society, and succeeded in developing a thriving Catholic middle class. The other major factor was the impact of the Second Vatican Council which encouraged greater openness towards, and engagement with, the wider world.

It was against this background that the predominantly Irish working-class, Catholic community located in the poorer parts of the inner cities began to change and an increasingly large Catholic middle class developed within the emerging pluralistic, secular and multi-cultural society. Nevertheless, in the more turbulent social climate that has developed in England during recent years, there still exists, at the beginning of the 21st century, what can be described as a sense of Catholic tribalism, though it may no longer exhibit the very distinctive, homogeneous identity of the 1940s and 1950s, and its members are likely to exhibit increasingly individualistic and more personalised forms of Catholic adherence. Consequently, the context in which Catholic schools operate has also changed. Whereas when the original 'Case for Catholic Schools' was written, the bishops might reasonably take the social attitudes, beliefs and commitment of parents and their children for granted, today, the educative task of Catholic schools takes place within much more fluid circumstances. An increase in social and religious mobility, greater cultural and ethnic diversity and the emerging plurality of religious belief and opinion means it is no longer possible to discuss Catholic schools as serving a single homogeneous faith community[13] (even in schools which may be fully subscribed with baptised Catholic pupils).

Nor can the bishops necessarily rely upon the unwavering support of the laity in educational matters as might have once been the case.[14]

EDUCATION AND SOCIAL COHESION

The educational debates of the late 19th and early 20th centuries concerned competing claims of Christian denominations in a Christianised country. Now the socio/political circumstances are very different. We live in a multi-cultural, multi-ethnic and determinedly secular culture in which concerns about the potential for racial tension, and possible conflict, have loomed large in government thinking following well-publicised disturbances in some northern towns and cities during 2001.[15] While there are various, and sometimes conflicting, explanations of the essential causes of the unrest, government has argued "tensions can grow where ethnic groups have segregated themselves from each other - whether by choice or circumstance - in housing, work, leisure and education."[16] To counter those social ills, it has sought to promote ethnic, religious and cultural tolerance and respect between different groups of people living and working together through legislation and the education system, arguing that schools have a key statutory role in promoting social cohesion. That belief has now been translated into statutory requirements in respect of all existing and proposed new schools.[17]

While the Catholic Church has argued that it seeks to play a positive role in promoting the common good of society,[18] it would be foolish to ignore the fact that there is some political opposition to the concept of diversity of educational provision. Some oppose the very existence of church or faith-based schools, and are particularly hostile to the Catholic sector. Perhaps such opposition is inevitable since the role of Catholic schools in supporting Catholic parents in transmitting Catholic culture within a post-Christian and highly secularised society highlights tensions between secular and religious values. An apparent increasing level of intolerance of religious communities wishing to operate in the public sphere means that the bishops find themselves considering the future of the Catholic sector in much less benign circumstances than has been the case in the relatively recent past.

Claims are made that schools provided by, and for, the adherents to a particular faith are, by their very nature, socially divisive.[19] Such assertions are rooted in a particular perspective of how the inherent tensions between the rights of individual parents and the responsibilities of the state acting on behalf of all parents might be resolved. It is a view that places excessive weight upon the (legitimate) interests of the state compared to the rights of individuals in a way that seems to be contrary to the thrust of human rights legislation and Catholic social teaching. In the particular case of education, they both take the stance that the normal function of the state is not to teach but to assist parents in their educative function. In other words, teachers, and therefore schools, should always be acting *in loco parentis*, not *in loco civitatis*.

Schools in England have, traditionally, aimed both to serve a community and to be communities in their own right. The model of 'school as community' has been generally accepted as wholly beneficial, promoting effective learning within a nurturing environment that engendered mutual trust and loyalty between taught and teachers. The value of the concept, however, depends greatly upon our understanding of community and its essential characteristics.

> *"... Communities offer the promise of a sense of belonging or membership ... are held together by shared values - but not any shared values will do. ..[F]or a school. shared values should bind people together in the pursuit of a shared conception of a good education - and not any shared conception ... will do. If, for example, the conception shared was that the central purpose of education was to enable students to get the best jobs or get into the best colleges, students would find they were competing for scarce goods. The values shared [of a good education]then, should lead students to pursue at least some non-positional goods where the achievements of each contributes to the good of all."*

(Strike, K., 2003, pp. 171-172)

The Catholic Church would argue that the founding principles of its schools provide, precisely, the sort of beneficial societal glue that Strike alludes to. Nevertheless, it would be foolish to argue that religious beliefs can never be a source of social unrest, though equally erroneous to suggest that it is always so, since history shows us that they are, paradoxically, associated both with tolerance and intolerance towards contrary views and life-styles. Consequently, there is clearly a role for legislators to determine the balance to be struck between the good of society as a whole and rights of families to choose what is good for them. Those who have responded to recent incidents of social unrest by assuming that (Catholic) faith schools are part of the problem rather than part of the solution, are making judgements in the absence of supportive empirical evidence. In the case of Catholic schools, the weight of evidence is against their critics. Nevertheless, it is held by many to be self evident that a Catholic school educating Catholic pupils cannot, of itself, either generate or promote social harmony, but must have some different, but undefined, focus, if it is to be of general benefit to the community. Needless to say, it is not an opinion that the bishops accept, but it is the climate within which they must now secure the future of Catholic education as much of the building stock established in the 1950s and early 1960s is modernised, rebuilt, and in some cases, replaced by new schools.

SCHOOLS FOR CATHOLICS

In a matter of just over half a century, government attitudes towards Catholic schools has moved from a grudging acceptance that they could be provided, but for the Catholic community only, to an aspiration that they reserve up to a quarter of their capacity for non-Catholic pupils.[20] This significant change in attitude seems, in large measure, to be connected with their perceived success in providing the educational conditions and outcomes so valued by successive governments. However, the desire for the fruits of a Catholic education by (some) non-Catholic parents and by government does not seem to be connected to an understanding or appreciation of the (likely) reasons why they are able to achieve the outcomes they seek.[21]

In the immediate post-war years, apart from those directly involved in their provision and use, the Catholic school system in England received remarkably little attention from politicians, Her Majesty's Inspectors (HMI), academics or the general public. Their relative effectiveness as academic institutions was not a matter of particular interest or concern.[22] Most Catholic parents seemed happy to send their children to Catholic schools and the main problem for the bishops was not the quality of education provided in them, but to ensure there were sufficient places to meet Catholic demand. The Education Act 1944 reaffirmed the dual system of education of state and voluntary provided schools. The settlement was designed, in part, to ensure that those parents who wanted an education for their children that was compatible with their own religious beliefs could do so, provided they built their own schools (with some financial assistance from central government) to meet the demand. Neither legislators nor the bishops ever considered that Catholic schools would be provided for anyone other than their own congregations; or that anyone who was not a member would want their children educated in them.[23] Consequently, the Church adopted a strategy designed to secure, over time, a place in a Catholic school for every Catholic pupil of compulsory school age, through which parents would be helped to fulfil their role in bringing up their children within the Catholic faith and culture.

Despite the apparent clarity of the 1944 Act, the bishops' plans were occasionally obstructed by both government and local education authorities.[24] Nevertheless, the 1950's and early 1960s saw a vast expansion of provision as the Church responded to the rapidly increasing Catholic population who wanted their children to receive a Catholic education. Unfortunately, just as that building programme seemed to have resolved the problem, the birth-rate began to decline, and from the mid-1960s onwards, the bishops had to grapple with problems arising from excess capacity and an increasing demand for places for non-Catholic pupils.[25] The challenges presented by these new circumstances are expressed, in slightly differing ways and in different contexts, in the comments below. The first was made while legislation enabled governors and local education authorities to agree to keep places unfilled in Catholic schools if there were fewer Catholics seeking places than the available school capacity. The second was made after its repeal.

> "A Catholic school must in some way be a community of faith in which worship is appropriate, possible and wholly acceptable. If it were not catechesis and evangelisation would be impossible. This has implications for admissions and forces us to think very carefully about who should and should not be admitted to our schools. The answer to that can never be cut and dried. The situation of each school is different. Local factors must be taken into account. It is not simply a matter of applying percentages."
>
> (Konstant, D., 1996, Briefing, 26. 4. pp. 26-29)

> "The presence of pupils from other faiths in Catholic schools makes the cultural question of how to profess the truth of the Gospel into a social one too. How should one relate to members of other faiths in a Catholic school? The option of retreating to moral education and avoiding the cultural question, the claim to truth, can seem attractive again in a post-modern context. Yet, it is becoming clear that in order to foster the Catholic identity of a school, this cultural question cannot be avoided altogether. The challenge is to avoid, on the one hand, a fundamentalism that fails to face up to the modern world and, on the other, a liberalism that effectively denies the specific identity of a Catholic school and leaves in its place an empty secular shell."
>
> (Hanvey, J. & Carroll, A., Heythrop Institute, 2005, pp. 78-79)

Legislation enacted in 1980 included new provisions affecting, among other things, school governance and pupil admissions. The changes to admissions were designed to enhance the scope for parental choice of school and have continued to be a feature of successive Education Acts. Initially, Catholic schools (i.e. those having aided or special agreement status) were not required to comply with parents' preference where an agreement to limit the number of non-Catholic pupils had been made with the local education authority, though the grounds upon which such an agreement might be reached were not specified.[26] Subsequent legislation[27] made it clear that the basis of any agreement should be for the purpose of "preserving the religious character of the school". This clause remained in force until, with the agreement and support of the bishops exercised through the Catholic Education Service,[28] it was abolished under the provisions of the Education Act 2002, section 216 (4).

PATTERNS OF SCHOOL PROVISION

Falling pupil rolls was first recognised as a national problem during the late 1970s.[29] For the Catholic sector, the problem was exacerbated by a general movement of Catholic communities away from the inner cities towards the suburbs. If the Church retains the education of Catholic children as its prime educational purpose, some dioceses may need to reduce the number of Catholic schools that they currently provide, many of which are located in the inner cities. In many cases, that reduction will be managed by closing or amalgamating existing provision to create new (smaller?) schools, either on existing sites or, possibly, on a new site more suitably placed to serve two or more existing parishes. Any such proposals will be made in the light of the most recent Statutory Guidance,[30] in which the government's aspiration to encourage diversity in educational provision has to be balanced against fears that it may encourage social division. For example:

> "Promoters of new schools should include in their proposals information about how the school will tackle religious, racial and cultural division, and meet the statutory duties to promote community cohesion and well-being across the community." ... The Decision Maker will need to consider the views of the local community, the commitment of the new school promoters and their own assessment of the robustness of the proposed means for achieving inclusiveness. Proposals for new faith schools should be judged on the same basis as proposals for other schools."
>
> (DfES, 2007, Part C, §§55; 57)

In some, still fairly rare, circumstances, diocesan planners may consider amalgamating one or more of their schools with those of another faith group. Where this has happened the chosen partner has, at the time of writing, always been with the Anglican Church. Sometimes, Catholic schools are located in areas where there is no longer any form of Catholic community to serve but the places that they provide are still needed. In such instances, diocesan schools might be transferred to a local authority or ownership of another denomination or faith group. On the other hand, where proposals to close a school are brought forward by governors or, more usually, the local authority[31] it is most unusual for them to be accepted without parental opposition; sometimes extremely vociferous. In each of the possible responses to falling rolls outlined above, there have been, in different dioceses, much hurt and bitterness directed at those who have brought such proposals to fruition. Managing expansion is clearly much easier than securing the future of Catholic schools at a time of falling pupil numbers. Whether the arrival of significant numbers of Polish, Portuguese and other mainly Catholic immigrants in the UK will reverse this downward trend is an open question.[32]

STAFFING CATHOLIC SCHOOLS

For a school to be declared Catholic by the diocesan bishop under the provisions of canon law[33] it is not necessary that it be full of Catholic pupils. In fact, truly Catholic institutions can provide services where there are no baptised Catholics (think of the work of missionaries in non-Catholic countries). For any Catholic school to fulfil its purpose, however, its leadership at least must comprise people who are committed to the person of Christ and seeking to work for His purposes. In its most recent statement on education, the Congregation for Catholic Education argues:

> "By reason of its identity, the Catholic school is a place of ecclesial experience which is moulded in the Christian community."

> "... what is taught has greater influence on the student's formation when placed in a context of ... coherence of attitudes, life-styles and day-to-day behaviour."

> "... the prime responsibility for creating this unique Christian school climate rests with the teachers, as individuals and as a community ... it depends chiefly on them whether the Catholic church school achieves its purpose."

(The Catholic School on the Threshold of the Third Millennium, §§12; 18; 19)

This necessity has always presented difficulties, especially during the 18th and early 19th centuries when the poverty of financial and human resources hampered the development of universal Catholic schooling. At that time, religious orders of priests and nuns provided the backbone of the Church's educational enterprise. Despite their prodigious efforts,[34] for all but a tiny minority of exceptionally able and lucky working class Catholic children there were no Catholic secondary schools available to them until well after the Second World War. In consequence, there were never enough qualified Catholic teachers to meet the necessary demand to work in either the primary or, more particularly, in the expanding secondary sector created by the Education Act 1944. The position has not improved over the past quarter of a century; indeed it is becoming more problematic. In 1974, when pupil numbers in the maintained primary sector peaked, some 9.8% of teaching posts were filled by non-Catholics. In secondary schools at their peak (1980), the proportion of non-Catholic teachers was nearly 34%. It has continued to rise in both phases as the sector overall has reduced in size over the years.

This is not to denigrate in any way the positive contribution non-Catholic teachers make to the mission of Catholic schools, but simply serves to highlight the difficulties in providing and recruiting sufficient Catholics teachers to the evangelistic and catechetical vocation of teaching. Though there will be Catholic staff witnessing to their faith and proclaiming the gospel both through their teaching and their very presence in secular schools, there is no record of their number. It is most unlikely, however, that even if it were possible for them all to be employed in Catholic schools, they would meet the current need for suitably able and committed Catholic teachers within the Catholic sector.

TEACHING STAFF IN MAINTAINED CATHOLIC SCHOOLS[+]						
	Primary			Secondary		
Year	Total	Non/RC	% Non/RC	Total	Non/RC	% Non/RC
1974/80	18880	1855	9.8	21776	7396	33.9
1993	16741	2039	12.2	18089	7439	41.1
2001	16870	3086	18.3	19596	8950	45.7
2005*	14821	3136	21.2	15857	7578	47.8

SOURCE: CATHOLIC EDUCATION SERVICE

[+] Excluding Sixth Form Colleges
* At the time of writing these are latest figures available from the Catholic Education Service. Data collected January 2005

In one sense, therefore, the position has not changed in fifty years. The objective remains to ensure that those who lead and teach in Catholic schools are able and willing to make them communities of faith, meeting places for those who wish to express Christian values in education.[35] Given the actual pattern of teacher employment in their schools, dioceses (and the governors they appoint) have to grapple with three related pedagogical and religious issues if Catholic schools are to fulfil their mission.

The most important is to work towards securing sufficient numbers of suitable Catholic teachers entering the profession. Realistically, it is most unlikely that Catholic schools can be staffed exclusively with appropriately qualified and committed Catholic teachers, especially in the secondary phase. It is imperative, therefore, that governing bodies adopt selection and appointment processes to ensure candidates are aware of the demands that will legitimately be made of them if they are appointed, so that they can, to the limits of their ability, make a positive contribution to the maintenance and development of the school's religious character. Secondly, all staff, irrespective of their religious adherence, should be provided with appropriate induction programmes, access to professional development and, where appropriate, the personal religious formation that will help them meet the demands of being educators in a Catholic school. Anecdotal evidence suggests there is room for improvement in both these areas.[36] Finally, (and this is not simply a problem for the Catholic sector) since all research of school effectiveness highlights the importance of leadership, ways must be found to prepare and encourage teachers to take on leadership roles within their schools and, for some, to become successful Catholic head and deputy-headteachers. Research suggests the task has become more rather than less difficult in recent years.[37] That these difficulties exist does not, of course, imply that the Church authorities are not trying to address them.[38] However, given the relatively small size of the potential and actual number of Catholic teachers in comparison to the size of the sector, it is little wonder that the difficulties facing the dioceses and governors are more acute than for the nation generally.

THE CHANGING CHARACTER OF EDUCATION - SCHOOLS IN THE MARKET PLACE

Education is generally regarded as both a public and private good with parents and the state having a legitimate interest in the nature of its content and provision. In 1967, James Callaghan, the then Prime Minister, made what many regard as a seminal speech at Ruskin College, Oxford. He called for a national debate about the purpose of education and the standards that should be achieved by the nation's schools. Though his remarks calling for a rational discussion noted the collaborative character of the educational enterprise, he counselled:

> "If everything is reduced to such phrases as educational freedom versus state control, we shall get no-where."
>
> (Callaghan, J., October 18th 1976, Ruskin College)

This is, however, an essential dynamic of the (legitimately) coercive character of the English educational system that cannot be ignored. The task is always to ensure an appropriate balance between the differing interests of parents, educators and the state.

Callaghan's speech was intended to further the interests of greater personal equity and increase national prosperity. Whether or not he envisaged the outcome of his intervention, it marked the beginning of a significant change in the existing relationship between the parents and the state in post-war England[39] and began what might be termed the marketisation of education, a process that successive governments have extended and refined over the past twenty-five years. Beginning in the 1970s, successive governments have sought to improve schools' academic standards by introducing a form of market economy into the education sector.[40] Schools were given greater freedoms from local authority control, but made more accountable for their performance through inspection and the publication of test and examination results in, what have been popularly termed, league tables, the first of which appeared in 1992.[41] Parents have been encouraged to see education as a consumer product and use such public data to inform the exercise of their (limited) ability to choose the schools in which they wish their children to be educated. By encouraging parents to 'shop around' to find the 'best deal' schools have been forced to 'compete for market share', i.e. for pupils.

Proponents argue that the strategy has been successful in improving levels of pupil attainment for the benefit both of pupils and the British economy. Critics say that the process has made education a purely instrumental commodity rather than a communal involvement in, and commitment to, the nurturing of human beings[42] without bringing the claimed economic benefits. Whatever the relative merits of the opposing views, there is no doubt that the character of schooling has been reformed along commercial/

industrial lines having measured inputs and outcomes, standardised content and processes, with staff being subject to performance management and inspection. It has become, arguably, the most centralised and bureaucratic system in the Western world. The changing emphasis has had a twofold effect on the Catholic sector schools. The new competitive environment is regarded by many as inimical to their underlying principles and purposes[43] while, ironically, under its regime they have become remarkably successful on the outcome measures chosen by government.[44] Both circumstances bring new challenges for the bishops.

Throughout the fifteen years during which league tables have been published, Catholic schools have appeared to be particularly successful compared to similar schools in the maintained sector on each of the various measures used by government during that period. Given the market orientation of education and the drive by successive governments to increase the ability for parents to exercise choice as to where their children are educated, that relative success has, undoubtedly, increased the popularity of Catholic schools. This has led to an increase in demand for places, and claims that non-Catholic parents are being unfairly discriminated against because Catholic parents are given priority. Both were contributory factors in the ill-judged attempt by the Secretary of State for Education & Skills in 2006 to require new, so called, faith schools take a quota of non-adherent pupils.[45] In addition, their apparent success in marketing terms has created tensions between the traditional values and perspectives of the essentially religious mission that is integral to Catholic schooling, and the demands of 21st century educational consumerism.[46]

> *"On the one hand Catholic schools formally acknowledge their mission to the service of troubled youth and proclaim a Christian message of forgiveness and reconciliation and yet, on the other hand, they have to survive in an educational marketplace where compassion does not feature among performance indicators [of success]."*
>
> (Grace, G., 2002, p. 201)

CURRICULUM CONTROL

The Church recognises and acknowledges that the state has a legitimate interest in the education of its citizens. That will lead, perhaps inevitably, towards the state wanting some degree of control over the content of the curriculum. In any democratic country, the extent and character of that control will be a matter of debate. For many years the school curriculum was a matter for educators not politicians. The Ruskin College Speech marked the first stage of a process culminating in today's highly centralised, state controlled and inspected curriculum[47] that, some argue, has become a vehicle for the achievement of secular social policy and values rather than being truly educative.[48]

After twenty years of increasing centralisation, the current government has introduced a new curriculum designed, partly, to enable a degree of individualised teaching and learning (tailoring the curriculum to the perceived needs of the individual pupil) but also to return to teachers some measure of professional control over the content of some twenty-five percent of curriculum time. Together with this slight loosening of its own control, however, the government has added new elements to the curriculum (including personal well-being, economic well-being and financial capability) and placed two new duties on governors, to promote community cohesion and the well-being of pupils at the school.[49] Successive governments have, so far, resisted the temptation to control the content of the religious curriculum, leaving it to be determined by individual governing bodies (of voluntary aided and foundation schools having a religious character) or by local agreement albeit within a national framework (for voluntary controlled schools and community schools). However, there are those who believe there should be some measure of controlling legislation in this area of the curriculum, though their recommendations have not changed government policy.[50]

CAPACITY TO RESPOND

Given the scope of this paper, there is insufficient space to explore, even tentatively, the many matters that are likely to have a significant impact on the future pattern and well-being of the Catholic sector. The following examples serve to illustrate the range of challenges facing the Church as the world of education becomes increasingly complex and bureaucratic. (1) The bishops depend upon an army of volunteer governors to secure the distinctive religious character of Catholic schools. Their extensive statutory responsibilities were summarised in chapter seven. It is increasingly difficult to find clergy and lay people with the time and ability to effectively fulfil the demands of the post.[51] (2) The mooted extension of the school leaving age to eighteen will, if implemented, present a range of new challenges, including that perennial question of financing any additional building. (3) It is not clear whether the provisions of home to school transport contained in the Education and Inspection Act 2006 will be implemented in ways that will benefit or hinder the sector's development.[52] (4) The long-term effects of linking schools together in loose or permanent form of federation are simply unknown, as is the future of joint-faith institutions and Academies.

What does seem clear is that the current tide of educational legislation shows little sign of abating. Since 1980 there have been sixteen major Acts of Parliament and, at the time of writing, over five hundred Statutory Instruments relating specifically to education. Other legislation, such as the Race Relations Act (1976) (as amended by the Race Relations (Amendment) Act 2000); the Children Act 2004; the Disability Discrimination Act (1995) (as amended by the Disability Discrimination Act 2005); the Equality Act 2006 and the various Employment Acts also impinge upon the world of education.

It is becoming apparent that the agencies established by the bishops to implement their educational strategies, at both national and local diocesan level, are finding it difficult to respond to the ever-increasing administrative burdens created by new and additional legislation. The prime purpose of the Catholic Education Service is to influence the legislative framework in which Catholic schools operate. Whether the necessary funds are available to the bishops' to enable them to employ sufficient staff with the expertise to engage effectively with the legislature is open to doubt. In the same way, individual dioceses, particularly the smaller ones, are finding it difficult to provide and manage the range of services required by their schools to enable them to effectively fulfil their four-fold purpose set out at the beginning of this chapter. If they cannot effectively mediate secular legislation, there is a real danger that Catholic sector schools will become simply an arm of government, clones of Community schools with a slight leavening of religious faith, rather than an integral part of the Church's salvific missionary activity.

SUMMARY

All institutions face challenges as they adapt to changing circumstances. For self-funding charitable organisations, such as the Catholic Church, securing the necessary resources to adequately finance its objectives is a perennial problem.

Catholic schools are one element in its strategy for fulfilling those objectives. They also serve to assist parents who are the primary educators of their children, to assist the local Church in its parochial activities and, by fulfilling those purposes, serve the wider community. Following the settlement contained in the 1944 Education Act, financing the post-war demand for school places was the major challenge facing the bishops. Over the years, government has raised the level of grant aid considerably, so alleviating that particular concern to a significant degree. However, the increase in public funding can seem to legitimate the progressive involvement by successive governments in seeking to control the content and outcomes of the national education system, compromising the autonomy of Catholic schools and inhibiting their religious purposes.

In addition, changes in social circumstances generally, and in the character of the Catholic community have brought a range of challenges to be faced by the Church as it seeks to maintain the religious character and purposes of its schools in a socio/political environment that is increasingly hostile towards religion and its public manifestation. This chapter has tried to outline the major challenges at the start of the 21st century, just over fifty years since the 'Case for Catholic Schools' was first published. A more complete list, linked to the four purposes of Catholic sector schools, is attached as an appendix. What the best responses to them might be falls outside the scope of this narrative.

NOTES

1   This shorthand version of the Church's educative mission is explored and explained in detail in the encyclical *Divini Illius Magistri* [The Christian Education of Youth] 1929, the Vatican II document *Gravissimum educationis* [Declaration on Christian Education] (1965) and subsequent post-conciliar documents prepared by the Sacred Congregation for Catholic Education, The Catholic School (1977); *Lay Catholics in Schools: Witnesses to Faith* (1982); *The Religious Dimension of education in a Catholic School* (1988); *The Catholic School on the Threshold of the Third Millennium* (1997).

2   For a detailed examination of the effects of this market philosophy upon individual Catholic schools and the Catholic sector generally see Grace, G. (2002) *Catholic Schools: Mission, Markets and Morality*, London, RoutledgeFalmer; also, Sullivan, J. (2000) Wrestling with managerialism, in: M. Eaton, J. Longmore & A. Naylor (eds) (2000) *Commitment to Diversity: Catholics and Education in a Changing World*, London, Cassell.

3   See chapter 12 of St. Paul's First Letter to the Corinthians.

4   Inspectors from the Office of Standards in Education (OfSTED) need to have an inclusive definition of spirituality that is meaningful and acceptable from a religious, agnostic, or atheistic perspective with "a common denominator with which most can agree". The OfSTED guidance document, HMI 2125, (2004) *Promoting and evaluating pupils' spiritual, moral, social and cultural development*,

www.ofsted.gov.uk/, suggests that pupils who are developing spiritually will exhibit [human] characteristics, among others, such as:

- a set of values, principles and beliefs … which inform their perspective on life and their pattern of behaviour;

- an awareness and understanding of their own and others' beliefs;

- a respect for themselves and for others;

- a respect for insight as well as knowledge and reason;

- an expressive and/or creative impulse;

- an ability to think in terms of the 'whole' – for example concepts such as harmony, interdependence, scale, perspective

- etc., etc.' - see page 13 of document.

In comparison, a Catholic understanding of spirituality will have a much more specific and transcendental perspective. For example, the Archdiocese of Birmingham document *Section 48: Guidance for Inspectors* (2005) says, "Spiritual and moral development are essential features of the Catholic life of the school … Inspectors should assess [in relation to spirituality] the extent to which the school provides opportunities to:

- develop a sense of the transcendent and reflect on the presence of God in their lives;

- know there is more to life than facts and seek answers to questions of purpose and meaning;

- reflect on their own experience, attitudes and values in the light of Scripture and the teaching of the Church;

- interpret and respond to the world in a Christian way;

- develop the range, depth and quality of their prayer life;

- become aware of how people of other faiths respond to the spiritual dimension of life.

For a fuller exploration of this complex educational issue see, for example, Carr, D. (1996) Rival conceptions of spiritual education, *Journal of Philosophy of Education*, 30. 2. 159-178; Hand, M. (2003) The meaning of 'spiritual education', *Oxford Review of Education*, 29. 3. 391-401; Plunkett, D. (1990) *Secular and Spiritual Values: Grounds for Hope in Education*, London, Routledge, particularly chapter 5, 'The transcendent perspective'.

5   See, for example, Allegations of a veto on the appointment of Catholics to the 'Warnock Committee' studying embryology in: Graffius, C. (1994) When persecution was a real and vicious fact, *Catholic Times*, April 24th; Haldane, J. (2007) Address at the CTS Conference, 14th July, London, Westminster Cathedral; also the moral dispute between Church and (secular) state over the impact of the Equality Act 2006 in: N. Robinson (2007) A matter of principle, *http://www.bbc.co.uk/ blogs/nickrobinson/2007/01/24*, accessed 21st February 2007. There are also claims that the BBC has developed an institutional bias against religion generally and the Catholic Church, see British Broadcasting Corporation Trust (2007) *From seesaw to wagon wheel; safeguarding impartiality in the 21st century*, London, BBC Trust, http://www.bc.co.uk/bbctrust/, accessed 22nd June 2007; Aitken, R. (2007) *Can We Trust the BBC?*, London, Continuum, chapter 8; Jay, A. (2007) *Confessions of a Reformed BBC Producer*, London, Centre for Policy Studies. For an understanding of the phenomenon but in an American context see, Jenkins, P. (2003) *The New Anti-Catholicism: The Last Acceptable Prejudice*, Oxford, Oxford University Press.

6   Longley, C. (1995) Dialogue at St. James, *The Tablet*, 15th April, p. 485; Williams, I., et al. (1996) *The economic Needs of the Irish Community in Britain*, Birmingham, Birmingham City Council; Hickman, M. & Walter, B. (1997) *Discrimination and the Irish Community in Britain*, London,

Commission for Racial Equality; Robinson N. (2007) No blanket exemption, *http://www.bbc. co.uk/blogs/nickrobinson/2007/01/25*, (accessed 21st February 2007).

7   See, for example, Department for Education & Employment (2001) *Schools achieving success*, London, Her Majesty's Stationery Office; Department for Education & Skills, (2005) *Higher standards, better schools for all*, London, Her Majesty's Stationery Office ; Depratment for Children, Schools and Families (2007) Faith in the System, Nottingham, DCSF Publications

8   It is reported that, when he was Secretary of State for Education, David Blunkett expressed the wish that the government could "bottle" the ethos of faith schools. See, Facts about Faith Schools, (2001) Guardian Unlimited, Wednesday November 14th, *http://education.guardian.co.uk/print/0,,4299025-110908,00.html*, (accessed 7th June 2007).

9   The provisions of the Education Act 2006 requires that all proposals for new schools are required to show (a) how the school will promote and contribute to community cohesion; (b) increase inclusion and equality of access for all social groups; and (c) collaborate with other schools, ... colleges and training providers. See, Statutory Instrument 2007/1288, Schedule 2 (17), Schedule 3 (20). The above provisions, when first published in the Education Bill, applied only to, what were termed, faith schools. The Bill's drafters assumed that they were the only educational institutions that needed to have such demands placed upon them. Following representations made to the Secretary of State for Education by Archbishop Nichols, Chairman of the Catholic Education Service, the relevant clauses were amended as the Bill progressed towards enactment to apply to all schools.

10 The Charities Act 2006, section 3, removes the existing presumption that organisations for the promotion of religion, education or the relief of poverty are of public benefit. At the time of writing, a new 'test of public benefit' to be determined by the Charity Commission remains undefined but, when established, it will set out the parameters within which charities will have to demonstrate the good that they do. Whether the removal of the presumption and the terms of the new test become a threat to the activities of the Church is a matter of some debate. The Chairman of the Charity Commission believes there is no potential secularist threat – see her letter to the *Catholic Herald*, June 22nd 2007 – others are much less sanguine – see Editorial (2007) Charity Law is being Used as a Weapon Against the Church, *Catholic Herald*, June 15th, p. 11; Caldwell, S. (2007) Bishops grow nervous over charity reforms, *Catholic Herald*, June 15th, p. 3.

11 See, for example, Gwynn, D. (1950) The Irish Immigration; Gwynn, D. (1950) Growth of the Catholic Community, both in: G. A. Beck (ed) (1950) *The English Catholics 1850-1950*. See also, Hornsby-Smith, M. P. & Dale, A. (1988) The assimilation of Irish immigrants in England, *British Journal of Sociology*, 39. 4. 519-543; Hornsby-Smith, M. P. (ed) (1999) *Catholics in England 1950-2000, historical and sociological perspectives*, London, Cassell;

12 A comprehensive collection of studies of the changing character of the Catholic community over the past fifty years can be found in: Hornsby-Smith, M. P. (ed) (1999) *Catholics in England 1950-2000: Historical and Sociological Perspectives*, London, Casssell; Eaton, M., Longmore. J. & Naylor. A. (eds) (2000) *Commitment to Diversity: Catholics and Education in a Changing World*, London Cassell; and McClellend, V. A. & M. Hodgetts, M. (eds) (1999) *From Without the Flaminian Gate: 150 Years of Roman Catholicism in England & Wales 1850-2000*, London, Darton, Longman & Todd.

13 See Francis, L. J. (2002) Catholic schools and Catholic values? A study of moral and religious values among 13-15 year old pupils attending denominational and Catholic schools in England and Wales, *International Journal of Education and Religion*, 3. 1. 69-84. The study used data from 33,982 adolescents in order to profile the distinctive identity of pupils attending Catholic secondary

schools within the state maintained sector. In addition to (varying) numbers of non-Catholics, Francis identified three distinct communities of values held by pupils who are what he labels (a) active Catholics, (b) sliding Catholic and (c) lapsed Catholics.

14 See, for example, Arthur, J. (1995) *The Ebbing Tide*, Leominster, Gracewing, chap. 5.

15 Cantle, T. (2003) *Community Cohesion: A Report of the Independent Review Team* (The Cantle Report), London, Home Office, Her Majesty's Government.

16 DfES (2003) Decision Makers Guide, *http://www.dfes.gov.uk/Guidance,* para. 39, (accessed 8th August 2005).

17 DfES (2003) Decision Makers Guide, *http://www.dfes.gov.uk/Guidance*, paras. 40-41, (accessed 8th August 2005). See also the new duty placed on all schools to promote social cohesion the implementation of which will be inspected by OfSTED under by the provisions of the Education and Inspection Act 2006, section 154.

18 See, for example, Sacred Congregation for Catholic Education (1982) *Lay Catholics in Schools: Witnesses to Faith*, London, Catholic Truth Society, §19. *"The vocation of every Catholic educator includes the work of ongoing social development: to form men and women who will be ready to take their place in society, preparing them in such a way that they will make the kind of social commitment which will enable them to work for the improvement of social structures ... make[ing] human society more peaceful, fraternal, and communitarian."*

19 See discussion in chapter 2.

20 Proposed amendments by the MP for Holborn & St. Pancras, Mr. Frank Dobson, to the then Education Bill 2002 were debated. Among other things he advocated a quota system requiring "all religious schools to admit 25 per cent of their pupils from families of other faiths or of no faith" (Hansard, 6th February 2002, column 868). It was defeated by 405 votes to 87. One member voting against was Alan Johnson (who was subsequently appointed Secretary of State for Education in 2006). In July 2004, the government response in Parliament to the Office of the Deputy Prime Minister Select Committee Report on Social Cohesion published earlier that year stated unequivocally that "The government does not hold them [faith schools] responsible for ethnic or social segregation" and that "forced admission quotas would not work." (Cm 6284, page 12). In October 2006, following an attempt by Lord Baker to introduce an amendment very similar to the rejected Dobson amendment, but for new faith schools only, the Secretary of State, without any warning or consultation, made public his intention to introduce a clause based on the Baker amendment to the Education and Inspection Bill 2006. It is not clear why, though it may have much more to do with government pre-occupation with Islamic maintained schools than the Catholic sector. Church leaders conducted a successful campaign against the proposed amendment, on the basis that, if enacted, it may well prevent Catholic parents from obtaining a Catholic education in a new Catholic maintained school because it would be forced, either, to accept a quota of non-Catholic pupils or retain empty places to accommodate up to 25% non-Catholic pupils. The compromise agreement, though not enacted in primary legislation, was that when plans were developed to establish a new Catholic school, with the agreement of the local authority and with Government capital support over and beyond the 10% governor liability, the Church would provide enough places to meet the Catholic demand and **additional places for non-Catholic pupils** up to a maximum of 25% of the total intake. See letter to Archbishop Nichols from the Secretary of State, Alan Johnson, dated 26th October 2006, published on the Catholic Education Website, *www.cesew.org.uk/news&events/;* also, Department for Children, Schools & Families (2007) *Faith in the System: the role of schools with a religious character in English education and society*, www. teachernet.gov.uk/publications, p. 17 (accessed 11th November 2007).

21 Hargreaves, D. (1994) *The Mosaic of Learning: Schools and Teachers for the Next Century*, London, Demos; Strike, K. (2003) Towards a liberal conception of school communities, *Theory and Research in Education*, 1. 2. 171-193; Morris, A. B. (2005) Academic standards in Catholic schools in England: indications of causality, *London Review of Education*, 3. 1. 81-99.

22 There is a suggestion that, in the 1960s, in some areas of the country at least, Catholic schools were providing a poorer standard of education than similar county institutions. See, for example, Wake, R. (1986) Catholic Education in School, *The Month*, July/August, pp. 248-250. He states *"When I was appointed to the Inspectorate in 1960 and sent to the north west I was given generally to understand by my new colleagues that Catholic schools were inferior to the rest"*. However, it is argued there is no hard quantitative evidence of them generally having a significantly lower academic or intellectual orientation than other schools in the maintained sector at that time – see Hornsby-Smith, M. P. (1972). Wake also reports in his article in *The Month* that, whatever the situation may have been in the 1960s by the 1980s, *"A systematic reading of recently published HMI reports will certainly not show that Catholic schools are 'worse' than any others."*

23 Unlike the Catholic Church that only provided schools for its own minority community, the Church of England, simply because of its position as the established Church has sought (in principle) to provide a suitable education for all children living within the immediate locality, albeit grounded in the principles of Christianity, with religious teaching subject to a 'conscience clause' allowing parents to withdraw their children if they so wish. See, Dennis, N. (2001) *The Uncertain Trumpet: A History of Church of England School Education to AD 2001*, London, Civitas; Barnes, L. P. & Kay W. K. (2002) *Religious education in England & Wales: Innovations and Reflections*, RTSF Monograph, Leicester, Religious and Theological Studies Fellowship.

24 The Ministry of Education Circular No. 245 subordinated the need for denominational places to the overall need for school places within a local authority. In effect, if the authority met, what was termed *absolute need*, there would be sufficient places for all the pupils living within the LEA including the Catholics, thus removing any need for Catholic provision. For further details see records of correspondence noted in *'The Case for Catholic Schools'* (1955) pp. 46-49. Although the obstructive effects of Circular 245 were subsequently withdrawn, it has remained the case to the present day that legislation requires that Catholic schools can only be built where there is demonstrable demand from Catholic parents – see, in relation to new schools, *Statutory Instrument 2007/1288*, Schedule 2 (11), Schedule 3 (14), Schedule 5 (19); in relation to any proposed changes to an existing school, *Statutory Instrument 2007/1289*, Schedule 3 (24).

25 When the number of pupils in Catholic maintained primary schools peaked in 1974, less than 2% were non-Catholics. In the secondary sector peak numbers came in 1980. At that time there were just over 3% non-Catholics on roll. By 2004, despite the removal of surplus places by various strategies including school closures and amalgamations (occasionally with schools provided by other Christian denominations), some 19% of pupils attending Catholic primary schools and nearly 21% of pupils attending Catholic secondary schools were non-Catholics. In 1974 there were 0.49 million baptised Catholic pupils in maintained Catholic primary schools. In 1980 there were 0.35 million baptised Catholic pupils in maintained Catholic secondary schools. In contrast to those peak figures, by 2004, the numbers of baptised Catholic pupils on roll in Catholic schools across both phases, had declined to a total of some 0.52 million. See Catholic Education Service, School Census Data 1994, 2004.

26 The exceptions to the duty to comply with a parent's expressed preference for a place in an aided school are set out in the Education Act 1980, Section 6(3).

27 Section 6(3) of the 1980 Education Act, was amended by the Education Reform Act 1988, Section

30 - which became Section 413 in the consolidating Education Act 1996 - and was re-affirmed in the School Standards & Framework Act 1998, Section 91.

28 Hansard (2002), House of Lords debate on the Education Bill 2002, 19th June, Col. 851-852. Baroness Ashton of Upholland, in moving the clause to repeal Section 91 of the School Standards & Framework Act 1998 on behalf of the government, said:

"... where, for example, fewer Roman Catholics apply for a Catholic school place than there are places available ... a Section 91 arrangement would allow the school to keep places it cannot fill with Catholic pupils empty – even though there may be demand for those places from non-Catholic families. ... We have discussed this proposal to end Section 91 agreements with the Roman Catholic Authorities ... and the Catholic Church is happy that the benefits of Catholic schooling to be extended to other families who appreciate and want those benefits as long as demand from Roman Catholics can continue to be met. I beg to move."

The Bishop of Blackburn added:

"My Lords, I support the amendment. I do so with the full backing of the Catholic Education Service, as the Minister has said."

29 See, for example, Briault, E. & Smith F. (1980) *Falling Rolls in Secondary Schools*, Slough, National Foundation for Educational Research. The report was commissioned by the (then) Department of Education & Science in 1977. It considered the effects of falling rolls for individual schools, their pupils and staff and also for local authorities. Perhaps significantly, there was no-one representing the Catholic sector involved in the Project Team, the Steering Committee or the bodies consulted. All the schools from which data for the study were collected were County (i.e. Community) schools. The Report made no recommendations about the voluntary sector. However, some Catholic dioceses, the Archdiocese of Birmingham is one example, began discussions with its schools about reorganising diocesan secondary provision around this time independently of local authority schemes.

30 DfES (2007) *Establishing a New Maintained Mainstream School: A Guide for Local Authorities*, Section C Decision Makers' Guidance, Darlington, School Organisation Unit.

31 Legislation does not allow a diocese to close a school. Those powers remain with the governors or the local authority. In both cases the diocese can oppose the proposal. It would be unusual, though not impossible, for such a proposal to succeed against the (well-founded) wish of the bishop concerned. For example, there was an unsuccessful attempt by a local authority to close an academically successful, fully subscribed, socially, ethnically and religiously inclusive Catholic school, albeit with few Catholic pupils on roll, against the wishes of the bishop, and subsequently reopen it as a Community school – see Stoke-on-Trent School Organisation Plan (2002), sections 5.16 & 5.17; also the Minutes of Stoke-on-Trent Education Executive Committee Meeting, 28th January 2002. In other words, the local authority needed the places but did not want them to be in a school having a religious character.

32 There have been suggestions that new Catholic schools will be needed in some areas of the country to accommodate Polish immigrants – see reported comments of the (then) Home Secretary, John Reid, in: Potts, J. (2007) Call for more Catholic schools to cater for migrants from Poland, *The Catholic Herald*, June 29th, p. 2. Accurate data is not yet available to show whether it will, in fact, be necessary, but it is the case that a number of dioceses have translated information about admissions to their schools into different languages for use by individual immigrants, parishes and local authorities. This suggests that the numbers are significant. A fairly typical example of this type of diocesan documentation is available at *http://www.bdsc.org.uk/home*.

33 Canon Law for the Latin Rite (1983), Canon 603 (1) & (3). The role and jurisdiction of the bishop in this respect is fully recognised by the state, see, for example, the Explanatory Note to the Statutory Instrument, SI 1999/2432 *The Designation of Schools Having a Religious Character Order 1999*.

34 This is not the place to outline the history of the involvement of religious orders in all aspects of education from founding and running primary schools to teacher training colleges. Excellent accounts are available in: G. A. Beck (ed) (1950) *The English Catholics 1850-1950*, London, Burns Oates, chps. 10, 11, 12; M. Eaton, J. Longmore & A. Naylor (eds) (2000) *Commitment to Diversity: Catholics and Education in a Changing World*, London, Cassell, chaps 1, 4, 5, 6 & 7.

35 Pope Paul VI, Alloction to the Ninth Congress of the O.I.E.C, reported in: *L'Osservatore Romano*, June 9th 1974, and quoted in: Sacred Congregation for Catholic Education (1977) *The Catholic School*, Abbotts Langley, Catholic Information Office, para. 53.

36 See, for example, Morris, A. B. & Marsh, A. (2002) Motives of newly qualified teachers for choosing to work in Catholic schools in England, *Networking*, 3. 5. 8-13; Manning, S. (2007) A question of faith, *Times Educational Supplement Magazine*, 6th July, p. 8.

37 Howson, J. (2007) *22nd Report on Senior Appointments in Schools*, Oxford, Education Data Surveys Ltd.

38 Catholic Higher Education Institutions, such as St. Mary's, Twickenham and the Maryvale Institute, have offered a variety of Masters level degree courses in Christian Educational Leadership since the mid 1980's. More recently, a number of dioceses in regional clusters have collaborated with the National College for School Leadership to develop and deliver leadership courses, including the National Professional Qualification for Leadership, specifically tailored for the Catholic sector.

39 The Ministry of Education was established in 1944 with limited powers to intervene in what and how schools taught their pupils. In 1964 the Ministry was renamed the Department for Education and Science (DES) which has now metamorphosed into the Department for Children, Schools and Families – an interesting change in emphasis about the extent of the legitimate exercise of state power. In one sense this mirrors the Church's understanding of a threefold interlinking organic structure that underpins civic society (home-school-parish) without the Church's emphasis on the primacy of parents.

40 For an analysis of the early stages of the marketisation of education from a governmental perspective, see: Baker, K. (1993) *The Turbulent Years*, London, Faber & Faber, chapters 8-10 inc. See also, Plunkett, D. (1990) *Secular and Spiritual Values in Education: Grounds for Hope in Education*, London, Routledge, chp. 2; Pring. R. (1996) Markets, Education and Catholic Schools, in: McLaughlin, T. H., O'Keefe, J. & O'Keeffe, B. (eds) (1996) *The Contemporary Catholic School: Context, Identity and Diversity*, London, Falmer Press.

41 See DfES School Achievement and Attainment Tables, available at *http://www.dfes.gov.uk/*

42 See, for example, the reported comments of pupils, parents and school staff presented in: Alexander R. & Hargreaves, L. (2007) *Community Soundings: The Primary Review, regional witness sessions*, Cambridge, University of Cambridge Faculty of Education.

43 See Grace, G. (2002) *Catholic Schools: Mission, Markets and Morality*, London, RoutledgeFalmer.

44 See Morris, A. B. (1998) Catholic and Other Schools: an analysis of OFSTED inspection reports 1993-95, *Educational Research*, 40. 2. 181-190; (2001) Patterns of Performance of Catholic Schools in England, *Networking*, 3. 1. 17-21; (2005) Diversity, Deprivation and the Common Good: Pupil Attainment in Catholic Schools in England, *Oxford Review of Education*, 31. 2. 311-330; (2007)

Post-16 Pupil Performance in Catholic Secondary Schools in England 1996-2001, *Educational Review*, 59. 1. 55-69. Morris. A. B. (2008) Academic Standards in Catholic Schools in England, presentation at the *21st Congress of the German Corporation for Educational Science*, Dresden, March 18th; Morris A. B. (forthcoming) Contextualizing Catholic Schools Performance in England. See also, Morris, A. B. & Godfrey, R. (2006) *A statistical survey of attainment in Catholic schools in England with particular reference to secondary schools operating under the trust deed of the Archdiocese of Birmingham*, Canterbury, National Institute for Christian Education Research.

45 See endnote 20 above. The Secretary of State suggested that the arrangements in the amendment to the Education & Inspection Bill 2006 which applied to new faith schools was simply a first step in a process that would be extended to cover all faith schools not just new ones. See Alan Johnson's Speech to LGA/ADSS Conference – Brighton, 18th October 2006, *www.des.gov.uk/speeches/speeches.cfm?/SpeechID=392*.

46 Grace, G. (2002) *Catholic Schools: Mission, Markets and Morality*, London, RoutledgeFalmer, chp 8. See also, Foley, J. & Grace, G. (2001) *The Birmingham Catholic School Partnership: Holding to common good values in a market competitive age*, London, Centre for Research and Development in Catholic Education. Grace and his colleague provide one startling example of the way in which the Catholic sector has sought to resolve the tension. They describe a collective voluntary programme by Birmingham Catholic Secondary schools designed to combat social exclusion and reduce instances of permanent exclusion from mainstream school of disruptive pupils. The Zacchaeus Centre, an educational support unit, was established by the ten Catholic secondary schools in Birmingham in 1995 under a collaborative voluntary structure very similar to that which was subsequently formalised by government in the Statutory Instrument, SI 2003/1962 School Governance (Collaboration)(England) Regulations 2003. The Centre's purpose was to support pupils at risk of exclusion with a variety of short courses designed to overcome their particular difficulties in coping with mainstream schooling, so ensuring that they completed their compulsory education successfully. It proved to be most effective. However, changes in the government's funding regime have made it increasingly difficult for the Centre to retain financial viability and it may well be forced to close. If so, it will be a casualty of market forces despite the undoubted benefits it has provided over the last twelve years for individual pupils and their families, as well as the schools that they attend and the local authority concerned.

47 The Education Reform Act 1988 first defined the curriculum that was to be taught in maintained schools. The Education Act 1992 established the Office for Standards in Education (OfSTED) with a remit, among other matters concerned with quality assurance, to ensure schools complied with the new centrally determined curriculum. See an account of the governing body's gradual loss of control in curriculum matters in: Arthur, J. (1995) *The Ebbing Tide*, Leominster, Gracewing, pp. 173-186.

48 Whelan, R. (ed) (2007) *The Corruption of the Curriculum*, London, Institute for the Study of Civil Society.

49 The Education and Inspection Act 2006, section 38, inserts into section 21 of the Education Act 2002 a new duty requiring the governing body to promote the well being of pupils (as defined in section 10(2) of the Children Act 2004) and to promote community cohesion. The school's contribution to community cohesion will be inspected and reported on under the provisions of the Education Act 2005, section 5, as amended by section 154 of the Education and Inspection Act 2006.

50 In its scrutiny report on the Sexual Orientation Regulations, the Joint Committee on Human Rights recommended that the curriculum of all schools, including religious education, should be subject to the moral relativism embodied in (this particular) government legislation. The government did

not accept the recommendation. See, Joint Committee on Human Rights, *Sixth Report of Session 2006-07, HL Paper 58, NC 350*, 28th February 2007, London, The Stationery Office Limited.

51 For a general view of the problems of school governance see, Dean, C., et al. (2007) *Schools, Governors and Disadvantage*, York, Joseph Rowntree Foundation; also Ranson, S., et al. (2005) The participation of volunteer citizens in school governance, *Educational Review*, 57. 3. 357-371.

52 Local authorities are under an obligation not to discriminate against anyone on the basis of their religion and belief. The duty, however, does not apply to the exercise of an authority's functions in relation to transport (Section 51(2)(b) of the Equality Act 2006), though in its guidance on Home to School Transport, government warn local authorities that they *"will need to be aware of their obligations under human rights legislation"* and *"... ensure they do not discriminate contrary to Article 14 of the European Convention on Human Rights."* Para. 134 – see Department for Education and Skills (2007) *Home to School Travel & Transport Guidance*, www.teachernet.gov. uk/publications, para. 133. The Guidance indicates the wish of the Secretary of State that local authorities should provide transport that supports families to choose a school in accordance with their religious beliefs while the Parliamentary Under Secretary of State for Children, Young People and Families, Parmjit Dhanda, says that the exemption contained in s. 51 is necessary *"to ensure that this practice [providing transport for pupils attending faith schools] could continue."* (Stated in private correspondence between the Under Secretary and the author's MP, 12th March 2007). The warnings in the Guidance, and the reason given for the legal exemption, imply a degree of legal uncertainty and possible conflict of interpretation which may, at some stage, require the court's adjudication. As it stands, Catholic parents cannot be sure that suitable transport for their children to their nearest Catholic school will be provided by local authorities – see Hetherington, T. (2007), details in bibliography.

Chapter 9 Appendix – Summary of Contemporary Challenges

This summary is adapted and developed from information provided in a presentation made to the Diocese of Middlesbrough in 2007 by Fr. Marcus Stock, Director of Schools for the Archdiocese of Birmingham. I am most grateful for his permission to use and adapt his analysis of the current challenges faced by the Catholic Church in fulfilling its educative mission.

Challenges in the Political, Cultural and Legal Context			
To assist the Church in its mission	To assist parents in their educative role	To serve the local Church community	To contribute to the well-being of society
Broad Challenge	Broad Challenge	Broad Challenge	Broad Challenge
Countering the prevailing secular culture whose values and philosophy are market driven and utilitarian: based on the individual's contribution to economic prosperity not their transcendental dignity as human persons Engaging effectively in contemporary cultural debate – rehabilitating theological language & concepts Securing the charitable status of the church's educational activities Effectively influencing the content of, & responding to, the increasing level of education related legislation	Providing a religious based alternative to a state monopoly of education Articulating & promoting the rationale for Catholic schools (including their specific religious purposes) to parents, legislators, bureaucrats, intellectuals and media Managing the tension between the demands of statutory performance indicators and the Church's intentions for, and expectations of, its schools	Proclaim the religious activity of the Church in society Providing a forum for engaging parents in communal activity and endeavour, developing a sense of social commitment and solidarity Encouraging & maintaining social cohesion Developing & sustaining internal community cohesion (social bonding capital)	Developing effective partnerships with local and national strategic bodies Providing beneficial social and educational services, e.g. nursery provision, extended schools, collaborative ventures, pupil support Developing productive and civic minded citizens Promoting social cohesion; helping develop & sustain personal & social identity, & inter-community support (social bridging capital)

Challenges in the Canonical and Ecclesial Context

To assist the Church in its mission	To assist parents in their educative role	To serve the local Church community	To contribute to the well-being of society
Broad Challenge	Broad Challenge	Broad Challenge	Broad Challenge
Providing a clear exposition of the Church's teaching on education Ensuring all understand the essentially religious purpose and ethos of Catholic schools Recruiting & retaining a knowledgeable Catholic workforce, committed to Catholic education Securing and providing effective Catholic leadership programmes Appointing and training sufficient foundation governors to secure the Catholic mission and ethos of its schools	Providing sufficient school capacity to meet Catholic need Managing the changing demand in the overall numbers and location of Catholic communities The increasing demand for places in Catholic schools from non-Catholic parents Ensuring admission arrangements are clear, fair and give priority to baptised Catholic children Securing active parental involvement in, and understanding of, the religious and catechetical life of the school	Ensuring that the school involves parents and their children in parish activities Ensuring that the school supports, promotes and collaborates in the pupils' sacramental preparation, actively engaging parental participation Securing pupil involvement in the liturgical and social activities of the parish Ensuring the school facilities are made available for the purposes of the parish and its activities through preferential lettings etc	Articulating, representing and providing a religious perspective of human endeavour and communal solidarity Providing a high quality and effective Catholic RE, PHSE, SRE and citizenship curriculum Ensuring schools are engaged in local and communal activities showing the Church working for the common good Ensuring schools promote social justice for the common good

Financial Challenges

To assist the Church in its mission	To assist parents in their educative role	To serve the local Church community	To contribute to the well-being of society
Broad Challenge	Broad Challenge	Broad Challenge	Broad Challenge
The limitations of diocesan resources (specially small dioceses or those with declining communities) Ensuring a secure, viable and equitable system is in place to fund diocesan wide building costs Securing funding for an effective education service in individual dioceses some of which are relatively small Securing sufficient funding for a national education service able to engage effectively with legislators to influence primary legislation	Securing parental understanding of the financial implications of the voluntary nature of Catholic schools Ensuring parental understanding of the benefits of the voluntary aided status of Catholic schools Encouraging Catholic parents (and others who send their children to Catholic schools) to contribute towards meeting the financial liabilities of governing bodies Providing high quality school buildings and facilities	Demonstrating the role and benefit of the cost of Catholic schools in supporting parish life Developing & sustaining parochial activities at intra-parish (primary phase) and inter-parish levels (secondary phase) Ensuring material and resource collaboration between Catholic secondary schools and their 'feeder' primaries Ensuring material and resource collaboration with other non-Catholic institutions	Contributing towards the state's expenditure on education (over and above general taxation) by providing 10% of the capital cost of school buildings and their maintenance

179

Chapter 10

CONCLUSION

The dual system, a mix of voluntary and state provided schools, established by the Education Act 1870 was a pragmatic response by the government of the day to a pressing need. Government recognised that education was such an important individual and social good that it should become available to all regardless of their financial circumstances. At the same time, however, the Act established that though it was appropriate for the state to insist that all children should be educated, governments should not have the right to override the wishes of parents as to where and how their children should receive that education.

That legal principle remains the position today. Parents retain the prime responsibility to educate their children in accordance with their beliefs and convictions and the reality of today's educational world sees an increase in parental demand for choice as to where and, perhaps to a lesser degree, how their children are educated. The dual system clearly supports the idea of a plurality in educational provision and provides the legal underpinning for the maintained Catholic sector. It is unlikely there will be the sustained political momentum necessary to repeal that longstanding settlement in the foreseeable future, despite what many see as a diminished commitment to the concept embodied in the 1944 Act of separate but collaborating bodies; dioceses being coordinate with, not subordinate to, local education authorities. In addition, the European Convention on Human Rights, incorporated into English law through the Human Rights Act 1998, which was designed to ensure plurality of religion and protect the expression of beliefs, would, probably, prevent the creation in England of a wholly secular educational system given the current existence and purpose of church schools generally and Catholic schools in particular. This opinion, however, remains untested.

Catholic schools existed well before the state became directly involved in the provision of education. Nevertheless, while striving to provide an education for all, they were far from universal in scope. Collaboration with the state provided a positive way forward, but one that had its attendant dilemmas. Without financial support from the state, a disproportionate financial burden is placed upon parents wanting their children educated in accordance with their own religious convictions. It might even result in the exclusion of their children from the possibility of a Catholic education.

While the state's financial support has enabled the bishops to provide schools for the poorest sections of society, rather than them becoming the sole preserve of those who could afford to pay, Catholic schools have, as a direct result, lost their operational, cultural and educational autonomy to some degree. One consequence of the Church's financial reliance upon the state has been an inability to resist governments' ever encroaching involvement in, and control of, for example, the funding and payment of staff, establishing standards of design for school buildings, apportioning funds for school maintenance, determining the curriculum, advising and inspecting its implementation, inspecting teacher activity and performance or approving their qualifications and continuing professional development.

Within such a financial framework it was almost inevitable that successive governments began to assume and behave as if the Church's schools were at its disposal, and for its political purposes, rather than for the religious purposes of the Church and parents. It is a tendency that the Church has found increasingly hard to resist, but one that must be effectively countered if Catholic schools are to fulfil their religious and ecclesial purposes.

We live in an avowedly, and some would ague an aggressive, secular society in which there is a great deal of popular confusion between culture, religion and race. It is not without ideology and is as confessional as any theocracy. It simply reflects and promotes secular, materialistic humanism through its cultural and legislative programmes rather than, for example, Confucian, Marxist, Islamic, Christian or other interpretation of human existence. In such circumstances, Catholic agencies that hold a specific religious world view cannot assume that their perspectives will be generally regarded as having any societal value. If they are to avoid absorption into the secular culture, or swept away by legislation intolerant of religious belief and motivation, they need an institutional embodiment that witnesses to the truths the Church holds, so that those truths can be effectively transmitted to future generations of believers and proclaimed to those who are not.

The available empirical evidence supports the view that Catholic schools make a positive contribution to society, though their religious character is a matter of considerable controversy and their successes as educational institutions, even when granted by opponents, is often seen in purely secular and materialistic terms. Given the role of Catholic schools within the Church's salvific mission it is important, therefore, to explain, affirm and defend the distinctive Catholic understanding of the nature and purpose of education in as diplomatically forthright a manner as possible, so that their religious character can be more readily understood by opponents and sceptics. Rather than shying away from controversy about their worth and the nature of the communities they seek to develop and sustain, it is important that the Church proclaims their mission in accessible theological terminology and does not succumb to making vague, generalised, and sentimentalised statements about Catholic schools that do not, in fact, describe the distinctiveness of their ecclesial nature and purpose. It would be an error for Catholic sector schools to accommodate themselves to, or allow themselves to be assimilated by, the contemporary secular view of the purpose of schooling, however seductive the short-term gains may appear to be. There are, of course, potential dangers in making such a religious case in an aggressively secular environment. It can appear deliberately confrontational and become counter-productive. However, if the Church does not offer a real alternative form of education to that of the secular state, then there is little point in continuing the enterprise.

The case for Catholic schools was expressed very clearly during the period of European history that witnessed the rise of the secular religions of fascism and communism.

> "Let it be loudly proclaimed and well understood by all, that Catholics, no matter what their nationality, in agitating for Catholic schools for their children, are not mixing in party politics, but engaged in a religious enterprise demanded by conscience. They do not intend to separate their children either from the body of the nation or its spirit, but to educate them in a perfect manner, most conducive to the prosperity of the nation. Indeed a good Catholic, precisely because of his Catholic principles, makes the better citizen, attached to his country, and loyally submissive to constituted civil authority in every legitimate form of government."
> (Divini Illius Magistri, [The Christian Education of Youth], 1929, §85)

While political and social circumstances may have changed in the intervening years, the same fundamental claims are still applicable. The problem is to find the words appropriate to today's circumstances and ensure the reality of Catholic sector schools in England matches the rhetoric. In particular, it is important that the Church responds effectively to (misconceived) concerns about alleged manifestations of harmful religious, racial and cultural division, by illustrating and affirming the contribution Catholic schools make to the well-being of society by their transmission of Catholic faith and culture from one Catholic generation to the next. Given the conflation by many of religion, culture and ethnicity, it is important to refute the claim that a single faith school must be mono-cultural. In this respect, the Church's claims can be supported by evidence that the variety and extent of ethnic groupings attending Catholic schools compares well with the national average [1].

Furthermore, the Church can claim with justification, that diocesan Catholic schools are inclusive in the sense that they are provided, essentially, for any and all children, irrespective of race, colour, class, intellectual ability or socio-economic status, who belong to the global Catholic Church and live locally to the school(s) in question.

Their value appears to have been affirmed by government in an unprecedented document published by the Department for Children, Schools and Families in September 2007. It acknowledges:

- the historic place of the dual system at the heart of educational provision in England;

- that faith schools provide parental choice and diversity;

- they make a valuable contribution *"to the way in which this country discharges its duties under Article 2, Protocol 1, of the European Convention on Human Rights"* (p. 3);

- the effective ways in which faith schools promote community cohesion.

Indeed, this last item represents the main thrust of the twenty page document.

The Church can also reflect on its success in integrating successive waves of Irish immigrants. As such, the Catholic sector could well be a model for other religious groups seeking to establish themselves in British society.

Indeed, if one looks back on contemporary records relating to Irish immigration in the nineteenth century and substitute 'Muslim' for 'Irish' the parallels are striking.

Although it is disappointing, therefore, that there still seems to be the need, some fifty years after the original case was made, to proclaim Catholic schools as a general benefit to society, nevertheless, to those with an open mind and who are willing to listen, there is good news to tell; the evidence in their favour is overwhelmingly strong.

NOTES

1   See Catholic Education Service, (2003) *Ethnicity, Identity & Achievement in Catholic Education,* London, Catholic Education Service; Phillips, T. (2005) *After 7/7: Sleepwalking into Segregation,* speech to the Manchester Council for Community Relations, 22nd September, http://cre.gov.uk. In addition to the majority category of White British, Catholic schools have greater numbers of Irish, Black Caribbean, African and pupils from other minority ethnic backgrounds than other schools. Note that the Statutory Code of Practice on the Duty to Promote Racial Equality (para 5.13) encourages organisations to use the same ethnic categories as those in the 2001 national census, which includes Irish as a separate group.

Fifty Years On

BIBLIOGRAPHY

Adonis, A. (2006) *Social mobility and social justice,* speech given at the National Catholic Education Conference, 18th May.

Aitken, R. (2007) *Can We Trust the BBC?,* London, Continuum.

Alexander, H. A. (2005) Education in Ideology, *Journal of Moral Education,* 34. 1. 1-18.

Alexander R. & Hargreaves, L. (2007) *Community Soundings: The Primary Review, regional witness sessions,* Cambridge, University of Cambridge Faculty of Education.

Alexander, K. L. & Pallas, A. M. (1983) Private schools and public policy: new evidence on cognitive achievement in public and private schools, *Sociology of Education,* 56. 170-182.

Alexander, K. L. & Pallas, A. M. (1984) In defence of 'Private schools and public policy': reply to Kilgore, *Sociology of Education,* 57. 56-58.

Alexander, K. L. & Pallas, A. M. (1985) School sector and cognitive performance: when is a little a little?, *Sociology of Education,* 58. 115-128.

Allen G. (2006) Speech in: Hansard (2006), *Report of the Admission Policies of Faith Schools debate,* London, House of Commons, 14th February.

Allen, R. O. & Spilka, B. (1967) Committed and consensual religion: a specification of religious-prejudice relationships, *Journal for the Scientific Study of Religion,* 6. 191-206.

Allport G. W. (1950) *The individual and his religion: a psychological interpretation,* New York, Macmillan.

Allport G. W. (1954) *The Nature of Prejudice,* Cambridge, Massachusetts, Addison-Wesley.

Allport G. W. (1959) Religion and Prejudice, *Crane Review,* 2. 1-10.

Allport G. W. (1960) *Personality and Social Encounter,* Boston, Beacon Press.

Allport G. W. (1966) Traits Revisited, *American Psychologist,* 21. 1. 5-7.

Altena, P., Hermans, C. A. M. & Van Der Ven, J. A. (2000) Towards a narrative theory of religious education. *International Journal of Education and Religion,* 1, 2, 218-247.

Altena, P., Hermans, C. A. M. & Scheepers, P. L. H. (2004) Dependent autonomy: towards a contextualised and dialogic aim for moral education, *Journal of Empirical Theology,* 17. 2. 172-196.

Anscombe, G. F. M. (1981), *Collected Philosophical Papers Volume III,* Oxford, Blackwell.

Archdiocese of Birmingham (2005) *Section 48: Guidance for Inspectors,* Coleshill, Department of Religious Education (Schools).

Argyle, M. (1958) *Religious Behaviour,* London, Routledge & Kegan Paul.

Arthur, J. (1995) *The Ebbing Tide: Policy and Principles of Catholic Education,* Leominster, Gracewing.

Arthur, J. (1998) Communitarianism; what are the implications for education? *Educational Studies,* 24. 3. 253-368.

Arthur, J. & Godfrey, R. (2005) *Statistical Survey of the Attainment and Achievement of Pupils in Church of England Schools,* Canterbury, Christ Church University, National Institute for Religious Education Research.

Ashworth. J. & Farthing I. (2007) *Churchgoing in the UK,* Teddington, Tearfund.

Association of Teachers and Lecturers (2007) Faith Schools Position Paper, *http://www.atl.org.uk/atl_ en/* (accessed 26th March 2007).

Astley, J., Francis, L., Wilcox, C. & Burton, L. (2000). How different is religious education in Catholic schools? A study of teacher aims in England. *International Journal of Education and Religion,* 1, 2, 267-281.

Atkins, P. (2001) The Church school – good or evil: Against, *The Independent - Education Supplement,* p. 7, 1st March.

Augustine of Hippo (1467) *Concerning the City of God Against the Pagans,* (2003 Edition) English translation by Bettenson, H. (1972) London, Penguin Books.

Baker, K. (1993) *The Turbulent Years,* London, Faber & Faber.

Balls, E. (2007) Faith in the System, speech by the Secretary of State for Children, Schools and Families, 10th September, *www.dcsf.gov.uk/speeches/speech.cfm?SpeechID=677* (accessed 11th September 2007).

Ball, W. & Troyna, B. (1993) Resistance, rights and rituals: denominational schools and multicultural education, in: L. J. Francis & D. Lankshear (eds) (1993) *Christian Perspectives on Church Schools,* Leominster, Gracewing.

Banks, O. (1968) *The Sociology of Education,* London, Batsford.

Barnard, H. C. (1961) *A History of English Education From 1760 (Second Edition),* London, University of London Press.

Barnes, L. P. (2002) World religions in the Northern Ireland curriculum, *Journal of Beliefs and Values,* 23. 1. 19-32.

Barnes L. P. (2005) Religion, education and conflict in Northern Ireland, *Journal of Beliefs and Values,* 26. 2. 123-138.

Barnes, L. P. & Kay W. K. (2002) *Religious education in England & Wales: Innovations and Reflections,* RTSF Monograph, Leicester, Religious and Theological Studies Fellowship.

Barrow R. & Woods, R. (1975) *An Introduction to Philosophy of Education,* London, Methuen.

Battersby, W. J. (1950) *Secondary Education for Boys,* and *Educational Work of the Religious Orders of Women*; in: G. A. Beck (ed) (1950) *The English Catholics 1850-1950,* London, Burns Oates.

Beales, A. C. F. (1950) The Struggle for the Schools in: G. A. Beck (ed) (1950) *The English Catholics 1850-1950,* London, Burns Oates.

Beck, G. A. (ed) (1950) *The English Catholics 1850-1950,* London, Burns Oates.

Beck, G. A. (ed) (1951) *The Case for Catholic Schools,* London, Catholic Education Council.

Beck, G. A. (ed) (1955) *The Case for Catholic Schools (Revised Edition)*, London, Catholic Education Council.

Beck, G. A. (1955) *The Cost of Catholic Schools*, London, Catholic Truth Society.

Becker, H. S. & Greer, B. (1960) Latent culture: a note on the theory of latent social roles, *Administrative Science Quarterly*, 5. 304-313.

Beckett, F. (2001) Holier than thou, *The Guardian*, Tuesday 13th November.

Belcham, J. (1999) Class, creed and country: the Irish middle class in Liverpool, in: R. Swift & S. Gilley (eds) (1999) *The Irish in Victorian Britain: the Local Dimension*, Dublin, Four Courts Press.

Benton, T., Hutchinson, D., Schagen, I. & Scott, E. (2003) *Study of the Performance of Maintained Secondary Schools in England – Report for the National Audit Office*, Slough, National Foundation for Educational Research.

Berlin, I. (1969) *Four Essays on Liberty*, Oxford, Oxford University Press.

Bernt, F. M. (1989) Being religious and being altruistic: a study of college service volunteers, *Personality and Individual Differences*, 10. 663-669.

Bibby, R. W. (1985) Religious encasement in Canada: an argument for Protestant and Catholic entrenchment, *Social Compass*, 16. 285-303.

Bibby, R. W. & Posterski, D. C. (1985) *The Emerging Generation*, Toronto, Irwin.

Bishops Conference of England and Wales (1997) *Catholic Schools & Other Faiths*, London, Department for Catholic Education and Formation.

Bishops Conference of England and Wales (1997) *A Struggle for Excellence: Catholic Secondary Schools in Urban Poverty Areas*, London, Catholic Education Service.

Bishops Conference of England and Wales (1999) *Foundations for Excellence: Catholic Primary Schools in Urban Poverty Areas*, London, Catholic Education Service.

Blunkett, D. (2000) *Transforming Secondary Education*, speech to the Social Market Foundation, 15th March, London, Social Market Foundation.

Bossey, J. (1975) *The English Catholic Community 1570-1850*, London, Darton, Longman & Todd.

Bouma, G. D. (1992) *Religion: meaning, transcendence and community in Australia*, Melborne, Longman Cheshire.

Bourne, F. (1906) *The Catholic Attitude on the Education Question*, (transcript of an address delivered at Blackburn, 25th September 1905), London, Catholic Truth Society.

Bourne, F. (1929) *The Catholic Attitude on the Education Question*, London, Catholic Truth Society.

Bourne, F. (1929) *Declaration by the Archbishops and Bishops of England and Wales on the Subject of Education*, Essex, Catholic Parents Association.

Bowlby, J. (1988) Changing theories of childhood since Freud, in: E. Timms & N. Segal (eds) (1988) *Freud in Exile*, New Haven, Yale University Press.

Bowlby, J. (1953) *Child Care and the Growth of Love*, Harmondsworth, Penguin.

Briault, E. & Smith F. (1980) *Falling Rolls in Secondary Schools*, Slough, National Foundation for Educational Research.

Brighouse, H. (2005) Faith-based schools in the United Kingdom: an unenthusiastic defence of a slightly reformed status quo, in: R. Gardner, J. Cairns, D. Lawton (eds) (2005) *Faith Schools: Consensus or Conflict?*, London, RoutledgeFalmer.

British Broadcasting Corporation Trust (2007) *From seesaw to wagon wheel; safeguarding impartiality in the 21st century*, London, BBC Trust.

British Humanist Association (2001) *Religious Schools: the case against*, London, British Humanist Association.

Breckenridge, M. E. & Vincent, E. L. (1955) *Child Development*, London, W. B. Saunders Company.

Brown, C. G. (2001) *The Death of Christian Britain*, London, Routledge.

Bruce, S. (1995) *Religion in Modern Britain*, Oxford, Oxford University Press.

Bruce, S. (2002) *God is Dead: secularisation in the west*, Oxford, Blackwell.

Bryk, A. & Lee, V. (1992) Is politics the problem and markets the answer? *Economics of Education Review*, 11. 4. 439-451.

Bryk, A., Lee, V. & Holland, P. (1993) *Catholic Schools and the Common Good*, Cambridge, Massachusetts, Harvard University Press.

Burleigh, M. (2005) *Earthly Powers: Religion and Politics in Europe from the Enlightenment to the Great War*, London, Harper Collins.

Burleigh, M. (2006) *Sacred Causes: Religion and Politics from the European Dictators to Al Qaeda*, London, Harper Collins.

Burn, J., Marks, J., Pilkington P. & Thompson, P. (eds) (2001) *Faith in Education. The Role of the Churches in Education: a response to the Dearing Report on Church Schools in the Third Millennium*, London, Institute for the Study of Civil Society.

Burtonwood, N. (1998) Liberalism and communitarianism: a response to two recent attempts to reconcile individual autonomy with group identity, *Educational Studies*, 28. 3. 295-304.

Burtonwood, N. (2000) Must liberal support for separate schools be subject to a condition of individual autonomy? *British Journal of Educational Studies*, 48. 3. 269-284.

Burtonwood, N. (2002) Political philosophy and the lessons for faith based schools, *Educational Studies*, 28. 3. 239-252.

Burtonwood, N. (2003) Social cohesion, autonomy and the liberal defence of faith schools, *Journal of Philosophy of Education*, 37. 3. 415-425.

Caines, J. (1994) *St. Philip's Roman Catholic Sixth Form College, Report of an Enquiry into the Governance and Management of the College*; Coventry, Further Education Funding Council.

Caldwell, S. (2007) Bishops grow nervous over charity reforms, *Catholic Herald*, 15th June, p. 3.

Callaghan, J (1976) Towards a National Debate, Speech at the foundation stone-laying ceremony at Ruskin College, Oxford. 18th October, *http://education.guardian.co.uk/print/0,,4277858-109002,00. html* (accessed 6th July 2007).

Cantle, T. (2003) *Community Cohesion: A Report of the Independent Review Team* (The Cantle Report), London, Home Office.

Carr, D. (1996) Rival conceptions of spiritual education, *Journal of Philosophy of Education*, 30. 2. 159-178.

_____ *Catechism of the Catholic Church*, (1994) London, Geoffrey Chapman.

_____ *Catholic Directory of England and Wales*, (2005) Manchester, Gabriel Communications Ltd.

Catholic Education Service (1994) *School Census Returns*, London, Catholic Education Service.

Catholic Education Service (1997) *The Common Good in Education*, London, Catholic Education Service.

Catholic Education Service (2002) *School Census Returns*, London, Catholic Education Service.

Catholic Education Service (2003) *School Census Returns*, London, Catholic Education Service.

Catholic Education Service, (2003) *Catholic Education: A CES Position Paper on Catholic Education in Schools and Sixth Form Colleges*, London, Catholic Education Service.

Catholic Education Service (2004) *School Census Returns*, London, Catholic Education Service.

Catholic Education Service (2004*) Analysis of Pupil Level Annual School Census for all Catholic Schools in England 2003/2004*, London, Catholic Education Service.

Catholic Education Service (2005) *School Census Returns*, London, Catholic Education Service.

Catholic Education Service (2006) *Quality and Performance: A Survey of Education in Catholic Schools*, London, Catholic Education Service.

Central Advisory Council for Education (1959) *15-18 (The Crowther Report)*, London, Her Majesty's Stationery Office.

Central Advisory Council for Education (1963) *Half Our Future (The Newsom Report)*, London, Her Majesty's Stationery Office.

Central Advisory Council for Education (1966) *Children and their Primary Schools (The Plowden Report)*, London, Her Majesty's Stationery Office.

Chadwick, P. (1994) *Schools of Reconciliation*, London, Cassell.

Chadwick, P. (1997) *Shifting Alliances: Church & State in English Education*, London, Cassell.

Chamberlain, T., Rutt, S. & Fletcher-Campbell, F. (2006) *Admissions: Who goes where? Messages from the statistics*, Local Government Association Research Programme Report 4/05, Slough, National Foundation for Educational Research.

Chubb, J. E. & Moe, T. (1988) Politics, markets and the organisation of schools, *American Political Science Review*, 82. 4. 1065-1087.

Chubb, J. E. & Moe, T. (1990) Should market forces control educational decision making?, *American Political Science Review*, 84. 2. 558-565.

Cibulka, J., O'Brien, T. & Zewe, D. (1982) *Inner City Private Elementary Schools: A Study*, Milwaukee, Wisconsin, Marquette University Press.

Coleman, J. S., Hoffer, T. & Kilgore, S. B. (1982) *High School Achievement*, New York, Basic Books.

Coleman, J. (1988) Social Capital in the Creation of Human Capital, *American Journal of Sociology*, 94. Supplement S95-120.

Coman, P. (1977) *Catholics and the Welfare State*, London, Longman.

Conroy, J. C. (ed) (1999) *Catholic Education: Inside Out/Outside In*, Dublin, Lindisfarne Books.

Copson, A. (2006) Why education should not divide on faith, Westminster Forum, 24th April, *http:// Ekklesia.co.uk/content/features/article_060428faithschools,* (accessed 14th December 2006).

Crone, R. & Malone, J. (1979) *Continuities in Education: the Northern Ireland schools curriculum project 1973-78,* Slough, National Foundation for Educational Research.

Croll, P. (2004) Families, social capital and educational outcomes, *British Journal of Educational Studies,* 52. 4. 390-416.

Cunningham, R. (2000) Church and state in education in England and Wales 1833-1975, in: M. Eaton, J. Longmore & A. Naylor (eds) (2000) *Commitment to Diversity: Catholic and Education in a Changing World,* London, Cassell.

Curtis, S. J. (1967) *History of Education in Great Britain (Seventh Edition),* London, University Tutorial Press.

Davie, G. (1994) *Religion in Britain since 1945,* Oxford, Blackwell.

Dawkins, R. (2001) Children must choose their own beliefs, *The Observer,* Sunday 30th December.

Dawkins, R. (2004) Appeal for an end to state-subsidised faith schools, London, National Secular Society, *http://www.secularism.org.uk/32999.html* (accessed 30th June 2005).

Dawkins, R. (2001) No faith in the absurd, *Times Educational Supplement,* p. 17, 23rd February.

Dean, C., Dyson, A., Gallannaugh, F., Howes, A. & Ruffo, C. (2007) *Schools, Governors and Disadvantage,* York, Joseph Rowntree Foundation.

De Jong, J. & Snik, G. (2002) Why should states fund denominational schools?, *Journal of Philosophy of Education,* 36. 4. 573-587.

Dennis, N. (2001) *The Uncertain Trumpet: A History of Church of England School Education to AD 2001,* London, Institute for the Study of Civil Society.

Dennis, N. & Erdos, G, (2000) *Families Without Fatherhood,* London, Institute for the Study of Civil Society.

Department for Children, Schools & Families (2007) *Faith in the System: the role of schools with a religious character in English education and society,* Nottingham, DCSF Publications.

Department for Education & Employment, (1998) *The Learning Age: a renaissance for a new Britain,* London, Her Majesty's Stationery Office.

Department of Education & Science (1985) *Education for All* (Swann Report)), London, Her Majesty's Stationery Office.

Department for Education & Skills (2001), *Schools Achieving Success,* London, Her Majesty's Stationery Office.

Department for Education & Skills (2002) *Education and Skills: Investment for Reform;* London, Her Majesty's Stationery Office.

Department for Education & Skills (2003) Statutory Proposals: Decision Makers Guidance, *http://www. dfes.gov.uk/schoolorg/Guidance* (accessed 12th January 2004).

Department for Education & Skills (2003*) Education and Skills: the Economic Benefit,* London, Her Majesty's Stationery Office.

Department for Education & Skills (2003) *A New Specialist System: Transforming Secondary Education,* Nottingham, DfES Publications.

Department for Education & Skills (2004) *Five Year Strategy for Children and Learners,* London, Her Majesty's Stationery Office.

Department for Education & Skills, (2004) *Statistic of Education: Schools in England,* London, Her Majesty's Stationery Office.

Department for Education & Skills (2005) *14-19 Education and Skills,* London, Her Majesty's Stationery Office.

Department for Education & Skills, (2005) *Higher standards, better schools for all,* London, Her Majesty's Stationery Office.

Department for Education & Skills, (2007) School Achievement and Attainment Tables, *http://www.dfes.gov.uk/* (accessed 15th September 2007).

Department for Education & Skills (2007) *Establishing a New Maintained Mainstream School: A Guide for Local Authorities,* Darlington, School Organisation Unit.

Department for Education & Skills (2007) *Home to School Travel and Transport Guidance,* Nottingham, DfES Publications.

Donnelly, C. (1999) *Differences in Schools: a question of ethos,* paper presented at the British Education Research Association Annual Conference, University of Sussex, 2nd–5th September.

Donnelly, C. (2004) What Price Harmony? Teachers' methods of delivering an ethos of tolerance and respect for diversity in an integrated school in Northern Ireland, *Educational Research,* 46. 1. 3-16.

Donnelly, C. (2004) Constructing the ethos of tolerance and respect in an integrated school: the role of teachers, *British Educational Research Journal,* 30. 2. 263-278.

Duffy, E. (1992) *The Stripping of the Altars,* New Haven & London, Yale University Press.

Dunn, S. (2000) Northern Ireland: education in a divided society, in: D. Phillips (ed) (2000) *The Education Systems of the United Kingdom,* Oxford, Symposium Books.

Eaton, M., Longmore, J. & Naylor, A. (eds) (2000) *Commitment to Diversity: Catholics and Education in a Changing World,* London, Cassell.

Editorial (2007) Charity law is being used as a weapon against the Church, *Catholic Herald,* 15th June, p. 11.

Egan, J. (1986) Religious education in Catholic schools: some recent findings, *British Journal of Religious Education,* 8. 155-160.

Egan, J. & Francis, L. J. (1986) School ethos in Wales: the impact of non-practising Catholic and non-Catholic pupils on Catholic secondary schools, *Lumen Vitae,* 41. 2. 159-173.

Eliot, T. S. (1939) *The Idea of a Christian Society,* London, Faber & Faber.

Etzioni, A. (1964) *Modern Organisations,* New York, Prentice Hall.

Evans, M. D. R. (2004) Do Catholic schools and independent schools enhance educational success?, *Australian Social Monitor,* 7. 3. 53-69.

Evennett, H. O. (1944) *The Catholic Schools of England and Wales,* Cambridge, Cambridge University Press.

Everett, S. (1993) *GCSE examination performance in Nottinghamshire, Nottingham*, Nottinghamshire County Council, private correspondence re: Jesson et al., (1992), Jesson & Gray, (1993).

Fagan, P. (2001) *Family and faith: the roots of prosperity, stability and freedom*, Washington, DC, The Heritage Foundation.

Feheney, J. M. (ed) (1998), *From Ideal to Action: The Inner Nature of a Catholic School Today*, Dublin, Veritas.

Finan, J. (1975) *Struggle for Justice*, Stoke-on-Trent, Catholic Teachers' Federation.

Fiorenza, F. S. (1990) Redemption, in: J. A. Komonchak, M. Collins & D. Lane (eds) (1990) *The New Dictionary of Theology*, Dublin, Gill & Macmillan, pp. 836-851.

Flannery, A. (ed) (1981) *Vatican Council II: The Conciliar and Post Conciliar Documents*, Leominster, Fowler Wright.

Flannery, A. (ed) (1982) *Vatican Council II: More Post Conciliar Documents*, New York, Costello Publishing Company.

Flynn, M. (1985) *The Effectiveness of Catholic Schools*, Sydney, St. Paul Publications.

Flynn, M. (1993) Religious commitment and school achievement: is there a relationship? *Catholic School Studies*, 66. 2. 21-27.

Flynn, P. F. (1974) *Some Catholic Schools in Action: A Survey of Sixth Form Students at 21 Catholic Boys' High Schools in New South Wales and the A.C.T.*, Unpublished M. A. thesis, Macquarrie University, Sydney, Australia.

Foley, J. & Grace, G. (2001) *The Birmingham Catholic School Partnership: Holding to common good values in a market competitive age*, London, Centre for Research and Development in Catholic Education.

Fortin, J. (2003) *Children's Rights and the Developing Law*, London, Lexis Nexis, 2nd edition.

Frabutt, J. M. (2001) Parenting and child development: exploring the links with children's social, moral and cognitive competence, in: T. C. Hunt, E. A. Joseph & R. J. Nuzzi (eds) (2001), *Handbook of Research on Catholic Education*, Westport, Connecticut, Greenwood Press.

Francis, L. J. (1979) School influence and pupil attitude towards religion, *British Journal of Educational Psychology*, 49, 107-123.

Francis, L. J. (1980) Paths of holiness: attitudes towards religion among 9-11 year old children, *Character Potential*, 9. 129-138.

Francis, L. J. (1983) *School influence and pupil attitude: a decade's progress*, Abingdon, Culham College Institute.

Francis, L. J. (1984) Roman Catholic schools and pupil attitudes in England, *Lumen Vitae*, 39. 99-108.

Francis, L. J. (1986) Denominational schools and pupil attitudes towards Christianity, *British Journal of Educational Research*, 12, 145-152.

Francis, L. J. (1986) Roman Catholic secondary schools: falling rolls and pupil attitudes, *Educational Studies*, 12. 119-127.

Francis, L. J. (1987) Measuring attitudes towards Christianity among 12-to-18 year old pupils in Catholic schools, *Educational Research*, 29. 3. 231-233.

Francis, L. J. (1992) The influence of religion, gender and social class on attitudes towards school among 11-year-olds in England, *Journal of Experimental Education*, 60. 4. 339-348.

Francis, L. J. (2001) Religion and Values: A Quantitative Perspective, in: L. J. Francis, J. Astley & M. Robbins (eds) *The Fourth R for the Third Millenium*, Dublin, Lindisfarne Books.

Francis, L. J. (2002) Catholic Schools and Catholic Values: a study of moral and religious values among 13-15 year old pupils attending non-denominational and Catholic schools in England and Wales, *International Journal of Education and Religion*, 3. 69-84.

Francis L. J. (2005) *Faith and Psychology*, London, Darton, Longman & Todd.

Francis, L. J. & Kaldor, P. (2002) The relationship between psychological well-being and Christian faith and practice in an Australian population sample, *Journal for the Scientific Study of Religion*, 41. 1. 179-184.

Francis, L. J. & Kay W. K. (1995) *Teenage Religion and Values*, Leominster, Gracewing.

Francis, L. J. & Robbins, M. (2005) *Urban Hope and Spiritual Health: The Adolescent Voice*, Peterborough, Epworth.

Frankel, B. G. & Hewitt, W. E. (1994) Religion and well-being among Canadian University Students: the role of faith groups on campus, *Journal for the Scientific Study of Religion*, 33. 1. 62-73.

Fulton, J. (1999) Young adult core Catholics, in: M. P. Hornsby-Smith (ed) (1999) *Catholics in England 1950-2000: Historical and Sociological Perspectives*, London, Cassell.

Fulton, J. (2000) Contemporary young adult Catholics in England: faith and education, in: M. Eaton, J. Longmore & A. Naylor (eds) (2000) *Commitment to Diversity: Catholics and Education in a Changing World*, London, Cassell.

Gallagher, A. M. (1995) *Education in a Divided Society: A Review of Research and Policy*, University of Ulster, Centre for the Study of Conflict.

Gallagher, E. & Worrall, S. (1982) *Christians in Ulster 1968-1980*, Oxford, Oxford University Press.

Gallagher, J. (1996) The Catholic School and Religious Education: meeting a variety of needs, in: T. H. McLaughlin, J. O'Keefe & B. O'Keeffe (eds) (1996) *The Contemporary Catholic School: Context, Identity and Diversity*, London, Falmer Press.

Gardner, P. (1991) Personal autonomy and religious upbringing: the 'problem', *Journal of Philosophy of Education*, 25. 1. 69-81.

Gardner, P. (1992) Propositional attitudes and multicultural education or believing others are mistaken, in: J. Horton & P. Nicholson, (eds) (1992) *Toleration: Philosophy and Practice*, Avebury, Aldershot.

Gardner, R., Cairns, J. & Lawton, D. (eds) (2005) *Faith Schools: Consensus or Conflict?* London, RoutledgeFalmer.

Gaudium et spes [Pastoral Constitution of the Church in the Modern World] (1965), in: A. Flannery (ed) (1981) *The Conciliar and Post Conciliar Documents*, Leominster, Fowler Wright.

Gibbons, S., Machin, S. & Silva, O. (2006) *Competition, Choice and pupil Achievement*, London, Centre for the Economics of Education, London School of Economics.

Gibson, H. M. (1989) Measuring attitudes towards Christianity among 11-to-16 year old pupils in non-denominational schools in Scotland, *Educational Research,* 31. 3. 221-227.

Gilbert, A. D. (1980) *The Making of Post-Christian Britain*, London, Longman.

Gillard, D. (2002) Glass in their snowballs – the faith school debate, *Forum*, 44. 1. 15-23.

Goldstein, H. (1993) Review: 'Politics, Markets and America's Schools', *British Educational Research Journal*, 19. 1. 116-118.

Goodman, P. (1972) *Compulsory Miseducation*, Harmondsworth, Penguin.

Grace, G. (2002) *Catholic Schools: Mission, Markets and Morality*, London, RoutledgeFalmer.

Grace, G. (2003) Educational Studies and Faith Based Schooling: Moving from prejudice to evidence-based argument, *British Journal of Educational Studies*, 51. 2. 149-167.

Graffius, C. (1994) When persecution was a real and vicious fact, *Catholic Times*, 24th April.

Gravissimum educationis [Declaration on Christian Education] (1965) in: A. Flannery (ed) (1981) *Vatican Council II: The conciliar and post conciliar documents*, Leominster, Fowler Wright, 725-737.

Grayling, A. C. (2001) Keep God out of public affairs, *The Observer*, Sunday, 12th August.

Greeley, A. (1982) *Catholic High Schools and Minority Students*, New Brunswick, N. J., Transaction Press.

Greeley, A. (1998) Catholic schools at the crossroads: an American perspective, in: J. M. Feheney (ed) (1998), *From Ideal to Action: The Inner Nature of a Catholic School Today*, Dublin, Veritas.

Greenslade, L. (1992) White skin, white masks: psychological distress among the Irish in Britain, in: P. O'Sullivan (ed) *The Irish in the New Communities, Volume 2*, Leicester, Leicester University Press.

Greer, J. (1985) Viewing 'the other side' in Northern Ireland: openness and attitudes to religion among Catholic and Protestant adolescents, *Journal for the Scientific Study of Religion*, 24. 275-292. [Also in: L. Francis and D. Lankshear (eds) (1993) *Christian Perspectives on Church Schools*, Leominster, Gracewing.]

Greer, J. E. & Francis, L. J. (1991) Measuring attitudes towards Christianity among pupils in Catholic secondary schools in Northern Ireland, *Educational Research*, 33. 1. 70-73.

Groothuis, D. (2004) On not abolishing faith schools: a response to Michael Hand and H. Siegel, *Theory and Research in Education*, 2. 2. 177-188.

Gwynn, D. (1950) Growth of the Catholic Community, in: G. A. Beck (ed) (1950) *The English Catholics 1850-1950*, London, Burns Oates.

Gwynn, D. (1950) The Irish Immigration, in: G. A. Beck (ed) (1950) *The English Catholics 1850-1950*, London, Burns Oates.

Guardian Unlimited (2001) Facts about Faith Schools, 14th November, *http://education.guardian.co.uk/* (accessed 7th June 2007).

Haldane, J. (1985) Individuals and the Theory of Justice, *Ratio*, 27. 2. 189-96.

Haldane, J. (1986) Religious education in a plural society, *British Journal of Educational Studies*, 34. 2. 161-181.

Haldane J. (1996) Catholic Education and Catholic Identity, in: T. H. McLaughlin, J. O'Keefe, & B. O'Keeffe (eds) (1996) *The Contemporary Catholic School: Context, Identity and Diversity*, London, Falmer Press.

Haldane, J. (2004) *Faithful Reason: Essays Catholic and Philosophical,* London, Routledge.

Haldane, J. (2007) Address at the CTS Conference, 14th July, London, Westminster Cathedral.

Halstead, M. (1995) Voluntary apartheid? Problems of schooling for religious and other minorities in democratic societies, *Journal of Philosophy of Education,* 29. 2. 257-272.

Hancox, N. (2005) *The Selective Funding of Faith Schools: A Legitimate Exercise of State Power?,* Unpublished LL.M thesis, University of East Anglia.

Hand, M. (2002) Religious upbringing reconsidered, *Journal of Philosophy of Education,* 36. 4. 545-557.

Hand, M. (2003) The meaning of 'spiritual education', *Oxford Review of Education,* 29. 3. 391-401.

Hand, M. (2003) A Philosophical Objection to Faith Schools, *Theory and Research in Education,* 1. 1. 89-99.

Hand, M. (2004) The problem with faith schools: a reply to my critics, *Theory and Research in Education,* 2. 3. 343-353.

Hand, M. (2006) Against autonomy as an educational aim, *Oxford Review of Education,* 32. 4. 535-550.

Hansard (2002) *Report of the Education Bill 2002 debate,* Columns 577 to 587, London, House of Lords 17th June.

Hansard (2002) *Report of the Education Bill 2002 debate,* Columns 851 to 852, London, House of Lords, 19th June.

Hansard (2006) *Report of the Admission Policies of Faith Schools debate,* London, House of Commons, 14th February.

Hansard (2006) *Report of the Faith Schools Expansion debate,* Columns 720-737, London, House of Lords, 8th February.

Hansard (2006), *Report of the Education and Inspection Bill debate, Third Reading,* Columns 17-130, London, House of Lords, 30th October.

Hansard (2006) *Report of the Education and Inspection Bill debate,* Column 481, London, House of Commons, 2nd November.

Hanvey, J. & Carroll, A. (2005) *On the Way to Life,* London, Catholic Education Service.

Hargreaves, D. (1994) *The Mosaic of Learning: Schools and Teachers for the Next Century,* London, Demos.

Hargreaves, D. (1996) Diversity and Choice in School Education: a modified libertarian approach, *Oxford Review of Education,* 22. 2. 131-141.

Hastings, P. (1996) Openness and Intellectual Challenge in Catholic Schools, in: T. H. McLaughlin, J. O'Keefe & B. O'Keeffe (eds) (1996) *The Contemporary Catholic School: Context, Identity and Diversity,* London, Falmer Press.

Hay, D. (1985) Suspicion of the spiritual: teaching religion in a world of secular experience, *British Journal of Religious Education,* 7. 3. 140-147.

Her Majesty's Government (1973) Northern Ireland Constitutional proposals (White Paper, Cmnd 5259), London, HMSO, quoted in: McGrath, M. (2000) *The Catholic Church and Catholic Schools in Northern Ireland: The Price of Faith,* Dublin, Irish Academic Press.

Her Majesty's Government (2004) Treasury Minutes on the Nineteenth Report from the Committee of Public Accounts 2003-04, *Making a Difference: Performance of maintained secondary schools in England*, presented to Parliament by the Financial Secretary to the Treasury, June 2004 (Cm 6244).

Herson, J. (1999) Migration, 'community' or integration? Irish families in Victorian Stafford, in: R. Swift & S. Gilley (eds) (1999) *The Irish in Victorian Britain: the Local Dimension*, Dublin, Four Courts Press.

Hetherington, T. (2007) Spaghetti Junction: The new school transport provisions, *Education, Public Law & the Individual,* 10. 3. 9-15.

Hickman, M. J. (1997) *Religion, Class and Identity: The State, the Catholic Church and the Education of the Irish in Britain*, Hampshire, Avebury.

Hickman, M. J. (1999) Alternative historiographies of the Irish in Britain; a critique of the segregation/assimilation model, in: R. Swift & S. Gilley (eds) (1999) *The Irish in Victorian Britain: The Local Dimension*, Dublin, Four Courts Press.

Hickman, M. J. (2000) Catholicism and the nation-state in nineteenth century Britain, in: M. Eaton, J. Longmore & A. Naylor (eds) (2000) *Commitment to Diversity: Catholics and Education in a Changing World*, London, Cassell.

Hickman, M. J. & Walter, B. (1997) *Discrimination and the Irish Community in Britain*, London, Commission for Racial Equality.

Hill, P., Foster, G. & Gendler, T. (1990) *High Schools with Character*, Santa Monica, Rand Corporation.

Hillard, P. (1993) *Suspect Community: Peoples experience of the Prevention of Terrorism Act in Britain*, London, Pluto Press.

Hirst, P. H. (1981) Education, catechesis and the Church school, *British Journal of Religious Education*, 3. 3. 85-101. [Also in: L. J. Francis and D. Lankshear (eds) (1993) *Christian Perspectives on Church Schools*, Leominster, Gracewing].

Hoffer. T. (2000) Catholic school attendance and student achievement: a review and extension of research, in: J. Youniss & J. J. Covey (eds) (2000) *Catholic Schools at the Crossroads: survival and transformation*, New York, Teachers College Press.

Hoffer, T., Greeley, A. & Coleman, J. (1985) Achievement growth in public and Catholic schools, *Sociology of Education*, 58. 74-97.

Holloway, D. (2005) *Understanding the Northern Ireland Conflict: A summary and overview of the conflict and its origins*, Belfast, Community Dialogue.

Holmes (1992) *Educational Policy for the Pluralist Democracy: The Common School, Choice and Diversity*, London, Falmer Press.

Hooper, W. (1996) *C. S. Lewis: A Companion and Guide*, London, HarperCollins.

Hornsby-Smith, M. P. (1972) A sociological case for Catholic schools, *The Month*, October, 298-304.

Hornsby-Smith, M. P. (1978) *Catholic Education: The Unobtrusive Partner*, London, Sheed & Ward.

Hornsby-Smith, M. P. (1999) English Catholics at the New Millenuem, in: M. P. Hornsby-Smith (ed) (1999) *Catholics in England 1950-2000: Historical and Sociological Perspectives*, London, Cassell.

Hornsby-Smith, M. P. (ed) (1999) *Catholics in England 1950-2000: Historical and Sociological Perspectives*, London, Cassell.

Hornsby-Smith, M. P. (2000) The changing social and religious context of Catholic schooling in England and Wales, in: M. Eaton, J. Longmore & A. Naylor (eds) (2000) *Commitment to Diversity: Catholics and Education in a Changing World*, London, Cassell.

Hornsby-Smith, M. P. & Dale, A. (1988) The assimilation of Irish immigrants in England, *British Journal of Sociology*, 39. 4. 519-543.

Hostler, P. (1959) *The Child's World*, Harmondsworth, Penguin.

Horton, J & Nicholson, P. (eds) (1992) *Toleration: Philosophy and Practice*, Avebury, Aldershot.

House of Commons (2006) *Education and Skills Select Committee Report (HC 633-1)* on the White Paper 'Higher Standards, Better Schools For All', London, Her Majesty's Stationery Office.

Howson, J. (2007) *22nd Report on Senior Appointments in Schools*, Oxford, Education Data Surveys Ltd.

Hughes, P. (1950) *The English Catholics in 1850*, in: G. A. Beck (ed) (1950) *The English Catholics 1850-1950*, London, Burns Oates.

Hulmes, E. (1999) Faith in crisis: from holocaust to hope 1943-2000, in: V. A. McClellend & M. Hodgetts (eds) (1999) *From Without the Flaminian Gate*, London, Darton, Longman & Todd.

Humanist Philosophers Group (2001), *Religious Schools: The Case Against*, London, British Humanist Association.

Hume, B. (1988) *Towards a Civilisation of Love*, London, Hodder & Stoughton.

Hume, B. (1994) Education since the 1994 Act, in: *Partners in Mission: a collection of talks by Bishops on issues affecting Catholic education* (1997), London, Catholic Education Service and Briefing.

Hume, B. (1995) The Church's mission in education, *Briefing: Education Special, June*, London, Catholic Media Office.

Hunt, T. C., Ellis, E. A. & Nuzzi R. J. (eds) (2002) *Catholic Schools Still Make a Difference: Ten Years of Research 1991-2000*, Washington, National Catholic Educational Association.

Hyde, K. (1990) *Religion in Childhood and Adolescence: A Comprehensive Review of the Research*, Religious Education Press, Alabama.

Hyper, P. A. (1996) Catholic Schools and Other Faiths, in: T. H. McLaughlin, J. O'Keefe & B. O'Keeffe (eds) (1996) *The Contemporary Catholic School: Context, Identity and Diversity*, London, Falmer Press.

Illich, I. (1971) *Celebration of Awareness*, Harmondsworth, Penguin.

Image, F. (2005) *Management of change: evolving leadership and ethos in a federated secondary school*, Unpublished M.Ed thesis, Open University.

Jackson, R. (2003) Should the state fund faith based schools? A review of the arguments, *British Journal of Religious Education*, 25. 2. 89-102.

Jay, A. (2007) *Confessions of a Reformed BBC Producer*, London, Centre for Policy Studies.

Jenkins, P. (2003) *The New Anti-Catholicism: The Last Acceptable Prejudice*, Oxford, Oxford University Press.

Jencks, C. (1985) How much do high school students learn?, *Sociology of Education*, 58. 128-135.

Jesson, D., Gray, J, & Tranmer, M. (1992) *GCSE Performance in Nottinghamshire 1991: Pupil and School Factors*, Nottingham, Nottinghamshire County Council.

Jesson, D. & Gray, J. (1993) *GCSE Performance in Nottinghamshire 1992: Further Perspectives*, Nottingham, Nottinghamshire County Council.

Jeynes, H. K. (2000) *The effects of attending a religious school on the academic achievement of children*, paper presented at the Annual Conference of the American Educational Research Association, 27th April, New Orleans.

Jeynes, H. K. (2003) The learning habits of twelfth graders attending religious and non-religious schools, *International Journal of Education and Religion*, 4. 2. 145-167.

Johnson, A. (2006) Speech at the Local Government Association/Association of Directors of Social Services Conference – Brighton, 18th October 2006, *www.des.gov.uk/speeches/speeches.cfm?/SpeechID=392* (accessed 16th January 2007).

Johnson, A. (2006) Letter to Archbishop Nichols from the Secretary of State, 26th October, Catholic Education Service, *www.cesew.org.uk/news&events/* (accessed 16th January 2007).

Johnson, K. A. (1999) *Comparing math scores of Black students in D.C.'s public and Catholic schools*, Washington DC, Heritage Foundation, Centre for Data Analysis.

Johnson, H., McCreery, E. & Castelli, M. (2000). The role of the headteacher in developing children holistically: perspectives from Anglicans and Catholics, *Education Management and Administration*, 28. 4. 389-403.

Judge, H. (2001) Faith-based schools and state funding: a partial argument, *Oxford Review of Education*, 27. 4. 463-474.

Judge, H. (2002*) Faith Based Schools and the State: Catholics in America, France and England*, Oxford, Education Symposium Books.

Kelley, J. (2004) Class, religion and education: who gains most from Catholic and independent schooling?, *Australian Social Monitor*, 7. 3. 69-80.

Kendall, L. (1996) *Examination Results in Context: Report of the Analysis of 1994 Examination Results*, London, Association of Metropolitan Authorities.

Kendall, L. (1997) *Examination Results in Context: Report of the Analysis of 1995 Examination Results*, London, Association of Metropolitan Authorities.

Kendall, L. & Ainsworth L. (1997) *Examination Results in Context: Report of the Analysis of 1996 Examination Results*, London, Local Government Association.

Kennedy, P. (ed) (2001) *The Catholic Church in England and Wales 1500-2000*, Keighley, PBK Publishing Ltd.

Key, T. (2006) *The Performance of Catholic Schools and Sixth Form Colleges*, Presentation given at the National Catholic Education Conference, 18th May.

Kirby, J. 1996, *The Nationalisation of Childhood*, London, Centre for Policy Studies.

King, R. (1969) *Education*, London, Longman.

Komonchak, J. A., Collins, M. & Lane, D. A. (eds) (1987) *The New Dictionary of Theology*, Dublin, Gill and Macmillan.

King, A. J. C., et al. (1989) *Canada Youth and AIDS Study*, Ottawa, Ontario, Health & Welfare Canada, quoted in: Holmes (1992) *Educational Policy for the Pluralist Democracy: The Common School, Choice and Diversity*, London, Falmer Press.

Koenig H. G. & Cohen H. J. (2001) *The Link Between Religion and Health: Psychoneuroimmunology and the Faith Factor*, Oxford, Oxford University Press.

Konstant, D. (1996) 'Master Builders', address to the Catholic Teachers' Federation in Birmingham, March 1996, *Briefing*, 26. 4. 26-29, London, Catholic Media Office.

Kraemer, S. (1993) Domestic Organisation and Personal Identity, *Annual Review*, Windsor, St. George's House.

Lawton, D., Gordon, P., Ing, M., Gibby, B., Pring, R. & Moore, T. (eds) (1978) *Theory and Practice of Curriculum Studies*, London, Routledge & Kegan Paul.

Layard, R. (2005) *Happiness: Lessons from a New Science*, London, Allen Lane.

Leahy, M. (1990) Indoctrination, evangelisation, catechesis and Religious education, *British Journal of Religious Education*, 12. 3. 137-144.

Leavey, M. C. (1972a) *Religious education, school climate and achievement: a study of nine Catholic sixth form girls' schools*, Unpublished Ph. D. thesis, Australian National University, Canberra, Australia.

Leavey, M. C. (1972b) The transmission of religious and moral values in nine Catholic girls' schools, *Twentieth Century*, 27. 3. 167-184.

Lester-Smith, W. O. (1957) *Education*, Harmondsworth, Penguin.

Letwin, O. (2003) E pluribus unum – agreeing to differ, speech on Conservative philosophy on race and religion, 11ᵗʰ April, *http//www.conservatives.com* (accessed 28ᵗʰ March 2006).

Local Government Association (2002) *Education Bill, Education Policy Review Meeting*, March 2002, London, Local Government House.

Longley, C. (1995) Dialogue at St. James, *The Tablet*, 15ᵗʰ April, p. 485.

Mackenzie, J. (2004) Religious Upbringing is not as Michael Hand describes, *Journal of Philosophy of Education*, 38. 1. 129-142.

Manning, S. (2007) A question of faith, *Times Educational Supplement Magazine*, 6ᵗʰ July, p. 8.

Margo, J., Dixon, M., Pearce, N. & Reed, H. (2006) *Freedom's Orphans*, London, Institute for Public Policy Research.

Matthew, D. (1950) *Old Catholics and Converts*, in: G. A. Beck, (ed) (1950) *The English Catholics 1850-1950*, London, Burns Oates.

Marks, J. (2001) Standards in Church of England, Roman Catholic and LEA Schools in England, in: J. Burn, J. Marks, P. Pilkington & P. Thompson (eds) (2001) *Faith in Education. The Role of the Churches in Education: a response to the Dearing Report on Church Schools in the Third Millennium*, London, Institute for the Study of Civil Society.

Marples, R. (2005) Against faith schools: a philosophical argument for children's rights, *International Journal of Children's Spirituality*, 10. 2. 133-147.

Marples, R. (2006) Review: Faith Schools; Consensus or Conflict, *British Journal of Educational Studies*, 54. 2. 250-251.

Mason, M. (2001) Faith Based Schools: The Humanist View, debate at the Royal Society of Arts, 18ᵗʰ October, *http://www.humanism.org.uk/site/cms/contentarticle=1272*, (accessed 14ᵗʰ December 2006).

Mason, M. (2003) Religion in schools: a rights-based approach, *British Journal of Religious Education*, 25. 2. 117-128.

Mason, M. (2005) Religion and schools – a fresh way forward? A rights-based approach to diversity in schools, in: R. Gardner, J. Cairns & D. Lawton (eds) (2005) *Faith Schools Consensus or Conflict?*, London, RoutledgeFalmer.

Marshall, T. W. M. (1850) General Report on Roman Catholic Schools (1849), *The Catholic School*, 2. 1. 40, London, Catholic Poor School Committee.

McClellend, V. A. & Hodgetts, M. (eds) (1999) *From Without the Flaminian Gate*, London, Darton, Longman & Todd.

McGarry, J. & O'Leary, B. (1995) *Explaining Northern Ireland: Broken Images*, Oxford, Blackwell.

McGrath, M. (2000) *The Catholic Church and Catholic Schools in Northern Ireland: The Price of Faith*, Dublin, Irish Academic Press.

McLaughlin, T. H. (1995) Liberalism, education and the common school, *Journal of Philosophy of Education*, 29. 2. 239-255.

McLaughlin, T. H. (1999) Distinctiveness and the Catholic school: balanced judgement and the temptations of commonality, in: J. C. Conroy (ed) (1999) *Catholic Education: Inside Out/Outside In*, Dublin, Lindisfarne Books.

McLaughlin, T. H., O'Keefe, J. & O'Keeffe, B. (eds) (1996) *The Contemporary Catholic School: Context, Identity and Diversity*, London, Falmer Press.

McMahon, A. (2002) in: *Hansard Debate on the Education Bill 2002*, column 919, 6th February 2002.

Meegan, E. A., Carroll, J. B. & Ciriello, M. J. (2002) Outcomes, in: T. C. Hunt, E. A. Ellis & R. J. Nuzzi (eds) (2002) *Catholic Schools Still Make a Difference: Ten Years of Research 1991-2000*, Washington, National Catholic Educational Association.

Mitchell, B. (1900) *How to Play Theological Ping-Pong: Collected Essays on Faith and Reason*, London, Hodder & Stoughton.

Miskell, L. (1999) Irish immigrants in Cornwall: the Cambourne experience, 1861-82, in: R. Swift & S. Gilley (eds) (1999) *The Irish in Victorian Britain: the Local Dimension*, Dublin, Four Courts Press.

Moberg, D. O. (1962) *The Church as a Social Institution*, New Jersey, Prentice-Hall.

Moberg, D. O. (1965) Religiosity in Old Age, *Gerontologist*, 5. 78-87.

Moreira-Almeida, A., Neto, F. L. & Koenig, H. G. (2006) Religiousness and mental health: a review, *Revista Brasileira de Psiquiatria*, 28. 3.

Morgan, P. (1999) *Farewell to the Family? Public Policy and Family Breakdown in Britain and the USA (Second Edition)*, London, Institute of Economic Affairs.

Moore, T. (1978) The nature of educational theory, in: D. Lawton, P. Gordon, M. Ing, B. Gibby, R. Pring, & T. Moore (eds) (1978) *Theory and Practice of Curriculum Studies*, London, Routledge & Kegan Paul.

Morris, A. B. (1996) *School Ethos and the Academic Productivity: The Catholic Effect*, Unpublished Ph. D. thesis, Warwick University.

Morris, A. B. (1997) Same mission, same methods, same Results? academic and religious outcomes from different models of Catholic schooling, *British Journal of Educational Studies*, 45. 4. 378-391.

Morris, A. B. (1998) Catholic and other secondary schools: an analysis of OfSTED inspection reports 1993-95, *Educational Research*, 40. 2. 181-190.

Morris, A. B. (2001) Patterns of Performance of Catholic Schools In England, *Networking*, 3. 1. 17-21.

Morris, A. B. (2005) Diversity, Deprivation and the Common Good, *Oxford Review of Education*, 31. 2. 311-330.

Morris, A. B. (2005) Academic standards in Catholic schools in England: indications of causality, *London Review of Education*, 3. 1. 81-99.

Morris, A. B. (2007) Post-16 Pupil Performance in Catholic Secondary Schools in England 1996-2001, *Educational Review*, 59. 1. 55-69.

Morris. A. B. (2008) *Contextualizing Catholic School Performance in England*, presentation at the 21st Congress of the German Corporation for Educational Science, Dresden, March 18th.

Morris, A. B. (forthcoming) Contextualizing Catholic School Performance in England, *Oxford Review of Education*.

Morris, A. B. & Godfrey R. (2006) *A Statistical Survey of Attainment in Catholic Schools in England with Particular Reference to Secondary Schools Operating Under the Trust Deed of the Archdiocese of Birmingham*, Canterbury, National Institute for Christian Education Research. [Also available from *hppt://www.bdsc.org.uk*].

Morris, A. B. & Marsh A. (2002) Motives of Newly Qualified Teachers for Choosing to Work in Catholic Schools in England, *Networking*, 3. 5. 8-13.

Mullins, D. (1981) *Guidance for Governors*, Cardiff, Archdiocese of Cardiff & Diocese of Menevia.

Mullins, D. (1985) Address to the Catholic Teachers' Federation, Cardiff, *Catholic Education Today*.

Murphy, A. J. (2005) Learning together: the case for 'joint church' schools, in: R. Gardner, J. Cairns & D. Lawton (eds) (2005) *Faith Schools: Consensus or Conflict?* London, RoutledgeFalmer.

Murphy-O'Connor, C. (2007) *Religion and the Public Forum*, Address given at the Corbishley Lecture, Westminster Cathedral Hall, 28th March.

Murray, V. (1996) Other faiths in Catholic schools: general implications of a case study, in: T. H. McLaughlin, J. O'Keefe & B. O'Keeffe (eds) (1996) *The Contemporary Catholic School: Context, Identity and Diversity*, London, Falmer Press.

Musgrave, P. W. (1965) *The Sociology of Education*, London, Methuen.

Musick, M., Wilson J. & Bynum, W. B. (2000) Race and formal volunteering: the differential effects of class and religion, *Social Forces*, 74. 1. 1539-1570.

National Secular Society (2007) The public don't want more faith schools, and they will be divisive, *http://www.secularism.org.uk/thepublicdontwantmorefaithschool3.html*, (accessed 14th September 2007).

Nias, J. (1981) Commitment and motivation in primary school teachers, *Educational Review*, 33. 3. 181-190.

Nias, J. (1985) Reference groups in primary teaching; talking, listening and identity, in: R. Glatter, M. Preedy, C. Riches, & M. Masterton (eds) (1988) *Understanding School Management*, Milton Keynes, Open University.

Nichols, V. (1995) The Church's Mission in Education in a Multi-Faith Society, *Briefing Education Special Edition (June)*, London Catholic Media Office.

Nichols, V. (2002) Faith Schools and the Wider Community, *Briefing* 13th March, London Catholic Media Office.

Nichols, V. (2005) Proclaiming the Faith in a Pluralist Society, public lecture, University of Wales, Swansea, Tuesday December 6th, *http://www.birminghamdiocese/org.uk/archbishop/lectures&talks,* (accessed 16th January 2006).

Nichols, V. (2006) Oral Evidence taken before the Education and Skills Select Committee on citizenship education, Monday 11th December 2006, Questions 609-708, HC 147-I, Uncorrected transcript, *http://www.publications.parlaiment.uk/pa/cm200607/cmselect/cmduski/uc,* (accessed 9th January 2007).

Nichols, V. (2006) What is lawful is not necessarily moral, homily at St. Chad's Cathedral, Birmingham, Solemnity of Christ the King, 26th November, *http://www.birminghamdiocese/org.uk/archbishop/homilies*, accessed 9th January 2007.

Norman, E. (1986) *Roman Catholicism in England*, Oxford, Oxford University Press.

Norman, E. (2002) *Secularisation*, London, Continuum.

Nuffield Foundation (2002) *Integrated Schools and Faith Schools*, Nuffield Foundation Seminar Report, Friday 5th July.

Nuttall, D. (1990) *Differences in examination performance*, Research & Statistics Branch, RS 1277/90, London, Inner London Education Authority.

O'Donnell, E. E. (1977) *Northern Irish Stereotypes*, Dublin, College of Industrial Relations.

O'Keefe, B. & Zipfel, R. (2003) *Ethnicity, Identity & Achievement in Catholic Education*, London, Catholic Education Service.

O'Neill, R. (2002), *Does Marriage Matter?* London, Institute for the Study of Civil Society.

Office of the Deputy Prime Minister (2004) *Social Cohesion*, Sixth Report of Session 2003-04, London, House of Commons.

Office for Standards in Education (2000) *Improving City Schools: strategies to promote educational inclusion*, London, OfSTED.

Office for Standards in Education (2001) *Faith Schools*, Unpublished internal paper prepared by OfSTED Research & Analysis Division, September 2001, London, OfSTED.

Office for Standards in Education (2002) *Examination Entry Patterns in Catholic and other Schools*, Unpublished data – provided in private correspondence, Research & Analysis Division, London, OfSTED.

Office for Standards in Education (2002) *Achievement of Black Caribbean Pupils: Good Practice in Secondary Schools*, HMI 448, London, OfSTED.

Office for Standards in Education (2004) *Promoting and evaluating pupil's spiritual, moral, social and cultural development*, Guidance document, HMI 2125, www.OfSTED.gov.uk/

Office for Standards in Education (2008) *Reducing Exclusions of Black Pupils from Secondary Schools: examples of good practice*, London, OfSTED.

O'Keeffe, B. (1999) Reordering Perspectives in Catholic Schools, in: M. P. Hornsby-Smith (ed) (1999)

Catholics in England 1950-2000: Historical and Sociological Perspectives, London, Cassell.

Ottaway, A. K. C. (1953) *Education and Society: An Introduction to the Sociology of Education*, London, Routledge & Kegan Paul.

Ozorak, E. W. (2003) Love of God and neighbour: religion and volunteer service among college students, *Review of Religious Research*, 44. 3. 285-299.

Parker-Jenkins, M. (2005) The legal framework for faith-based schools and the rights of the child, in: R. Gardner, J. Cairns & D. Lawton (eds) (2005) *Faith Schools: Consensus or Conflict*, London, RoutledgeFalmer.

Parker-Jenkins, M., Hartas, D. & Irving B. A. (2005) *In Good Faith: Schools, Religion and Public Funding*, Aldershot, Ashgate.

Passmore, B. & Barnard, N. (2001) Voters oppose expansion of faith schools, *Times Educational Supplement,* 30th November.

Paterson, L. (1991) Socio-economic status and educational attainment: a multi-dimensional and multi-level study, *Evaluation and Research in Education*, 5. 3. 97-121.

Pettit, P. (1986), Social Holism and Moral Theory, in: *Proceedings of the Aristotelian Society*, Vol. LXXXVI.

Phillips, D. (ed) (2000) *The Education Systems of the United Kingdom*, Oxford, Symposium Books.

Phillips, T. (2005) After 7/7: Sleepwalking to segregation, speech given at the Manchester Council for Community Relations 22nd September, *http://www.cre.gov.uk*, (accessed 28th March 2006).

Plunkett. D. (1990) *Secular and Spiritual Values: Grounds for Hope in Education*, London, Routledge.

Pontifical Council for Justice & Peace (2004) *Compendium of the Social Doctrine of the Church*, London, Burns & Oates.

Pope Benedict XVI, (2007) *Jesus of Nazareth*, London, Bloomsbury.

Pope John-Paul II, (1979) *Catechesi tradendae* [Catechesis in Our Time], Apostolic Exhortation, 16th October, in: A. Flannery (ed) (1982) *Vatican Council II: More Post Conciliar Documents*, New York, Costello Publishing Company.

Pope John-Paul II, (1984) Address to Catholic educators, St. John's Basilica, Newfoundland, Canada, 12th September, *http://www.vatican.va/holy_father/john_paul_ii/speeches/1984*, (accessed 8th March 2006).

Pope John-Paul II (1992) Fidei Depositum [The Deposit of Faith], Apostolic Constitution on the publication of the Catechism of the Catholic Church, in: *Catechism of the Catholic Church* (1994), London, Geoffrey Chapman, pp. 2-6.

Pope John Paul II (1997) Address to Teachers and Students of the Catholic Villa Flaminia Institute, Rome, 23rd February, *http://www.vatican.va/holy_father/john_paul_ii/speeches/1997*, (accessed 8th March 2006).

Pope John-Paul II (1998) *Fides et Ratio* [Faith and Reason], London, Catholic Truth Society.

Pope Paul VI (1974) Alloction to the Ninth Congress of the Catholic International Education Office (O.I.E.C), reported in: *L'Osservatore Romano*, June 9th.

Pope Paul VI (1976) Discourse on Christmas Night, December 25th, Rome, *Acta Apostolica Sedis* 68, p. 145.

Pope Pius XI (1929) Divini Illius Magistri, [The Christian Education of Youth], Encyclical, Rome, 31st December, *http://www.vatican.va/roman_curia/congregations/documents* (accessed 28th April 2004).

Pope Pius XI (1931) Quadragesimo Anno, [Reconstruction of the Social Order], Encyclical, Rome, 15th May, *http://www.vatican.va/roman_curia/congregations/documents* (accessed 28th April 2004).

Popper, K. (1959) *The Logic of Scientific Discovery,* London, Routledge.

Porteus-Wood, K. (2004) Scale down religious schools or face a disaster for race relations, National Secular Society, 9th June, *http//www.secularism.org.uk* (accessed 9th June 2004).

Potts, J. (2007) Call for more Catholic schools to cater for migrants from Poland, *The Catholic Herald,* 29th June, p. 2.

Power, M. (2001) *Home to School Transport: A Discussion Paper,* (unpublished internal CES document), London, Catholic Education Service.

Price, A. (1999) Turbulent Times – A challenge to Catholic education in Britain today, in: J. C. Conroy, (ed) (1999) *Catholic Education: Inside Out/Outside In,* Dublin, Lindisfarne Books.

Pring, R. (1978) Problems of justification, in: D. Lawton, P. Gordon, M. Ing, B. Gibby, R. Pring, & T. Moore (eds) (1978) *Theory and Practice of Curriculum Studies,* London, Routledge & Kegan Paul.

Pring. R. (1996) Markets, education and Catholic schools, in: McLaughlin, T. H., O'Keefe, J. & O'Keeffe, B. (eds) (1996) *The Contemporary Catholic School: Context, Identity and Diversity,* London, Falmer Press.

Province Of Westminster (1852) First synodal letter of the Roman Catholic Archbishop and Bishops of the Province of Westminster, 17th July, in: R. E. Guy (1886) *The Synods in English: Being the Texts of the Four Synods of Westminster,* London, St. Gregory's Press.

Ranson, S., Arnott, M., McKeown, P., Martin, J. & Smith P. (2005) The participation of volunteer citizens in school governance, *Educational Review,* 57. 3. 357-371.

Reese, C. M., Miller, K. E., Mazzeo, J. & Dossey, J. A. (1997) *NAEP 1996 Mathematics report card for the nation and the states,* Washington, DC, National Centre for Educational Statistics.

Redford, J. (2004) *Bad, Mad or God? Proving the Divinity of Christ from St. John's Gospel,* London, St. Pauls Publishing.

Regan, E. (2004) Catholic education: past and present, *Briefing,* March, London, Catholic Media Office.

Regnerus, M. D. (2003) Religion and positive adolescent outcomes: a review of research and theory, *Review of Religious Research,* 44. 4. 394-413.

Reitsma, J., Scheepers, P. & te Grotenhuis, M. (2005) Dimensions of individual religiosity and volunteering in Europe, *Paper presented at the NCVO & VSSN 11th Researching the Voluntary Sector Conference,* University of Warwick.

Reynolds D. (1992) The effective school, *Managing Schools Today,* 1. 7. 16-18.

Reynolds D. (1992) School effectiveness and school improvement: An updated review of the British literature, in: D. Reynolds & P. Cuttance (eds) (1992) *School Effectiveness: Research, policy and practice,* London, Cassell.

Richmond, W. K. (1945) *Education in England,* Harmondsworth, Penguin.

Riley, D. (1990) Should market forces control educational decision making? *American Political Science Review*, 84. 2. 554-558.

Robinson, N. (2007) A matter of principle, *http://www.bbc.co.uk/blogs/nickrobinson/ 2007/01/24* (accessed 21st February 2007).

Robinson N. (2007) No blanket exemption, *http://www.bbc.co.uk/blogs/nickrobinson/2007/01/25*, (accessed 21st February 2007).

Romi, S. (2002) Disruptive behaviour in religious and secular high schools, *Research in Education*, 71. 81-91.

Sacred Congregation for Catholic Education (1977) *The Catholic School*, Abbotts Langley, Catholic Information Office.

Sacred Congregation for Catholic Education (1982) *Lay Catholics in Schools: Witnesses to Faith*, London, Catholic Truth Society.

Sacred Congregation for Catholic Education (1988) *The Religious Dimension of Education in a Catholic School*, London, Catholic Truth Society.

Sacred Congregation for Catholic Education (1997) *The Catholic Church on the Threshold of the Third Millennium*, Rome 28th December.

Sacred Congregation for Catholic Education (2002) *Consecrated Persons and their Mission in Schools: Reflections and Guidelines*, Rome, 28th October.

Saunders, L. (1998) *'Value added' measurement of school effectiveness: an overview*, Slough, National Foundation for Educational Research.

Saunders, L. (1999) *'Value added' measurement of school effectiveness: a critical review*, Slough, National Foundation for Educational Research.

Schagen, S., Davies, D., Rudd, P. & Schagen, I. (2002) *The Impact of Specialist and Faith Schools on Performance*, Local Government Association Research Report 28, Slough, National Foundation for Educational Research.

Scruton, R. (1998) *An Intelligent Person's Guide to Modern Culture*, London, Duckworth.

Sheehy, G., Brown, R., Kelly, & McGrath (eds) (1995) *The Canon Law: Letter & Spirit*, The Canon Law Society of Great Britain and Ireland, London, Geoffrey Chapman.

Shipman, M. D. (1968) *Sociology of the School*, London, Longman.

Short, G. (2002) Faith Based Schools: a threat to social cohesion? *Journal of Philosophy of Education*, 36. 4. 559-572.

Short, G. (2003) Faith Schools and Social Cohesion: opening up the debate, *British Journal of Religious Education*, 25. 2. 129-141.

Short, G. (2003) Faith schools and indoctrination: a response to Michael Hand, *Theory and Research in Education*, 1. 1. 331-341.

Siegel, H. (2004) Faith, knowledge and indoctrination: a friendly response to Hand, *Theory and Research in Education*, 2. 1. 75-83.

Singh, B. R. (1998) Liberalism, parental rights, pupil's autonomy and education, *Educational Studies*, 24. 2. 165-182.

Sinnott, J. (1992) *Analysis of the London Reading Test results, 1992,* London, Borough of Tower Hamlets, Policy and Performance Monitoring.

Smith R. K. M. (2003) *International Human Rights,* Oxford, Oxford University Press.

Snook I. A. (ed) (1972) *Concepts of Indoctrination,* London, Routledge & Kegan Paul.

Social Justice Policy Group (2006) *Breakdown Britain,* London, Social Justice Policy Group.

Spear, M. Gould, K. & Lee, B. (2000) *Who would be a teacher? A review of factors motivating and de-motivating prospective and practising teachers,* Slough, National Foundation for Educational Research.

Spencer, A. E. C. W. (2006) *Facts and Figures for the Twenty-First Century – An assessment of the statistics of the Catholic community of England and Wales at the start of the century,* Taunton, Pastoral Research Centre.

Stock, M. (2005) *'Christ at the Centre: a summary of why the Church provides Catholic schools',* Birmingham, Archdiocese of Birmingham Diocesan Schools Commission.

Stoke-on-Trent Local Education Authority (2002) *School Organisation Plan, (sections 5.16 & 5.17),* City Council, Stoke-on-Trent.

Stoke-on-Trent City Council (2002) *Minutes of the Education Executive Committee Meeting,* 28th January, City Council, Stoke-on-Trent.

Storr, C. (2007) Catholic School Governance in the Twenty-First Century: Continuity, Inconguity and Challenge, Unpublished Ph. D. thesis, Institute of Education, London University.

Strike, K. A. (1999) Can schools be communities? The tension between shared values and inclusion, *Education Administrative Quarterly,* 35. 1. 46-70.

Strike, K. A. (2000) Schools as communities: four metaphors, three models, and a dilemma or two, *Journal of Philosophy of Education,* 34. 4. 617-642.

Strike, K. A. (2003) Toward a liberal conception of school communities: community and the autonomy argument, *Theory and Research in Education,* 1. 2. 171-193.

Sullivan, J. (2000) *Catholic Schools in Contention,* Dublin, Lindiafarne.

Sullivan, J. (2000) Wrestling with managerialism, in: M. Eaton, J. Longmore & A. Naylor (eds) (2000) *Commitment to Diversity: Catholics and Education in a Changing World,* London, Cassell.

Swift, D. F. (1969) *The Sociology of Education: Introductory Analytical Perspectives,* London, Routledge & Kegan Paul.

Swift, R. & Gilley, S. (eds) (1985) *The Irish in the Victorian City,* London, Croom Helm.

Swift, R. & Gilley, S. (eds) (1989) *The Irish in Britain 1815-1939,* London, Pinter.

Swift, R. & Gilley, S. (eds) (1999) *The Irish in Victorian Britain,* Dublin, Four Courts Press.

Tan, C. (2004) Micheal Hand, indoctrination and the inculcation of belief, *Journal of Philosophy of Education,* 38. 2. 257-267.

Tanner, M. (2001) *Ireland's Holy Wars: the struggle for a nation's soul,* 1500-2000, New Haven, Yale University Press.

Taylor G. & Saunders J. B. (1976) *The Law of Education,* London, Butterworths.

Teachman, J. D., Paasch, C. & Carver, K. (1996) Social Capital and dropping out of school early, *Journal of Marriage and the Family*, 58. 3. 773-783.

Thiessen, E. J. (1993) Two concepts or two phases of liberal education, in: L. Francis and D. Lankshear (eds) (1993) *Christian Perspectives on Church Schools*, Leominster, Gracewing.

Thiessen, E. J. (1993) *Teaching for Commitment: Liberal Education, Indoctrination and Christian Nurture*, Leominster, Gracewing.

Thomas, S., Nuttall, D. & Goldstein, H. (1993) *Report on analysis of 1991 examination results*, Association of Metropolitan Authorities project on 'Putting examination results in context', London, University of London Institute of Education.

Toynbee, P. (2001) Keep God out of class, *The Guardian*, Friday 9th November.

Toynbee, P. (2006) This is a clash of civilisations – between reason and superstition, *The Guardian*, Friday 14th April.

Tweedie, J. (1990) Should market forces control educational decision making? *American Political Science Review*, 84. 2. 549-554.

Van Bueren, G. (1994) *The International Law on the Rights of the Child*, Boston and London, Martinus Nijhoff Dordrecht.

Wake, R. (1986) Catholic Education in School, *The Month*, July/August, pp. 248-250.

Weaver, A. J., Flannelly, L. T., Gabarino, J., Figley, C. R. & Flannelly, K. J. (2003) A systematic review of research on religion and spirituality in the Journal of Traumatic Stress, 1990-99, *Mental Health, Religion and Culture*, 6. 215-228.

Wells, R. A. (1999) *People behind the peace: community and reconciliation in Northern Ireland*, Grand Rapids, Eerdmans.

West A. (2006) School choice, equity and social justice: the case for more control, *British Journal of Educational Studies*, 54. 1. 15-33.

West, A. & Hind, A. (2003) *Secondary school admissions in England: exploring the extent of overt and covert selection*, London, Research and Information on State Education Trust.

West, A., Hind, A. & Pennel, H. (2003) *Secondary Schools in London: admission criteria and cream skimming*, London, Research and Information on State Education Trust.

Whelan, R. (ed) (2007) *The Corruption of the Curriculum*, London, Institute for the Study of Civil Society.

White, J. P. (1982) *The Aims of Education Restated*, London, Routledge & Kegan Paul.

Willis, P. (2002) in: *Hansard, Official Report, Standing Committee G*, 10TH January.

Willis, P. (2005) Faith Schools – we must seek to build on success not seek to destroy it, Speech given at the Catholic Association of Teachers, Schools and Colleges Conference, 2nd February 2005. *http://www. libdems.org.yk/edcation/faith_schools*, (accessed 10th March 2006).

Willms, J. D. (1985) Catholic school effects on academic achievement: new evidence from the 'High School and Beyond' follow-up study, *Sociology of Education*, 58. 98-114.

Wilson, J. & Musick, M. (1997) Who cares? Towards an integrated theory of volunteer work, *American Sociological Review*, 62. 5. 694-713.

Winnicott, D. W. (1964) *The Child, the family and the Outside World*, Harmondsworth, Penguin.

Whitbourn, S. (2003) *Education and the Human Rights Act 1998*, Slough, National Foundation for Educational Research.

Whitfield, R. (1995) Educating for Family Life: from advocacy to investment and action, *The Month*, December, 465-469.

Whitfield, R. (1996) Security of Attachment: a necessary objective in taking ourselves and our children seriously, *Annual Review*, Windsor, St. George's House.

Williams, K. (1998) Education and human diversity: the ethics of separate schooling revisited, *British Journal of Educational Studies*, 46. 1. 26-39.

Williams, I., Dunne, M. & Mac an Ghaill, M. (1996) *Economic Needs of the Irish Community in Birmingham*, Birmingham, Birmingham City Council.

Woods, P., Landry, C. & Broomfield, J. (2006) *Cultural Diversity in Britain*, York, Joseph Rowntree Foundation.

Working Party on Catholic Education in a Multicultural Society (1974) *Learning from Diversity*, London, Catholic Media Office.

Worlock, D. (1995) Address to the Annual Study Conference of the Catholic Teachers' Federation, March 4th, Liverpool, *Briefing*, 22nd April, London, Catholic Media Office.

Worlock, D. (1995) What the butler did not see: the changing face of education, in: *Partners in Mission: a collection of talks by Bishops on issues affecting Catholic education* (1997), London, Catholic Education Service and Briefing.

Youniss J. & Covey, J. J. (eds) (2000) *Catholic Schools at the Crossroads: Survival and transformation*, New York, Teachers College Press.